4W 350

Martin Luther
His Life and His Labor

LUTHER TRANSLATING THE BIBLE

Martin Luther
His Life and His Labor

By WILLIAM DALLMANN

*Speaking
the truth in love.*
Ephesians 4:15

CONCORDIA PUBLISHING HOUSE
Saint Louis

COPYRIGHT 1951 BY

CONCORDIA PUBLISHING HOUSE, ST. LOUIS, MO.

Printed in U.S.A.

FOREWORD

This revised edition of Luther's life (first edition 1917) is written for the people in their homes.

As much as possible the floor was given to Luther, to Catholics, and to non-Lutherans.

The reader may rest assured the Catholic Church has not been wronged; the writer's statements may be verified in the twelve volumes of the "History of the Popes" by Prof. Dr. Ludwig Pastor, a Catholic historian, whose work has been endorsed by Pope Leo XIII.

Recent research in this new edition has been used to make an up-to-date life of Luther.

W. D.

CONTENTS

1. YOUNG LUTHER   1
2. FRIAR MARTIN   15
3. A TRIP TO ROME   23
4. LUTHER'S CONVERSION   42
5. THE NINETY-FIVE THESES   59
6. CONTROVERSIES ABOUT THE THESES   80
7. THREE MONUMENTAL WRITINGS   100
8. LUTHER AT WORMS   113
9. LUTHER AT THE WARTBURG   132
10. LUTHER AND THE FANATICS   139
11. LUTHER AND THE PEASANT WAR   144
12. THREE PRECIOUS BOOKS   152
13. MORE BATTLES   165
14. LUTHER SAVED FROM BURNING CONFESSION, AND THE FIRST RELIGIOUS   180
15. THE FIRST PROTESTANTS, THEIR FIRST PEACE   193
16. MORE TALK OF A COUNCIL   211
17. LUTHER AT HOME   220
18. LUTHER'S DEATH   249

ILLUSTRATIONS

Luther Translating the Bible *(Frontispiece)*	
Eisleben	1
Mansfeld	2
Luther School in Mansfeld	3
Luther's Father	4
Luther's Mother	5
The Clergy in the Ship of the Church, the Laity in the Water	7
Luther Taken in by Ursula Cotta	9
Luther Finding the Bible	11
Erfurt Cathedral, Where Luther was Ordained as Priest	15
John Staupitz as Augustinian Prior	18
Library of the Cloister at Erfurt	20
Scene in Rome in Luther's Day	23
Augustinian Cloister and S. Maria del Popolo	25
Porta del Popolo, Church of S. Maria, Augustinian Cloister	26
S. Maria del Popolo	27
Many Popes Buried in the Catacombs of Calixtus	28
St. Veronica	29
Scala Santa, Pilate's Staircase	33
S. Maria dell' Anima, the German Church	36
The Augustinian Cloister	42
Castle, City Church, Wittenberg University	44
St. Mary's, or City Church	46
Luther Preaching Christ Crucified	55
Posting the Ninety-Five Theses	59
Tetzel	64
The Castle Church	70

XIII

Interior View of the Castle Church Before 1760	71
The Pleissenburg at Leipzig	80
Kaiser Maximilian I	82
Cajetan	84
Luther and Cajetan	87
John Eck of Ingolstadt	95
Luther Burning the Papal Bull	100
Ready to Face the Diet	113
Burning of Savonarola	120
Knight, Death, and the Devil	123
Luther's Entrance into Worms	125
Luther Before the German Reichstag	126
Luther Monument at Worms	128
The Wartburg in the Days of Luther	132
Luther Preaching in the Wartburg	136
Luther in the "Black Bear" at Jena	139
The Three Peasants	144
Melanchthon, Luther, Bugenhagen, Cruciger, Translating the Bible	152
Marburg	165
The Conference at Marburg	175
Martin Luther	180
Hans Sachs	184
Albrecht Duerer	185
Reading the Augsburg Confession	193
Philip Melanchthon	199
Elizabeth, Wife of Elector Joachim I of Brandenburg	209
St. Thomas Church in Leipzig	211
Luther at Home	220
The Wedding of Martin Luther	222
Luther's Daughter Magdalene	227
Luther's Son Paul	228
Luther's Daughter Margaret	229
Taking Down Luther's Table Talk	243
The Age of the Reformation	248
Where Luther Died	252
St. Andrew's Church	253

Martin Luther
His Life and His Labor

EISLEBEN

Chapter One

YOUNG LUTHER

"Blessed be the day of Martin Luther's birth! It should be a festival second only to that of the nativity of Jesus Christ," says Robert Southey, the crowned poet.

"And thou Eisleben art not the least among the cities of Germany, for out of thee shall come to my spiritual Israel a knight and the last prophet. The Eislebian Christian Knight," Micah 5:2; Matt. 2:6. So said Martin Rinkart, author of the great hymn "Now Thank We All Our God," in 1613.

Thomas Carlyle here thought of another birth, at Bethlehem.

Edwin D. Mead: "Luther is the most influential and significant man in the spiritual history of mankind since Christ."

The Catholic Friedrich von Schlegel says: "I think there are few, even of his own disciples, who esteem Luther highly enough."

"In the year 1483 I, Martinus Luther, was born [Nov. 10]. I do not remember this, but I believe my parents."

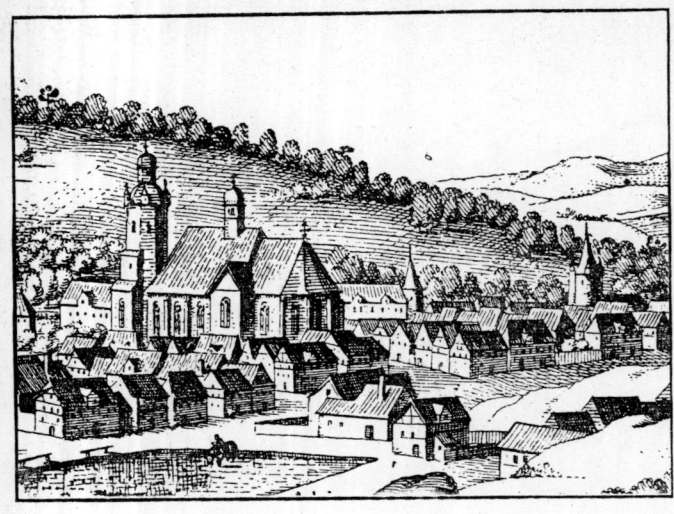

MANSFELD

The next day Pastor Bartholomaeus Rennebecker baptized him in the basement chapel of St. Peter's, and we were shown the font and the bowl.

He was named Martin for the saint of the day, Martin of Tours, the saint on horseback who with his sword halved his cloak to share it with a beggar — a thing Luther did all his life.

After about six months the family moved to the small city of Mansfeld, where Father Hans worked in the copper mines and Mother Margaret carried the firewood on her bent back to help make both ends meet and fill the mouths of the hungry children. Millet's "Angelus" may help us picture the parents.

Martin had at least two younger brothers and four sisters. Martin and James were such pals that neither enjoyed games and meals without the other. That is about all we know of the children.

Martin was not mollycoddled. "My father was a poor miner. My mother carried all her wood on her back.... Such a hard life makes people hard. On account of a miserable nut my mother once beat me till the blood flowed. My father once flogged me so severely that I fled and had a grudge against him till he wooed me back. But they meant heartily well."

That experience made Martin a great pedagog. "One must

LUTHER
SCHOOL
IN MANSFELD

punish so that the apple goes with the rod." Yea, verily; not the apple alone, nor the rod alone, but apple and rod in proper proportion and at the right time and in the right place. After four hundred years our educational congresses may still learn from Luther. No Hans Andersen's *Fairy Tales,* no *Alice in Wonderland,* no "Mother Goose Rhymes" for the youngsters in those days!

The Catholic Joseph Clayton writes: "Pope Innocent VIII at the end of 1484 issued a bull on witchcraft, and in 1486 Jacob Sprenger published the *Witch Hammer;* both encouraged persecution and did untold harm in Germany . . . reveal the low estate of Catholic faith and Christian morals." — *Luther,* pp. 22—25. If Luther became superstitious, whose the fault?

There was but one help against the infernal witches and cobolds — "Help, St. Anna!" Annaberg, a new mine, was placed under her protection by Duke George of Mansfeld. And yet Luther was far outstripped in superstition by enlightened Humanists of his day like Melanchthon, Johannes von Tritheim, and many others.

In these days, 1486, Bartholomaeus Diaz doubled the Cape of Good Hope.

Though it came hard, the hard-handed but softhearted Hans raised the needed *groschen* to send Martin to the city school, likely on St. Gregory's Day, March 12, 1488.

LUTHER'S FATHER

"My good old friend Nicolaus Oemler more than once carried me in his arms to school and back, when we both did not know one brother-in-law carried another." Happy school days! The rules forbade the children to throw snowballs and to skate! But during vacations? There were no vacations!

What did he learn? The Latin grammar. "In one morning I got fifteen stripes for not knowing what no one had taught me." Certainly a good prep school for the University of Hard Knocks to which he had to become used. He learned the Ten Commandments, Creed, Lord's Prayer, *Ave Maria,* or Hail Mary, and also moral maxims from Cato, the old Roman Stoic. He learned the calendar with Latin verses for the many saints' days and the legends of the saints.

Thomas Platter says there were no textbooks in 1510; the teacher dictated, and the pupils wrote and learned by rote.

Martin learned to sing in the daily religious exercises in school,

LUTHER'S MOTHER

and as a choir boy he sang the litany, Psalms, versicles, responsories in church on Sundays and the many festivals and processions.

When about twelve, Martin was confirmed. "I was so used from childhood up that I must turn pale and take fright when I heard the name of Christ called, for I was not otherwise taught than to hold Him for a severe and angry judge." So he prayed to St. George, the dragon killer, to the gentle Virgin, to her mother, St. Ann, and to others.

Did he show leadership? "My father said I would become a leader, mayor of a dorp, some sort of head servant over the others."

In these days, 1492 to be exact, Christopher Columbus discovered America. The most dissolute Pope, Alexander VI, as God on earth, in his bull *Inter Caelia Divinae* promptly presented it to Ferdinand and Isabella of Spain. Principal P. T. Forsyth of Hackney College, London, thinks America was discovered in order to be a refuge and a sphere for Luther's Reformation. "Where would English faith have been without America to fly to?"

MAGDEBURG

In the spring of 1496 Peter Reinecker sent his Hans to the "then famous school" at Magdeburg, and Martin marched along to the busy place of about fifteen thousand on the Elbe River.

Near the Dome was the school taught by the *Nullbrueder,* Lollards, Brethren of the Common Life, or rather Lot. Luther always spoke well of them.

Dr. Paul Mosshauer, an official of the archbishop, was of Mansfeld and gave shelter to his young countryman Martin. But for his bread the lad had to sing from door to door, a usual thing for students to do; they really gave the people a chance to do a "good work" for themselves.

"Was it here at Magdeburg or still at Mansfeld that this happened? As usual at *Fastnacht* we had sung at the doors for sausages, when a man joked with us and cried loud, 'What are you bad boys doing?' and ran towards us with two sausages. But I and my pal were scared by the loud cry and fled. He had to give us many good words till we at last went back and took the sausages from him."

"With these my eyes I saw a prince of Anhalt in the cap of the Barefooters walking on Broadway for bread, carrying the sack like a donkey, so that he had to bend to the earth; but his fellow brother walked empty alongside him, so that the pious prince alone had to show the world the highest example of the gray shorn holiness. And they had so cowed him that he did all the other work in the cloister like any other brother. He had so fasted, kept vigil, and mortified his body that he looked like a dead man, sheer skin and bone, so that he died soon after. Whoever looked on him was deeply stirred by his devotion and felt ashamed of himself." Let us remember this.

"They painted a big ship, called the holy Christian Church; therein sat no layman, neither kings nor princes, but only the pope with the cardinals and bishops in front under the Holy Ghost and the priests and monks along the sides with the oars and thus went to heaven. The laymen swam in the water around the ship, some drowned, some pulled themselves toward the ship on ropes tossed them by the holy fathers, graciously to share their good works to

THE CLERGY IN THE SHIP OF THE CHURCH, THE LAITY IN THE WATER
By a Venetian Monk

help them, that they drowned not but, clinging and hanging to the ship, also would get to heaven. No pope, cardinal, bishop, priest, or monk was in the water, but only lay people."

What an impression on the lad!

"Also at Magdeburg I was very sick. When I suffered great thirst, for water was forbidden during fever, it happened on a Friday that everybody after eating had gone to church and had left me alone in the house. When I could no longer stand the thirst, I crawled on hands and feet down to the kitchen, drank my fill of fresh water with great relish, and made my way back, weak, on hands and feet, to my room, which I barely reached before the folks came back from church. On this drink a sound sleep came over me, and the fever left me."

Perhaps this was the reason for leaving Magdeburg.

While Luther was at Magdeburg, Andreas Proles, vicar of the German Augustinians before John Staupitz, visited the city. He said, "Brethren, Christianity needs great and strong reformation, and I see it near at hand."

Why didn't he begin it?

"I am old, weak, lack the gifts, but the Lord will send a man excellent in age, power, endurance, learning, intellect, and eloquence, he'll begin it and oppose all errors; God will give him the heart to dare contradict the great lords."

EISENACH

About Easter, 1497, Martin went to school at Eisenach, where lived his mother's aunt, the wife of Conrad Hutter, sexton at St. Nicholas, whom Luther loved and invited to his first mass.

It seems, however, the poor sexton could not do much for the poor scholar, who again became a "crumb seeker," singing from door to door. Thus he came to "Henricianus," Heinrich Schalbe, consul in Eisenach 1495—99, who gave him meals in return for taking Henry junior to school.

"I found shelter with a pious matron, who had a hearty liking for me on account of my devout singing and praying." This was Ursula Cotta, born Schalbe, wife of Henry Cotta. She took in a stranger and entertained an angel unawares. On her deathbed, on November 29, 1511, the worthy matron said God had signally blessed her since taking Martin under her roof. God bless her! Her kindness to Martin made her immortal. In a note to Prov. 31:10 Luther later celebrated a saying of his hostess: "Nothing more lovely on earth than the love of a good woman." Let our ladies' aids be encouraged to become Ursula Cottas, and aid needy students for the holy ministry!

In the house opposite Cotta's was born the mightiest master of music, Johann Sebastian Bach, who poured out some of his genius on Luther's hymns. Two most interesting houses.

"I also received many kindnesses from John Braun, the vicar of St. Mary's." He often invited Luther and cultivated poetry, music, and singing. "His great and upright goodness is unforgettable."

At the foot of the Wartburg was the Franciscan cloister, much favored by the Schalbe family. These monks kept one of their number, John Hilten, in prison for having foretold the end of

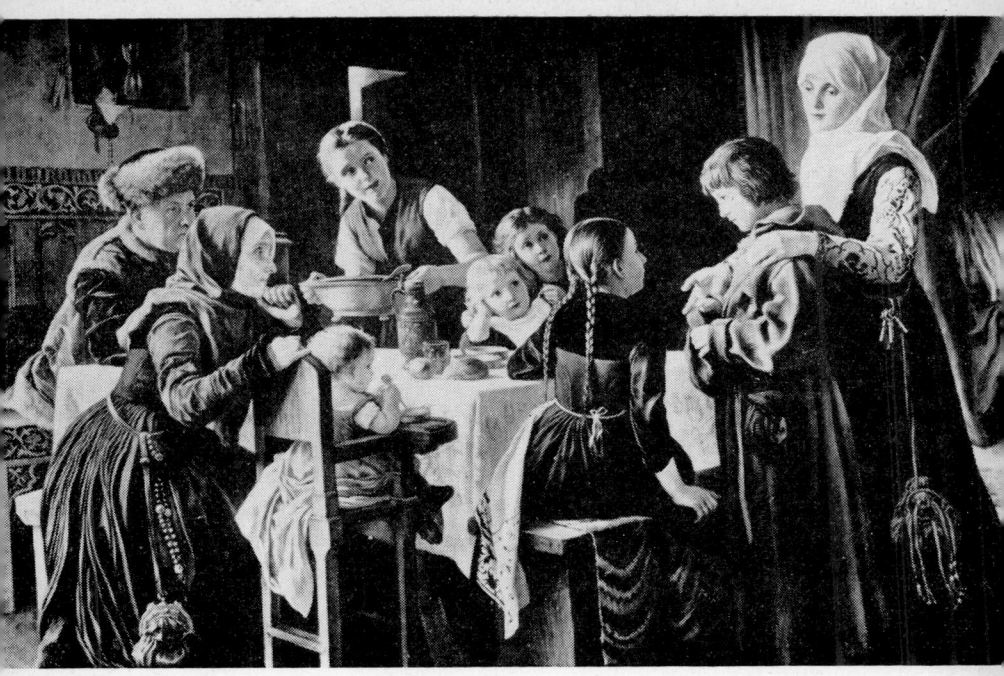

LUTHER TAKEN IN BY URSULA COTTA
After G. Spangenberg

the tyranny of the Roman Antichrist about 1514 or 1516. "At that time I did not think I would be that monk." "They served me in the highest degree."

In the church of St. Catherine's Monastery was the grave of Heinrich Raspe, a holy man, and a wonderful image of the Virgin and Child, which graciously viewed visitors with gifts, but turned away from those without gifts. Luther later tells how the hidden mechanism was worked by the monks. The pope's indulgence was granted to those who once a year visited this holy place.

"The rector of George's School was John Trebonius, a stately and learned man, whose gifts I must praise. As often as he stepped into the classroom, he doffed his hat till he took his chair. His colleagues had to do the same. When some at times forgot to do so, he earnestly talked to them. 'For among these young pupils sits many a one whom God can make one an honorable mayor, another a chancellor, a very learned doctor, or ruler, though you don't know them now; them you should show honor.'

"Another teacher, whom I have to thank much, was Wigand Guldenapf" — for whom he 1526 sought a decent pension.

"Was it here or later at Erfurt that a Bible fell into my hands? I happened to read the story of the mother of Samuel. The book pleased me very much, and I thought I would be happy if ever I could own such a book. I soon bought a postil. It pleased me much, because it had more Gospel lessons than usually were read during the year."

Here Luther finished his grammar and then took up the "arts of speaking and poetry," likely the rhetoric of Alexander de Villedieu.

While Luther was seeking an education at Eisenach, Vasco da Gama, on May 20, 1498, came to "Calicut" seeking "Christians and spices."

ERFURT

The English monk Winfrid took pity on the heathen Germans and brought them Christianity and enforced it by chopping down their holy oak at Geismar. In 741 the Apostle of Germany built a church on St. Mary's hill and founded a bishopric at Erfurt. Some would not take him for a Boniface, or Benefactor, and murdered him.

Erfurt became the many-towered, many-cloistered, the Garden City, "the lard mine," as Luther named it for its great wealth. It was known as "little Rome," for it had over a hundred buildings of religion, churches, chapels, monasteries, hospitals, and the like, for its 25,000 inhabitants. Also it had Germany's most famous university, instituted by Pope Clement VII in 1379, opened in 1392 with 523 students. It had many rich endowments and thirteen professors.

"Martinus Ludher ex Mansfeld," wrote Prexy Jodocus Trutvetter of Erfurt at the end of April, 1501, registering the eighteen-year-old Martin as number forty, also *"in Habendo,"* having funds. The funds were furnished by Father Hans, who had prospered in his mining ventures; and so Martin no longer had to work his way through college. He paid spot cash the full fee of twenty groats, one third of a gulden.

Luther moved into St. George's *bursa,* a sort of fraternity house,

LUTHER FINDING
THE BIBLE
Ward's picture hangs in the place of honor in the British and Foreign Bible Society in London

on the Gera at Lemann's bridge. It had a very good reputation, though its nickname was the *Biertasche,* "Beer Pocket."

He swore to obey the rector, and the rector was under oath to have the students lead a decent life in every respect in the university and also in town. To be seen with questionable women was severely punished. A servant fetched and carried the linen for washing and mending. The motto of the burse was: "Into a malicious soul wisdom shall not enter; nor dwell in the body that is subject unto sin." — Wisdom of Solomon 1:4.

The day began with prayers at 4 A. M., devotions at table, to bed at 8 P. M.

The rector of the college and the dean of the university visited the burse quarterly and inquired into the character of the students. No one was admitted to the final examination unless the rector testified to his solid character, confirmed by a special examiner.

On the street he had to wear a gown, price about 90 pennies, and a small cap, price about 18 pennies, on festivals a large cap, price nearly 50 pennies. In the burse he wore a doublet and a leather belt and long trousers, which cost about 18 pennies. The

11

bill of fare was probably like that of another burse — on Sundays, Tuesdays, Wednesdays, and Thursdays they had meat; on Mondays vegetables and boiled eggs; on Fridays and Saturdays dumplings and eggs fried in butter, and cheese; fish were too high for a steady diet. Very good bread was served, and beer in modest quantities.

What had Luther studied at the prep? The *Trivium* — grammar, logic, and rhetoric; to these was added singing in the religious instruction. What did he study at the university? The *Quadrivium* — arithmetic, geometry, astronomy, and music; as an elective there was a monthly lecture on the musical manual of the famous John de Muris. He studied Aristotle, Vergil, Cicero, Livy, Ovid, Plautus, Terence, Juvenal, the modern Baptista Mantuanus, and others. He praised his teachers Jodocus Trutvetter of Eisenach and Bartholomaeus Arnoldi of Usingen.

Cutting the fast set attending "the lectures of King Gambrinus and Knight Tannhaeuser," Luther studied hard so that at the earliest permitted time, in the autumn of 1502, he became a Bachelor of Philosophy and lectured on Aristotle.

Martin was jovial and popular; his nickname was "The Philosopher" — highly significant, for the instinct of students is uncannily inerrant.

On October 30 he saw Raymond von Gurk, cardinal and papal chancellor, ride into Erfurt to the Dome to sell indulgences. Nikolaus von Siegen heard doubts about them: they were harmful to many souls, and they led clerics with their concubines to sin freely and frankly, since they could be absolved so easily. Hm! A penny for the thoughts of the young Bachelor!

"On Tuesday after Easter [1504] I wounded myself in the leg with my sword. I was in great danger of death and cried, 'O Mary, help!' I would have died on Mary. During the night the wound broke open again, I was in danger of bleeding to death, and again I called on Mary."

While recovering, Luther taught himself to play the lute and all through life "Dame Musica" remained his best friend next to theology. He also learned to play the flute.

"The father of a friend of mine found me sick and said, 'Dear Bachelor, don't grieve; you'll become a great man.' Then I heard a prophet. And another old man said, 'There must come a change, and a great one. It can't go on like this.' I think it has come."

Again in the shortest time permitted, about January 7, 1505, Luther stood before the assembled university, second among seventeen. They placed on his head the brown biretta of a Master of Arts, and he delivered his initial lecture.

"What a great majesty and glory it was when they made Masters and carried torches before them and honored them! I hold no temporal, earthly joy was like to it. In the same way they made a great show and demonstration when they created Doctors; then they rode around town, specially dressed and jeweled for the occasion." In 1506 two graduates rode around town with 271 horses. After this "great majesty and glory" the Master had to set up an "honorable supper" to the faculty.

Martin was a proud boy, and Hans — was he a proud father! Now he no longer addressed him with *du,* but honored him with the respectful *Ihr,* as a sort of superior being. But what to do with this new superior being? Hans wanted Martin to study law, bought him the costly *Corpus Juris,* and even had an eye on an "honorable and rich marriage" for his clever boy.

The father proposes; God disposes.

Professor Martin Luther, A.M., on April 24 began to lecture, likely on Aristotle's *Ethics,* and even began to write a commentary on the first book. In addition, in May, he is registered in the school of law; whether civil or canon we do not know.

The summer semester began with a great celebration in the Dome on May 19, the day of St. Ives, the patron saint of the lawyers. The lectures began the next day in St. Mary's burse. Justus Jonas tells us Luther now moved into the lawyer's burse, the *Porta Coeli,* Gate of Heaven, founded in 1443 by Amplonius Rabingk de Fayo. The inmates were required to pray through the whole Psalter once every fifteen days, with other prayers, and at table the Bible was read and explained.

"When a young Master, through my Bible reading to my great sorrow I saw many errors in papacy through the bare text of the Bible. But there came thoughts like these: 'Why, see how great the authority of the pope and the Church! Should I alone be wise? You might err.' Through such considerations I let myself be hindered from reading the Bible and for long years remained a raving papist."

In the summer semester he heard a lecture on Reuchlin's drama *Sergius* by Jerome Emser of Ulm, later a fierce enemy of Luther.

One classmate had died suddenly just before becoming a Master, another, Jerome Buntz, died of pleurisy soon after taking his degree. "Today, red, tomorrow, dead; today to me, tomorrow to thee."

"Returning from Mansfeld on July 2, 1505, near Erfurt a terrific storm surprised me. The lightning struck near me, and terror of a sudden unrepentant death gripped me. Grasped by death, I cried, 'Help, dear Saint Ann, I'll turn monk!' I rued the vow, and many advised against it. But I insisted, and on the day before Alexius, July 16, I invited my best friends for a farewell so that they might accompany me to the cloister on the morrow. As they tried to keep me back, I said, 'Today you see me, and after never.' They led me with many tears."

"I made the vow not for the sake of the belly; but for the sake of my salvation." There was no other sure way, said St. Anselm. St. Thomas Aquinas held the monkish vow equal to a second Baptism, by which the monk was restored to innocence. St. Bernard counts nine joys which a monk has over other Christians, and he did not rest until he had gotten all his brothers and sisters into a cloister.

"I entered the spiritual state for no other reason than to serve God and please Him in eternity."

He sold all his books but Vergil and Plautus.

ERFURT CATHEDRAL (left)
WHERE LUTHER WAS ORDAINED AS PRIEST

Chapter Two

FRIAR MARTIN

THE PROBATIONER

A friendly friar led the newcomer to Prior Winand von Diedenhofen, who escorted him into the chapel and led in prayer. Luther was kept under observation in the guest house, to the right of the entrance. He wrote for leave to enter the cloister, but "my father almost went mad. He was bitterly disappointed and would on no account give his consent."

Two of his younger sons died of the pest, and Martin was also reported dead. Friends pleaded with the old man to make the sacrifice to the honor of God. "So be it, and God grant it may turn out well." But "his good will was lacking," adds Martin.

The prior and chapter held Luther fit for the monkish life. He had to make a general confession, "that the prior might learn the features of the new animal added to his herd."

The cloister bell knolled, the monks filed into the chapel, Luther threw himself down before the prior at the altar —

"What do you want?"

"God's mercy and your society."

The prior made clear the drudgery of the monkish life; the shame of begging for the cloister; the happy yoke of the threefold vow of poverty, chastity, and obedience.

Nothing daunted, Luther was ready to bear all, with the help of God, as far as human frailty permitted.

Stripped of his lay clothing, he received a white woolen shirt to wear in honor of the Virgin Mary; then the black gown with a short cowl and black leather belt; at last the scapular, a strip of white cloth hanging around the neck over the breast, and worn only in the cloister in place of the cowl, to remind him of the easy yoke Christ lays upon His people. Hymns, prayers, versicles, responsories, the kiss of peace from the prior and all the monks. He was led into a 7×9 cell with a chair, a table, a straw sack, and woolen blankets. It could not be heated and locked; the only window looked upon the cemetery, where lay the "militia of Christ," who had finished their crusade and reached the Promised Land.

The master of the novices — John Greffenstein? — "a really excellent man and doubtless under the cursed cowl a true Christian," took the new recruit in charge to teach him the manners of the "Knights of Christ" — not to contradict his superiors; not to say *mine* and *me,* but *ours* and *us;* how to enter the door; how to be seated; how to rise; how to walk with downcast eyes; how to carry the hands hid under the scapular, or shoved into the arms of the gown; how to eat; how to take up a glass; how to pass the dish of food; how not to lean on the elbows at table; how to pay attention; study the Bible. He had to sweep and dust and scrub, fetch wood and water, with sack on back go from door to door begging bread for the good of the order and promising the kind givers a share in the prayers and good works of the friars and the blessing of the holy relics of St. Catherine in the cloister, for which regular legal bills of sale were made out by the prior, a proper salesman of spiritual wares.

He had to learn the Rules of St. Augustine and many chapters of the fifty-one of the constitution. Talking was forbidden in choir, cell, and the common room between 8 P.M. and 6 A.M., only sign language was allowed. The silence of the meals was broken only by the reading from a sacred book. Private confession at least once a week; public confession of breaking the rules in full meetings of the chapter, and every breach of the rules was a sin, a *crimen;* for willful offenses, scourging before all, or even expulsion. Laughing was strictly forbidden.

In the constitution of 1287 there was an exhortation to read the Bible, which Staupitz put into the new in 1504. And so Luther was given a Bible bound in red leather. In time he knew on what page any passage stood.

THE CLERIC

After the shortened term of probation the master of the novices led Luther to the steps of the altar, where the prior told him to choose between leaving the cloister or staying forever. Luther would sacrifice himself to God and the order. After chants and prayer the prior stripped Luther with the words: "The Lord put off thy old Adam with all his works. Amen." Then he put on the blessed garments of the cleric with the words: "The Lord put on thee the new man, which is created after God in righteousness, holiness, and truth. Amen." The other monks sang the hymn "O great Father Augustinus." Given the Rules of Augustine, Luther drew near on bended knees, laid the Rules on the knees of the prior, laid his hands on the Rules, and vowed: "I, Friar Martin, make profession and pledge obedience to God Almighty, and to blessed Mary, ever virgin, and to thee, Friar Winand, prior of this place, in the name and stead of the prior general of the Order of the Eremite Brethren of the holy Bishop Augustine and his lawful successors, to live without property, in chastity, and after the Rules of Saint Augustine until death." Then he threw himself flat on the floor and spread out his arms in the form of a cross. The prior sprinkled him with holy water, gave him a lighted candle, and led him into the chancel. Here the new monk kneeled

JOHN STAUPITZ
AS AUGUSTINIAN
PRIOR

while they clipped his hair and shaved the tonsure — a bald spot on the top of his head. The other monks stood around singing; the mournful hymns symbolized the death of the old man, and the joyful ones the birth of the new man. He arose and gave each friar the kiss of peace. They assured him he was now as pure as a child just baptized.

An Augustinian light, Professor Zacharias, had led the argument against John Hus at Constance and won the pope's Golden Rose as a reward for his zeal and skill. He lay buried before the altar, his effigy carved on the gravestone, on his gown the carved Golden Rose. On this stone Luther lay flat when made monk.

Did those stony lips not preach eloquently, "Go and do thou likewise?"

"Had anyone then taught what I now through God's grace believe and teach, I would have torn him with my teeth."

When we stood on that stone, we thanked God for our Christian liberty.

The new cleric was ordered to study for the priesthood, under the direction of Dr. John Nathin.

Now Luther studied the Canon of the Mass by Gabriel Bill, the teacher of Staupitz and Nathin at Tuebingen. About December 19 Prior Winand made him subdeacon; on February 27, 1507, Bishop Johann von Laasphe made him deacon; on April 4 both made him priest in the great cathedral. On Cantate Sunday, May 2, the new priest read his first mass. He felt so unworthy he would have made a mess of it but for the help of the prior. "When I said my first mass at Erfurt, I was all but dead." It was a great day, and many friends were invited. Father Luther came in style — he headed twenty of the Luther sib on horseback and footed the whole bill for horses and horsemen.

The hardy miner had no use for lazy monks, who masted themselves on the sweat of other men's brows, but this day he would do himself proud, and he made to Martin, that is, to the cloister, a donation of twenty gulden!

Anything small about that horny-handed son of toil? He bore up bravely and plainly wished to prove he wished to forgive and forget. Why did they not let well enough alone?

On occasion the silent miner could talk, and talk quite to the point. At the banquet, Luther, Jr., tried to get Luther, Sr., to admit his wrong in opposing the entrance into the cloister by praising that life as a good, quiet thing. That put the father on his mettle, and he promptly fired back, "Have you never heard one is to obey parents?" The young priest was stunned into silence.

The monks tried to quiet their guest, but the sturdy old miner growled, "I've got to be here, eat and drink; would much liefer be away." Quite Lutheresque!

When the son came to again and defended himself by saying he had been called to become a monk by a voice from heaven, the father rapidly rejoined, "God grant it wasn't a spook of the devil!"

Seems Martin came by his repartee quite honestly. "They ought not to tease the dog," wrote he later about his own vehemence.

Come to think of it, this old Hans is quite an interesting character: against a host of strange and learned clergymen this plain layman, with his back to the wall, appeals to a simple Scripture! And he feels himself the victor! There is no answer to his unanswerable question. Again: that voice of God from heaven — it might have been a spook of the devil! Horrors! Blasphemy in

LIBRARY OF THE CLOISTER AT ERFURT

such a place on such an occasion! Certainly a case of private judgment.

Back to the mines for Hans; back to the books for Martin.

Now Luther was ordered to study theology in the good seminary of the cloister in close touch with the university — some professors taught in both. Dr. Johann Jenser von Paltz was the principal of this theological seminary and also a professor in the university. In 1502 he published his famous work on Indulgences — "a new sacrament." In his *Celifodina* he also practically says the soul springs from purgatory when the money clinks in the chest.

Professor Usingen also later entered the cloister.

Luther studied Lombard's *Sentences,* the dogmatic basis for theology, with Biel's commentary, the *Glossa Ordinaria,* and the *Questions* of Peter D'Ailli and William of Occam, perhaps also the *Summa* of Thomas Aquinas and the commentary of Duns Scotus. He heard lectures on a book of the Old Testament and on one of the New Testament. This kept him quite busy during the twenty months from May, 1507, till October, 1508.

He read John Gerson, Bonaventura, Hugo of St. Victor, the Englishmen Holywood, Biligam, and Thomas Maulveldt.

He read the Fathers — Athanasius, Augustine, Bernard, Ambrose, Jerome, Chrysostom, Hilary, Dionysius, Areopagita, Leo the

Great, Gregory the Great, Justin Martyr. He used the *Biblia cum glossa,* published at Basel in 1508, the commentary of Nicolas of Lyra, the commentary of the Hebraist Paul of Burgos, Reuchlin's Hebrew grammar and dictionary, and the Greek *Catholicon.*

He read the *Lives of the Fathers,* Cassian's *History of the Monks,* and also works of devotion, which promised indulgence and salvation for saying certain prayers and doing certain works, a mechanical process of debit and credit for evil and good works. This has been proved by A. V. Mueller, a former monk, who made a study of thirty-seven M. S. prayer books from 1450—1550.

Nathin said, "Brother Martin, leave the Bible alone. Read the old teachers. They give you the whole marrow of the Bible. Bible reading simply breeds unrest." When Luther kept on reading his Bible, Nathin commanded Luther on his vow of obedience to stop reading the Bible altogether. Staupitz, however, told him to read.

Luther came on sermons of Hus, which seemed quite sound — "perhaps he wrote them before he became a damned heretic" — and he laid the book aside, "wounded to the heart" at the dreadful company into which he had strayed. Still worse, Professor Johann von Greffenstein remarked to him the Council of Constance had condemned John Hus without instruction, without evidence, without conviction" — and he was not alone. Still worse, some things in the papacy seemed to be not in the Bible, and even against the Bible! "Should you alone be so wise? Nay, you may be sure you're wrong."

Suddenly, in October, 1508, Luther was ordered to Wittenberg to take the place of Wolfgang Ostermayr at the university in the professorship of the Bible and the lectureship in Aristotle's *Ethics.* But he heartily detested to thresh the dry straw of the mighty man of Stagira, for he was in love with theology, as he wrote John Braun at Eisenach on March 17, 1509, "that theology, mind you, which is the kernel of the nut, the core of the wheat, the marrow of the bone." This is the first robin. The ring is Lutheresque. To be sure, one swallow does not make a summer.

The twenty-five year old Luther was honored, but his honors were onerous. Four times a week he lectured at 2 P. M.; three nights a week he presided at the debates of the students; four times a week he attended at least two theological lectures, and also the theological exercises and disputations; in addition he lectured on the Bible since March 9, 1509, when he took the degree of Bachelor of the Bible, for which he did not pay — "because I had nothing." He at once prepared for the next degree, Sententiarius, and in the fall he held his disputation; but before he could hold his first lecture on the *Sentences* of Peter Lombard, the standard dogmatics, he was suddenly sent back to Erfurt.

The theological faculty of Erfurt declined to recognize the degrees of the new and not noted University of Wittenberg. It was only after the energetic representation of Dr. Nathin that they finally received Luther as a Sententiarius, after a formal inaugural lecture in the Heavenly Auditorium at the nave of the Cathedral. After this he lectured three or four times a week in the cloister on Lombard's *Sentences*.

Luther's copy was found in 1890, filled with his notes in an uncommonly clear, neat, even hand. And they already prove an uncommonly virile independence.

"Many famous teachers may think thus, nevertheless, because they have not Scripture on their side, I say with the Apostle, 'Though an angel from heaven, i. e., a teacher in the Church, teach otherwise, let him be accursed.'" Gal. 1:8.

As a higher critic he was the first to deny to Augustine the authorship of two works; and he was right.

The young professor now studied Greek, and Hebrew he learned from Reuchlin's *Rudimenta,* the first Hebrew grammar with glossary published in Germany.

1510 was "the crazy year." The worm turned. The little man drove out the city council in January and killed Mayor Heinrich Kellner on June 24. On August 14 they destroyed the main building of the university with the fine library.

SCENE IN
ROME IN
LUTHER'S
DAY

Chapter Three

A TRIP TO ROME

The Augustinian monks were incorporated by Pope Innocent IV in 1243 and by 1450 were grown to two thousand chapters. Like all the rest, in time they became corrupt. Seven cloisters fought Spalatin's reform by sending Dr. John Nathin and Master Martin Luther to Adolf von Anhalt at Halle to get the archbishop of Magdeburg on their side; they failed. A monk was sent to Rome with an appeal, with ten gulden to strengthen the appeal, and with Luther as the traveling companion, a rule of the order, and single file and in silence.

They set out in November, 1510. To trudge in winter is to drudge, especially if you must also fast — and during Advent you fast.

Likely they took the shortest way, the Nuernberg route, via Chur, the Septimer, Chiavenna, Como, Lecco, Monza, Milan.

The mighty Po is "the prince of rivers," quoting Vergil's *Georgics* I, 481. "There is a very rich cloister of the Benedictines [San

Benedetto Po]. That has a yearly income of 36,000 ducats. There is such gorging that they spend 12,000 ducats on entertaining, 12,000 on the buildings, and a third on the brethren. In this cloister I was treated royally. Divine worship does not consist in wealth, after the saying: 'Religion, the mother, has borne riches; then the daughter devoured the mother,' namely, through superstition."

The yellow Arno flowing by famous Florence, home of the elegant Medicis; Brunelleschi's marble cupola of the dome and Giotto's campanile and the doors of Ghiberti; the works of Donatello, Leonardo da Vinci, and Michelangelo. The principal hospital was the Spedale di Santa Maria Nuova, founded by Portinari, father of Dante's Beatrice, and Luther praises the skillful doctors, careful nurses, good kitchen, painted beds, and clean linen. Not far away the foundling hospital, Spedale degli Innocenti, over the portal the touching relief of the children by Della Robbia. Luther is pleased to see the uniformed orphans marching through the streets. He lodged near the Porta San Gallo in the splendid Augustinian cloister, a donation of Lorenzo the Magnificent.

At Siena he heard of Kaiser Friedrich's saying: "Who knows not to dissimulate knows not to dominate."

"The Italian night air is specially dangerous and pestilential and soon brings on a fever. It happened to me and my brother that one whole night we slept soundly by an open window till about 6 o'clock. When we awoke, our heads were full of vapor, very heavy, and awkward, so that on that day we could only walk a mile. And we suffered from thirst. Wine nauseated us, so that we could not even smell it, always wanted to drink water, which is deadly. At last we again refreshed ourselves with two pomegranates. With these God saved our lives."

A few years before, an open window gave Conrad Pellican also a fever, which tortured him for weeks and forced him to turn back. On to Bolsena, Montefiascone, Viterbo, with its evil-smelling sulphur springs and baths, Ronciglione — "only seven German miles" from Rome. At La Storta the old Via Clodia and Via Cassia joined and went down to the Campagna. Perhaps from the Monte Mario he went down to the Tiber.

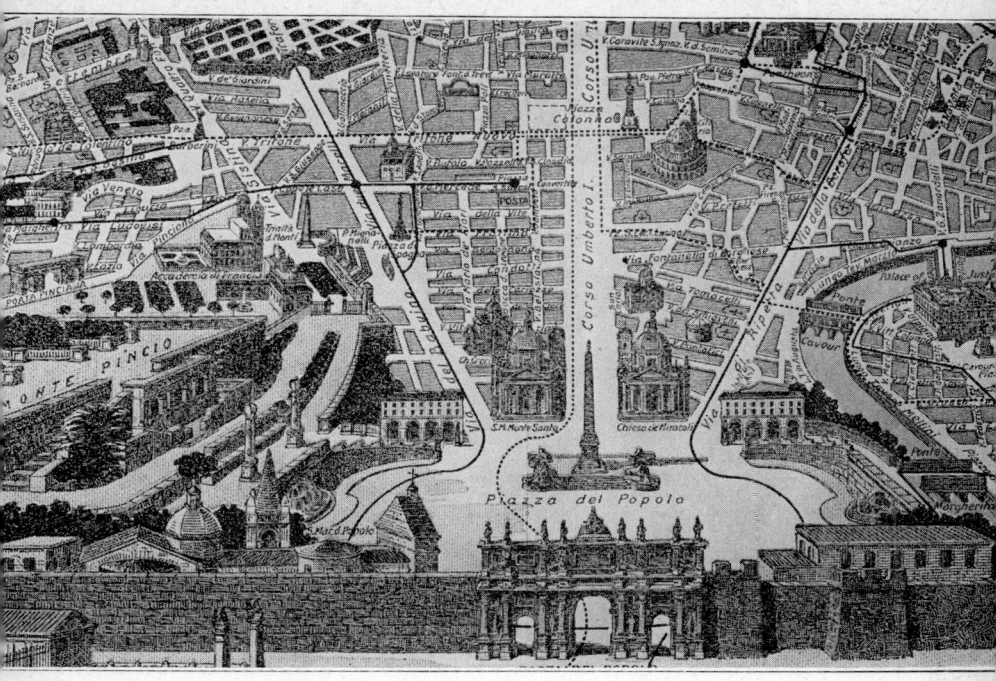

AUGUSTINIAN CLOISTER AND S. MARIA
DEL POPOLO TO THE LEFT OF
PORTA DEL POPOLO

"When I first saw Rome, I sank to earth, raised my hands, and said, 'Hail, holy Rome — yea, truly holy through the holy martyrs and their blood there shed!' "

On the Via Flaminia to the Porta Flaminia, also Porta del Popolo, where the victorious warrior Belisarius had stood blinded, begging his penny.

To the left, at the foot of the Monte Pincio, the Augustinian cloister of over forty friars adjoins the notable church of Santa Maria del Popolo. The weary way of about forty days is ended.

The next day, at S. Agostino, they presented the petition to appeal from the ruling of the Order, which was denied in January.

Nothing to do but see the sights, Luther went to see the sights — in the rain; it rained every day bar six from the end of October till the beginning of February. In order to prepare himself properly for this good work, he made a general confession, although he had already made two in Erfurt; but this third was the best, for it was

PORTA DEL POPOLO, CHURCH OF
S. MARIA, AUGUSTINIAN CLOISTER

in holy Rome. He came to priests that did not even know how to hear confession — in holy Rome! This was Luther's greatest grief in Rome. He said mass in Santa Maria del Popolo.

We rise quite early and have — no breakfast; holy things must be done fasting. We are off, personally conducted by a German Augustinian; such is the rule, though we are armed with a printed "Baedeker," the *Mirabilia Urbis Romae.* We cut across town, pass Paul's Gate, glance at the pyramid of Cestius, built before the days of Christ, tramp the Via Ostia to the magnificent Church of St. Paul, built by the Emperor Constantine, where Paul and Peter are buried, at least half of the body of each, and beyond the wall the bones of the three hundred Holy Innocents slain by King Herod at Bethlehem; the Crucifixus which had spoken to St. Bridget, and the pillar and the chain with which Paul had been chained to the pillar. Wonderful! Not far away the "Three Fountains," where Paul was beheaded. His head touched the ground three times, and at each place a fountain gushed up; hence the name.

On the old road delle sette Chiese to St. Sebastian's Church on the famous Via Appia, trod by St. Paul coming to Rome, the grave of St. Sebastian and that of the woman of Samaria, the well in which

S. MARIA DEL POPOLO

the bodies of Paul and Peter had lain for five hundred years, and the stone with the footprint of Christ when Peter said, *"Quo vadis, Domine?"* i. e., Whither art Thou going, Lord? In the catacombs of St. Calixtus the bones of 46 popes and 80,000 martyrs, and by walking through these caves five times during one mass we save a soul from purgatory; we can do the same blessed work more comfortably by a prayer at the high altar in the church. Two monks grumble for getting only six ducats a year for taking care of the caverns, while the rest of the huge income goes into the pockets of the pope. On January 21, all Rome and his wife visit St. Sebastian's, even "the grandest quantity of prostitutes," as Grossino wrote the noble lady Gonzaga in January, 1512. How lovely!

On to the Church of St. Lawrence with the graves of that saint and of St. Stephen and the stone that killed the first martyr.

Near by, on the Via Nomentana, the catacombs and the Church of St. Agnes. The lambs of St. Agnes furnish the wool of which the nuns of St. Agnes make a ribbon called the pall, which the pope blesses and then sells at a fancy figure; every new archbishop of Mainz, for instance, has to pay 27,000 gulden for this bit of wool. No, we did not crack the feeble joke of pulling the wool over the

MANY POPES BURIED IN THE CATACOMBS OF CALIXTUS

people's eyes, although good old Catholic Max did growl the pope's income was a hundred times greater than the Kaiser's.

We enter the southern section of the city. See the gleaming cross on St. John Lateran? That cross was wrought from the sword that beheaded St. Paul. Within is the grave of the Apostle John; the table at which he said mass on Patmos; the coat with which he raised two dead; the cup from which he drank poison without harm; the shears that sheared his first tonsure; crumbs of the five barley loaves that fed the five thousand; some branches of the burning bush Moses saw in the wilderness; the Ark of the Covenant with the two stone tables with the Holy Ten Commandments; the rod with which Moses smote the rock to give water to the thirsting Israelites in the wilderness; the table of Christ's Last Supper; the ointment bottle out of which Mary Magdalene anointed the body of our Lord; the hood of Joseph of Arimathea; a remnant of the Virgin's veil; the rod with which Christ was scourged; the knife for His circumcision, etc., etc.

In the Baptistry two columns of Mary's house in Nazareth; two

ST. VERONICA

alabaster pillars with leaden crosses that had served as torch holders on the house of Pilate; the red stone trough in which Emperor Constantine had planned to gather the blood of innocent children to cure his leprosy.

In the palace a door from Pilate's house through which Christ entered; on four columns stands the stone on which the thirty pieces of silver were counted out to Judas Iscariot for betraying our Savior; also the stone on which the soldiers divided among themselves the garments of Christ after His crucifixion. Under an arch the two oldest bells in the world.

On to Holy Cross Church, or Jerusalem, because of the pieces of the true cross of Christ, which Helena, mother of Constantine, had brought from Jerusalem; a piece of the cross of the penitent thief; the inscription on the cross; one of the nails of the cross; the sponge with which Christ was given drink on the cross; eleven thorns from His crown; the rope with which He was dragged to His passion; a sapphire with water and blood from His side; another with hair of the blessed Virgin Mary.

Here is the story the guidebook tells of Pope Sylvester II. When a poor boy, he made over his soul to the devil if made pope, to be delivered when he read mass in Jerusalem, to be captured with the help of the Emperor Otto III. Forgetting Holy Cross Church is also called Jerusalem, the pope goes in to read mass, the devil nabs him and carries him off, all except the heart.

Near Holy Cross Church Luther saw a statue of Popess Joanna, who had given birth to a boy in the open street in a public procession. This tale was confirmed by a favorite of Leo X and was considered history by papal scholars. What a light that throws on the morals of the popes! Luther wondered why the pope did not remove the scandalous statue. Pope Sixtus V did remove it in 1585.

Into the middle of the town, to Santa Maria Maggiore with a grave of St. Matthew; some relics of the Virgin Mary and of St. Jerome; the jawbone of Zacharias; an arm of St. Luke; a famous picture of the Virgin; the manger, the swaddling clothes, and hay from the stable in which Christ was born at Bethlehem. The panels were decorated with the first gold brought from America.

We cross the Tiber to the Vatican Hill, once the property of Nero, where was the circus in which Peter was crucified head down, as they say. On a portion of this circus wall Emperor Constantine reared St. Peter's Cathedral, rebuilding since 1506.

Thirty-eight steps up to the vestibule, and seven years' indulgence for each step gone up with devotion.

Right at the entrance one of the thirty pieces of silver for which Judas betrayed Christ; one reverent look at the coin instantly brings you indulgences for no less than 14,000 years! Have a look! To the left is the chapel in which Peter said his first mass in Rome; just give it one good look, and you get indulgence for 7,000 years. In the wall near the Golden Gate the stone rolled before Christ's grave. In the chapel to the left the graves of Simon and Jude; from a column hangs the rope with which Judas hanged himself. Silver stars show the place in the wall behind which is the sanctuary of Saints Peter and Paul; kiss these stars and get indulgences for 17,000 years! Above is the Holy Sacrament, turned into blood when Pope Gregory said mass. Next the brazen dish in which Pilate washed his hands; fourteen columns from Solomon's Temple;

the grave of Petronella, St. Peter's daughter; the altar with the other half of the bodies of Peter and of Paul.

In the Chapel of St. Martin the bronze statue of St. Peter "stretching out his foot to be kissed, and the one kissing that foot has all the grace he would have for kissing the pope's foot."

A stone with a groove as wide as two fingers — made by the tears Peter wept for denying Christ. We do not bat an eye.

"Two red marble columns that stood in Pilate's house in a window where he stood Christ after the scourging and showed Him to the Jews and said, *'Ecce homo,'* See the Man, and between the two columns a small window through which He looked upon St. Peter."

The Veronica. What's that? When Christ was bearing His cross through the streets of Jerusalem, a kindhearted woman wiped the sweat off His face and, lo and behold! His face was printed on the handkerchief; and this Veronica, which means true image, is right here and shown on a written permit of the Holy Father. How did it get here? The guidebook tells us. Emperor Tiberius had leprosy and sent messengers to Jesus for help, but Pilate had just crucified Jesus. Pilate was arrested, and St. Veronica was brought to Rome and cured Tiberius of his leprosy. We do not move a muscle and reverence the handkerchief, though all we can see is "a black board, with nothing on it."

"When they show the face of our dear Lord Jesus Christ, the Romans earn 7,000 years indulgence, those from around Rome 8,000 years indulgence, but those coming across the mountain or ocean earn 12,000 years indulgence as often as they see it."

That immense mansion over there? That is the Vatican, the pope's house. Just now the mighty master Michelangelo is putting his wonderful paintings on the ceiling of the Sistine Chapel, while the young genius Raphael, born in the same year as Luther, is painting himself immortal in the Stanza della Segnatura.

These four colossal columns, already arched? They are to bear the cupola of the new St. Peter's Church, on which Bramante is now at work for Pope Julius II. It will cost about $50,000,000. Ah! and oh! That is a lot of money; where does the pope get it? That is another story, which we shall hear anon.

At the end of our pilgrimage we receive Holy Communion at

St. Peter's and then drink from the fountain "whose water flowed through the ground holding the bones of the saints." A fine drink, holy and wholesome. To our cloister, weary, but happy.

Surely, those old-timers were not so slow. That fast pace on a fast day would do credit to your globe-trotter from U.S.A.

"St. John Lateran is the chief church of the whole world. The indulgence there can be counted by no one but God. I said a mass or ten at Rome and was almost sorry my father and mother were still living; for I would have gladly freed them out of purgatory with my masses and other good works and prayers. At Rome there is a saying [by Pope Boniface]: 'Happy is the mother whose son says a mass at St. John's on a Saturday'; how gladly would I have made my mother happy [out of purgatory]! But the crowd was too dense, and I could not get to an altar, and I ate a smoked herring."

But he saw the heads of the Apostles. "When they were shown, you had as much grace and indulgence as when they show the Veronica in Saint Peter's Minster." He saw the grave of John the Evangelist, "the purple dress our Lord Jesus Christ had on when Pilate said, *'Ecce homo,'* and the veil His dear mother had laid around Him on the cross, and the shirt of Christ, and the towel with which our Lord Jesus Christ dried the feet of His disciples." He saw the altar at which John read mass, the Ark of the Covenant of the Old Testament, the rod of Moses, the table of the Lord's Supper, the stone on which the soldiers gambled for the clothing of Christ. He heard "the first bells; the people say, 'Come from heaven.'"

In a chapel they showed a stone with an impression of a hand of Mary. "Mary, the mother of God, when told her Son, Jesus Christ, was a prisoner, fainted and would hold herself on the stone, and the mark remained in the stone." An old scoffer wrote, "She must have grabbed hard."

On the north side of the Lateran palace is the Chapel Sancta Sanctorum with the marble staircase from Pilate's house in Jerusalem. Jesus walked up these steps, and Luther crawled up on his knees. At every step he prayed the Lord's Prayer and had nine years' indulgence for every step — Pope Leo IV said so. The step on which Jesus broke down is marked with a cross, and on this step

SCALA SANTA,
PILATE'S STAIRCASE

Luther got a double indulgence, eighteen years. Twenty-eight steps to the top, and Grandfather Heine was out of purgatory. O joy!

Paul Luther says his father thought of "The just shall live by faith" when crawling up the stairs; but Paul was only eleven when he heard it in 1544, and he wrote it down thirty-eight years later. If so, it was only a passing thought and made no change in Martin at that time.

Did he admire the wonderful statue of Emperor Marcus Aurelius in front of the church? People thought it was Emperor Constantine.

St. Pancras on the Janiculus Hill, where "they showed the saint bodily and also martyrs without number."

Not far from his cloister is St. Silvestro in Capite, where the head of John the Baptist is revered. Later Luther read in Theodoret the heathen had burned the body of John the Baptist, and he is furious at having been led to reverence a fake.

Near by is S. Pietro in Montorio with the famous Tempietto by Bramante, built in 1502 by Ferdinand and Isabella in memory of the martyrdom of St. Peter.

"The mountain called Tarpejus is higher than the Aventine. The Theatrum is built round, fifteen steps high, seats 200,000 people. The walls and foundation still exist. The warm baths of Diocletian, led 25 German miles from Neapolis, a splendid house."

St. Mary's Church on the Ara Coeli, with a picture of the Virgin painted by St. Luke; near by another of her pictures by the same St. Luke in the San Francesca Romana at the Roman Forum; still another by the same diligent St. Luke in St. Augustine's Church, recently built by Cardinal d'Estoutville for Luther's order; still another by the same St. Luke in Santa Maria del Popolo, where Luther was living; still another, the most famous of all, the "Acheiropoiita," "Made without hands," for Luke but sketched it, and the next morning it was finished. Wonderful? Not at all; angels had done it, that's all.

"The building of the church, S. Peter's Minster, took over thirteen hundred years. A great sum of money was spent on it. The pope commanded the angels to take at once into heaven without sin the souls of those dying on the way to Rome. For this reason John Hus wrote against the pope he had no power to command the angels. So enormously grew the tyranny of the Roman popes."

"Tiberius, the heathen kaiser, a moral monster, as Suetonius writes, was an angel compared with the doings of the Roman court. . . . Therefore they said, 'If there is a hell, Rome is built on it.' Even courtiers said, 'It can't go on like this; it's got to break.' Among other loose talk at table I heard courtiers laugh and tell how some say mass and say of the bread, 'Bread you are, and bread you remain.' It nauseated me that they could say mass helter-skelter as if acting a farce. For before I got to the Gospel, the other priest had finished and bellowed, *'Passa, passa* — Away! Get out and return Mary's Son to her.' They could say six or seven masses before I one; they took money, I none. In summa, in Italy there is no disgrace but to be poor."

At the Porta Flaminia stood a big nut tree in which devils lived, who broke off the heads of people and animals that passed the gate, and all Rome was helpless. The Virgin Mary told Pope Paschalis to fell the tree and build a church in her honor.

In a huge procession the people went to the Porta Flaminia, the pope made the first axe stroke and "grubbed the whole tree out of the earth; there, under the tree they found a coffin, wherein lay the body of the bad Nero." Paschalis had Nero's body and the tree burned to powder, banned all devils that had lived in the tree, built a church, and called it Maria del Popolo, "because there were so many people there, and granted an indulgence of 2,000 years and 213 'karein.'" Sixtus V added to these graces.

The church had a wonderful treasure, a Madonna painted by St. Luke himself. It was "successfully invoked by Gregory XIII in a great plague and adored by the popes on September 8 till 1870. Pinturicchio decorated the church with his famous frescoes. The chaplain of the Cardinal of Sta. Sabina, the Florentine Francesco Albertini, in his guidebook calls attention to the paintings and statues in the many chapels of Maria del Popolo. Luther kneeled before these spiritual treasures, accepted graces, and edified himself with the legends.

Here, long ago, was buried Nero, worst of Roman emperors; and here, not long ago, was buried Alexander XI, worst of popes.

On Saturday, March 27, 1507, Pope Julius II slept in the cloister and on Sunday said mass in S. Maria del Popolo.

Naturally Luther was best pleased with the German church, Santa Maria dell' Anima, back of the Piazza Navona, on whose plans the great Bramante worked. On April 11, 1500, the cornerstone was laid by the Roman envoy Matthew Lang, whom we'll meet again as the archbishop of Salzburg. The parson was Heinrich Bode, assisted by a half dozen German chaplains. About forty German and Dutch papal employees attended here, and it naturally became the meeting place of all German and Dutch residents and visitors. What pleased Luther most was that here both clergy and worshipers were so much more reverent than in the Italian churches, where his serious soul was severely shocked by the levity of both.

This church is built on earth brought from Calvary and is the smallest independent country, its independence guaranteed by Germany, Italy, and the Vatican. Here the German visitor could hear stories, Italian cloister stories.

Though France and Genoa put up 300,000 ducats to elect Julius Rovere, Alexander bought the papal chair by enormous bribes.

Infessura says with stinging irony, "Directly he became pope,

S. MARIA DELL' ANIMA
the German Church

Alexander VI proceeded to give away all his goods to the poor" — to pay his election debts.

He got back his money. Eighty new offices were created and sold for 760 ducats each. Nine cardinals were made for 120,000 to 130,000 each.

The poet Pontanus Maximus warbled,
   "Alexander sells the keys, the altars, even Christ Himself.
   Well, he bought them, so he has a right to sell them."
Another trilled,
   "Rome was great under Caesar, greater far under Alexander;
   The first was only mortal, but the latter is a god."

This god on May 4, 1493, divided America between Spain and Portugal and in 1498 burned godly Jerome Savonarola at Florence, and in 1502 Bernardino went up in flames.

He made Alexander Farnese a cardinal for the price of his sister, the *bella Julia*.

Luther mentions the Campo di Fiore, where stands the most beautiful palace in Italy, now the Palazzo Sforza-Cesarini, where lived Vanozza Cantanei, since 1460 the mistress of Pope Alexander VI, though married to three other men. She died on November 26, 1518, at the age of 76. Her tomb, with the names of the four children she bore to Alexander, was in the church of Santa Maria del Popolo. Alexander had three or five more children by other women, seven or nine children in all for the Holy Father, who committed incest with his own daughter Lucretia; whom he married off with great pomp publicly in the Vatican.

The pope's official Burkard reports in 1501 the pope gave a banquet in the Vatican on a high church festival at which fifty public women danced with the servants, first in their clothes and then naked, while the pope, Cesare, and Lucretia looked on.

King Charles of France kissed the hand and foot of this monster.

Lanciani has an unpublished epigram by a witness of the god's deeds as a man, as a ruler, and as a priest, in which all the seven deadly sins are distinctly charged to him.

An archbishop wrote this "Nero of the Papacy": "We shall ever regard thee as a second god on earth," the Catholic Lord Acton tells us in the *North British Review,* October, 1869, p. 134.

Ollivier praises this monster of vice as a true follower of Christ, but the *Civilta Catholica* of March 15, 1873, admits his vices.

He tried to poison Cardinal Hadrian for his much money, but by mistake took the poisoned confectionery himself and died.

Guicciardini reports, when this monster died, "all Rome ran with indescribable gladness to visit the corpse. Men could not satiate their eyes with feeding on the carcass of the serpent who, by his unbounded ambition and pestiferous perfidy, by every demonstration of horrible cruelty, monstrous lust, and unheard-of avarice, selling without distinction things sacred and profane, had filled the world with venom." — *Hare's Walks,* p. 593. They said the devil had come to fetch his soul.

After this god came another god. Pope Julius II paved his way to St. Peter's chair with an enormous amount of gold gulden and then sold offices and benefices to fill his empty pockets and simply took to himself the great wealth of the late Cardinal Melchior of Meckau.

In April, 1510, the Venetian Ambassador Domenico Trevisano reckoned the pope's regular income at 200,000 ducats, his fees

150,000 more, about $5,000,000; that of the thirty-three cardinals at 18,000 ducats each; but some had much more. With all his costly wars, buildings, paintings, sculptures, Julius II left about 400,000 ducats.

"He made the indulgence business a financial operation," confesses the Catholic Ludwig Pastor.

He was likened to the Neptune of Vergil.

He boasted with his right hand he commanded the angels of heaven, and with his left hand he drew souls out of purgatory, and his person was mingled with that of the Godhead.

The custom of kissing the god's toe on Good Friday had to be given up. Why? The god's foot was covered with sores of "the disease of the Curia." What's that? Syphilis. Who says so? His master of ceremonies.

The poet Baptista Mantuanus, Mantovano, publicly charged him with sodomy and pederasty, and Pope Leo XIII blessed the poet. The Catholic historian Prof. Dr. Ludwig Pastor admits Pope Julius II had a venereal disease and three illegitimate daughters.

Pasquino wrote: "Julius is at Rome — what is lacking? Ye gods, give us Brutus! For whenever Julius is in Rome, the city is lost."

Christopher Marcellus addressed this pope as "Not a mere man, but, as it were, God on earth."

Luther did not see the god. The good shepherd was laying down the lives of his sheep for his greater glory in his war up north in the Romagna. He led his troops into battle and swore at God for giving victory to the French and said, "Holy Swiss, pray for us!" "The terrible pope" they called him. Everybody that was anybody, of course, had followed him; only two cardinals were in town, one lying on his deathbed, the other lying in prison.

Rome was a city of the dead and also a dead city, very much smaller than in 1527, when it had only 9,285 houses.

Morally Rome was rotten. The census of 1517 counted more prostitutes than respectable women. The Spanish priest Francesco Delicado says in 1524 there were 30,000 prostitutes and 9,000 panderers. When Luther was there, Rome's most famous lady was Imperia de Cugnatis, in a sumptuously furnished palace in the aristocratic district, at the St. Angelo Bridge. Her guests were bankers, ambassadors, poets, artists, the Pope's librarian, the Cardinals Cornaro, Gonzaga, Sadoleto. She died August 15, 1512, thirty-one years old, and was buried as a noble matron in St. Gregory's Church, and the inscription on her tomb told you she was worthy of the great name of a Roman.

Would you like to see her picture? You can see it in the Pope's Vatican, in the Stanza della Segnatura, the Calliope by Raphael.

Certain cardinals were regarded as living saints because they were merely fornicators and did not practice unnatural vices, as many did. The dissolute monk Lippo Lippi painted his mistress Lucretia Buti, as the Virgin Mary to be revered and adored by devout Catholics, says the Catholic Professor Pastor, V, pp. 196, 197.

Most of the twenty Benedictine convents were wholly, or almost wholly, deserted. Cardinal Contarini curtly calls the cloisters houses of ill fame, and the Council of Trent closed most of them.

Very many priests could not even read, much less say mass. Only the begging friars would preach — during Advent and Lent, as Loyola writes on December 19, 1538. Rodriguez says the Romans were utterly astonished when the Jesuits began to preach regularly.

Vices were acknowledged without shame, and men even gloried in their shame.

Admiral Philip of Burgundy was in Rome in the spring of 1509 and says: "The heathen are chaster and purer than these men who lay down the laws of religion to the Christian nations." When the relics of St. Peter were shown at Easter, he heard "the chief cardinals" crack the most indecent jokes. Priest and Monk Erasmus was at Rome about this time and says, "I have with mine own ears heard the most horrible blasphemies of Christ and His Apostles"; priests of the papal court during mass were guilty of this.

Good Catholics like Michelangelo, Wimpfeling, Tizio Senese, and others handed these bouquets to Rome, "The mother and nurse of all vices, the slaughterhouse of virtue, the dive of lust, the dump of filth," etc.

Luther quotes the good poet Baptista Spagnuolo of Mantua, who sang, "We can buy temples, priests, altars, prayers, heaven, and even God."

Jules Michelet, member of the Institute of France: "Rome presented something which has at no other time been exhibited in history: a systematic and scientific perversity; a magnificent ostentation of wickedness; in a word, the atheist priest proclaiming himself monarch of the universe."

Lawyer William Samuel Lilly, secretary of the Catholic Union of Great Britain, admits: "The deities of the ancient Pantheon once more asserted their empire. Venus and Bacchus, nay, Priapus and Silenus, were worshiped with the truest cult. . . . It was an age of unblushing grossness and unrestrained debauchery. Religion and liberty seemed to be departing from the earth." — *Renaissance Types.*

Jesuit George Tyrrell writes: "I do not wonder that to Savonarola, and the medieval mystics, Rome seemed Antichrist. At present Christ is thrown and Antichrist is upmost." — *Autobiography*, pp. 407, 413. Longmans. 1912.

Jesuit Hartmann von Grisar mildly admits: "The Rome of that day was the Rome of Julius II, the then pope, and of his predecessor Alexander VI . . . inwardly deeply debased. . . ." There was "anxiety lest the godless spirit of the world should poison the very heart of the Church," I, p. 32.

May we indulge the charitable hope Rome was a horrible exception? Candid Catholics will not let us do so.

Professor Pastor says: "It is a mistake to suppose that the corruption of the clergy was worse in Rome than elsewhere." "In many places matters were far worse than in Rome." (*History of the Popes,* V, pp. 171, 172.)

Men said generally that things could not go on like this, that a break must come.

The breaker left Rome about the end of January, 1511.

The yellow Tiber was crossed on the Milvian Bridge, where Constantine saw the flaming cross with the words "In this sign you will conquer" and then in bloody battle conquered the forces of paganism and then became the first Christian emperor. Like a better Constantine, Luther was to see the cross of Christ and by that Gospel overcome the paganism in the Roman Church. Over this bridge Caesar and his legions marched to conquer the Germans; over this bridge marched the Germans and destroyed Old Rome; over this bridge the papal Romans marched to enslave the German Church; over this bridge now marched a German Romanist who was to strike a smashing blow at the Roman Antichrist and free the German Church and all others that would be free, for all time to come.

Of old the Saxon leader Hermann destroyed the Roman legions, and Augustus wailed, "Varus, Varus, give me back my legions!" Anew the Saxon leader Luther was to destroy the minions of Rome, and still the pope is wailing for the fair provinces lost to the Protestants. Far worse than Hannibal and Alaric and Genseric was to be this pale and pious pilgrim.

On his return Luther would say mass in Milan's famed cathedral, but "the priests told us, 'We are Ambrosians, you cannot say mass here.'"

From the time of St. Ambrose they said mass in a manner different from Rome. Luther was greatly surprised at this lack of complete unity in the Church.

Grisar suggests that in order to avoid the wars in Northern Italy, Luther returned through France, saying mass at Nice on January 20, guest of the Augustinian cloister at Pernes near Avignon, up the Rhone Valley.

Crossing the Apennine Mountains, Luther wended his way eastward to Cento and Mirandola, to Mantua, over the Brenner Pass to Innsbruck and then to Augsburg — "nothing compared with Nuernberg."

Here he saw Ursula Lamenit, a living saint, living on nothing but the Host! He had his doubts. "Ursel, see that everything is straight!"

Curious! John Eck in 1513 had the same doubts.

Sure enough, the living saint was found a fraud, living on gingerbread hid under her apron. On the plea of the Duchess of Bavaria she was not killed, only exiled; and she could keep the 1,500 gulden dupes had given her, and also "a young fellow."

About the middle of March our pilgrim was back in Erfurt.

"Since our Lord has brought me into the ugly business and game to write against the pope, I would not take a thousand gulden not to have seen Rome. I should always have worried I was doing the pope an injustice. But we speak what we have seen. . . . I, too, was such a crazy saint, ran through all the churches and caves, believed all the stinking lies."

Good Martin was a "good Christian," as the Italians called a fool.

THE AUGUSTINIAN CLOISTER
Called the Black Cloister, because the
Augustinian garb was black. It was built
of red brick. Luther lived on the
second floor, to the right of the tower

Chapter Four

LUTHER'S CONVERSION

Wittenberg in 1513 had 172 burghers with brew rights, 184 cottagers, 26 in the suburbs, 382 taxpayers, barely 2,000 people.

There were unions of butchers, bakers, tailors, weavers, shoemakers, teamsters.

John Cochlaeus in 1524 found "the heretical new Rome a stinking hole, filthy houses, filthy streets, a barbarian people doing only beer business, an unhealthy, disagreeable climate, without vineyards, etc., etc." He would not be popular with the Chamber of Commerce.

Though the famed universities of Erfurt and Leipzig were near, Elector Frederick the Wise in 1502 built another at Wittenberg. In the charter he said he and the neighboring princes "would repair thither as to an oracle, so that when we have come full of doubt, we may, after receiving sentence, depart in certainty."

At the dedication Dr. Fleck said Wittenberg would become the "berg of wit, wisdom, and life, *vita.*" We can see the pleased people congratulating the eloquent orator.

Petrus Ravennas, professor of law, in his inaugural in 1503 proved the pope carries all laws in the shrine of his heart, and to appeal from his decisions is simply laughable.

No modernism here.

The school opened with 416 students; it sank to 40. What do? Advertise, of course. Here is the prospectus for 1507:

"Those who are eager for knowledge should come to Wittenberg. The air is excellent, the plague is entirely past, a living is cheap, costing only eight gulden a year. There one can learn not only science, but also the best manners. The university, moreover, has received from pope and emperor all the privileges and advantages enjoyed by the most ancient schools, and one may be assured that not even Padua or Bologna, the mother of them all, possesses a greater number of learned men."

And in the first years the degrees cost nothing! That ought help some.

Professor Andrew Meinhardi said the university breathed the spirit of old Rome. Roman language, Roman cultural ideals, Roman poets were studied exclusively. Why, were one to rise from the dead, he would think glorious ancient Rome had been transplanted to Wittenberg!

Professor Christopher Scheurl of aristocratic Nuernberg found his new fellow citizens "rude, drunken, and gluttonous," but from a wretched, muddy, unholy, fameless, boorish dorp Wittenberg had become a rich and famous city, yes, perhaps the most famous city. He dreamed to "make out of the academy a Bologna, out of the city a Nuernberg."

The famous Giordano Bruno later lectured here and found Wittenberg an Athens, Germany a Greece, and Luther the greatest ever.

Modern American real estate literature has nothing on that for — optimism.

Yet the vision came true.

Wittenberg was to become an ideal university, if President Gar-

Castle   City Church   Wittenberg University

field's idea of a university is correct — a log with Mark Hopkins at one end and himself at the other. In other words, a university does not consist of palatial buildings and broad athletic fields on Carnegie and Rockefeller foundations, but of men; and men were certainly coming to Wittenberg.

The greatest theologian of all times since the days of Paul came when Luther was sent there in 1511, and Philip Melanchthon, "the Preceptor of Germany," followed in 1518 — two stars of the first magnitude sparkling with undimmed brilliancy unto this present.

Luther found the people "unfriendly, impolite, without sense for finer and higher culture," and he writes of the "cold, high-minded, north wind of the Wittenberg learned world," and he wondered why a university should be planted "on the border of civilization."

In those rough times and among those rough people, the students were a rough lot. In 1511, the year Luther came, the city had to pay a fine of 2,000 gulden to remove the ban placed by the bishop of Brandenburg for insults offered his court by students. The year before, Rector Scheurl had to check drunkenness and forbid gun, sword, and dagger to the students. In 1512 another rector was assassinated by the students, and even the gentle Melanchthon once barely escaped with his life.

In September, 1511, Staupitz called Luther to sit by him under the pear tree in the cloister garden and said, "Herr Magister, you must preach, so that you'll get something to do."

Luther quickly had no fewer than fifteen reasons why he did not want to preach.

"My dear fellow, don't try to be wiser than the whole convent and the fathers."

Willy-nilly, Luther preached.

"No one believes how frightened one is the first time he enters the pulpit. He sees so many heads before him. Oh, how I feared the pulpit! Still I had to go in. They forced me to preach to the monks" in the dining hall. Such was the beginning of the world's greatest preacher.

Next he preached from the low pulpit of rough boards in the 20 by 30 frame chapel so rickety it had to be braced, reminding Myconius of the stable at Bethlehem.

During the illness of the pastor of St. Mary's, or the City Church, brother of the famous Chancellor Brueck, the city elected Luther to fill the pulpit, and he often preached daily, and even three and four times a day, and soon that became his happiest hour. Later on colleagues Martin Pollich, Jerome Schurf, Spalatin with his princely pupils, and Duke John were among his hearers; Elector Frederick heard him in 1512.

Again under the famous pear tree Staupitz ordered Luther to get his degree of Doctor of Theology.

"Herr Staupitz, you'll kill me; I'll not last a quarter of a year."

"That's all right, Martin. It seems our Lord is going to have big business. For that He will need good advisers. Should you die, you will get into His council, for He must also have some doctors."

How answer the unanswerable?

Willy-nilly, Martin had to study for his degree.

May 2—8 Brother Martin went to a meeting of his Order at Koeln and greatly admired the wonderful cathedral, built to house

ST. MARY'S, or CITY CHURCH

the relics of the Wise Men from the East, Caspar, Melchior, and Balthasar, which he reverently adored.

When we were there in 1927, the cleric was quite cautious. He said, "Tradition tells us these are the relics." He did not show us the relics, but only the jewel-encrusted reliquaries — for a fee.

Martin had a glass of Rhine wine — "smooth as oil and going to the fingertips." He was elected subprior, and as such the director of studies of the monks. For the first time he got a cell in the tower, which could be warmed — his study for the rest of his life. He studied Greek and read Augustine's *Trinity* and *City of God*.

On October 4 Luther was recommended for the doctor's degree. On the 8th he went to Leipzig to get the fifty gulden for the doctor's fee, given by the elector, induced by the promise of Staupitz. Luther would for life fill the "lectura in Biblia," hitherto held by Staupitz himself. On the 17th notices on the church doors told the promotion would take place on the 18th. At 1 P.M. in the Castle Church, Carlstadt presided over the great debate between the Bachelors of Arts and another between the Masters of Arts. The new

Licentiate swears to defend the Gospel. At 7 A. M. on the 19th the great bell is ringing, and the procession of professors and guests is wending its way through the decorated streets to the Castle Church. Carlstadt makes a speech; Luther takes the oath; Carlstadt gives him a closed Bible and then an open Bible; places the hat of pure wool on his head, a silver ring on his finger, and the kiss of peace on his cheek.

The new Doctor of Theology delivers an oration on the Glory of the Bible from Luke 21:15. His two "fighting cocks," Wenceslaus Link, prior of the Augustinians, and Nicholas Grueneberg, pastor of the City Church, debate in his honor. The benediction ends the celebration at 10 P. M.

On the 22d he was formally received into the Senate, the five professors of the faculty.

In a sermon on May 21, 1537, Luther said, "When I was made a Doctor, I did not yet know the light."

While Ponce de Leon was seeking the fountain of youth in Florida in 1512 and Vasco Núñez de Balboa from a peak in Darien was discovering the Pacific Ocean, Luther was seeking the divine fountain of eternal life and the ocean of divine love.

The monks rather prided themselves on the fact that their latest recruit was a Master of Arts from the great University, and converted by lightning from heaven like St. Paul, as Father John Nathin told the wondering nuns of Muehlheim.

On entering the cloister, Luther picked twenty-one saints, and daily prayed to three, and thus weekly made his rounds without slighting any. He received the Lord's Supper at least sixteen times a year.

He kept the canonical hours. At each hour there were Psalms or canticles; antiphons; responsories; hymns; lessons from the Bible, acts of the saints, fathers of the Church, legends of the saints; versicles; little chapters; collects — prayers.

All this was done at Prime, 6 A. M.; Terce, 9 A. M.; Sext, noon; None, 3 P. M.; Vespers, 6 P. M.; Compline, at nightfall; Vigils — watches or wakes — 9 P. M.; midnight; 3 A. M. — the three Nocturnes. Some recited the 150 Psalms every week, some every day.

"When I had much to do and could not keep these canonical hours, I locked myself in my cell for three days or a week, ate and drank nothing, till I had prayed to make up for the lost time, and prayed so long that I was sick unto death."

"In my cloister there was a Doctor who was absent a quarter of a year, and when he came back and the prayer debts had grown so large he could not manage, he hired two and gave each several gulden to help him pray, to get through with it the sooner. — Yes, it was a regular prison and purgatory in which we were tortured. About that you know nothing."

The other monks held Luther a living saint, says Dungersheim, an enemy. In 1549 Cochlaeus, "the Scourge of Luther," admitted Luther for four years at Erfurt "fought strenuously for God in studies and spiritual exercises." Erasmus, monk and priest, the leader of the literati, in 1519 wrote Cardinal Wolsey, the personal representative of Leo X, "God on earth," and himself "seven times more powerful than the pope": "The man's life is approved by the unanimous consent of all, and the fact that his character is so upright that even enemies find nothing to slander must considerably prejudice us in his favor."

On the word of three such men we may well believe Luther when he says: "It is true, I was a pious monk and kept the rules so strictly that I may say, If ever a monk got to heaven by his monkery, I, too, would have got there, as all monks knowing me will bear me witness; for, had it lasted longer, I should have killed myself with vigils, praying, reading, and other work."

And yet he wailed, "Oh! when will you be pious and do enough that God will be merciful to you?" All in vain! "Not once, with all masses, prayers, chastity, did I succeed in being able to say, 'Now I am sure God is gracious to me,' or, 'Now I have tried it and found that my order and my rigorous life has helped me on to heaven.'"

In a letter to Staupitz he wailed like a lost soul, "My sin, sin, sin!" Even Staupitz could not cure his conscience.

Luther was in despair. He could not be saved by his good works. Why could he not be saved by faith in Christ?

"I did not know Christ other than a severe judge, from whom I would flee and could not flee. . . . I so hated Christ that, when I saw His picture as hanging on the cross, I feared it, and cast down my eyes, and had rather seen the devil. For my heart was all poisoned by this papistic teaching that I had soiled my baptismal gown, and lost Christ and Baptism, and now had to save myself."

William Wetmore Story writes: *"Per Cristo* is the Italian's oath of hatred and revenge . . . and the reason is very simple. Christ is to him the judge and avenger of all, and so represented in every picture he sees, from Orgagna's and Michelangelo's *Last Judgment."* — *Roba di Roma,* p. 319.

This is the wretched pass to which Rome's false doctrine of salvation by good works brought the sincere soul of Luther; it drove him to despair and to the brink of hell. Being without Christ, he was without God and without hope. This is thy handiwork, O Rome! "When the need is highest, Then the help is nighest."

The new Doctor of Theology at once prepared himself to lecture on the Psalms, but at once was halted by "the righteousness of God."

Difficulties are made to be overcome. Labor conquers all things.

"With a burning desire to understand Paul, I took up the Epistle to the Romans. But in the very first chapter there opposed me the word: 'The righteousness of God is revealed in the Gospel.' (Rom. 1:16, 17.) You see I hated the word, 'the righteousness of God,' for, owing to the teaching of my former professors, I held it that attribute of holy God according to which He punishes the sinners. Though I lived a blameless monk, my restless conscience nevertheless told me I was a sinner before God. And for that reason I hated a righteous God punishing sinners. I rebelled against God. . . . My conscience was wounded, I gnashed inwardly, and yet ever came back to that verse, for I would by all means get the sense of Paul. At last, thinking over the matter for days and nights, God showed me mercy and the connection of these words with the sentence following: 'The just shall live by faith.' I began to understand the righteousness of God here is the one a pious man receives from God by faith as a gift. I saw the meaning of the verse to be: 'Through the Gospel is revealed that righteousness of God by which the merciful God declares the believers righteous.' For that is the sense given it by the words following: 'The one justified by faith shall live.' Now I felt myself newborn and in Paradise. All the Holy Scriptures looked different to me. And now I ran through it and sought similar expressions to confirm by them my understanding of the words, 'righteousness of God.' Ere this these words to me were hateful, now I embraced them with the intensest love. This passage in Paul appeared to me as the gate of Paradise."

The most important bit of autobiography since the days of Paul; ponder it.

1. "I hated a righteous God punishing sinners."

The carnal mind is enmity against God. Eph. 2:15; Rom. 8:7; 7:14.

Paul was a persecutor, but he obtained mercy. 1 Tim. 1:13-16; Tit. 3:3; Acts 9:4; 22:7; 26:14; Phil. 3:6.

2. "God showed me mercy."

According to His abundant mercy God hath begotten us again ... saved us. 1 Pet. 1:3; 1 Tim. 3:5.

"By grace are ye saved ...; and that not of yourselves; it is the gift of God, not of works, lest any man should boast." Eph. 1:7; 2:4-9; Rom. 3:24-30; 6:23; 2 Cor. 9:15.

Here is the great Lutheran principle — *Grace Alone!*

And we rejoice —

"By grace I'm saved, grace free and boundless."

"Grace, 'tis a charming sound."

3. "God showed me the connection of the words. . . ."

Luther was "taught of God," no one else. John 6:45; Is. 54:13.

Of his own will God begat us with the Word of truth ... born again by the Word of God ... the engrafted Word is able to save your souls. ... In Christ Jesus I have begotten you again through the Gospel ... the power of God unto salvation. ... Ye trusted in Christ, after that ye heard the Word of truth, the Gospel of your salvation. ... The holy Scriptures are able to make you wise unto salvation. 1 Pet. 1:3-5, 19, 23; 2:24; 3:18; 2 Tim. 3:15-17; Rom. 1:16; 8:2; Eph. 1:13; 1 Cor. 1:21; 4:15; 2 Cor. 3:6; Gal. 4:19; John 1:12, 13; 6:63. Faith cometh by the Word of faith, the Word of God. Rom. 10:8, 17; Gal. 3:2, 5, 6; 1 Cor. 1:2, 3; Acts 2:42; 14:27; 17:34; 28:28.

Luther studied that Word of faith and by it came to faith.

"It is in and through the Word that the Spirit comes and gives faith to whomsoever He wills."

"In the true preaching of the Word the Spirit is present and impresses the Word on the heart, so that every pious preacher is a parent who, by the ministry of the Word, generates and forms Christ in us through trust in Him."

Here is another great Lutheran principle — *Scripture Alone!*

And so we sing —

> Lord, open Thou my heart to hear,
> And through Thy Word to me draw near.
> Thy Word doth deeply move the heart,
> Thy Word doth perfect life impart,
> Thy Word my soul with joy doth bless,
> Thy Word brings peace and happiness.

4. "This passage in Paul appeared to me as the gate of Paradise. . . . I felt myself newborn and in Paradise."

"He that believeth . . . shall be saved." Mark 16:16; John 3:18; Rom. 10:9.

"Believe on the Lord Jesus Christ, and thou shalt be saved." Acts 16:31; 13:39; Rom. 1:16, 17; 3:22, 28; 4:24; Gal. 3:22.

Like Abraham, Luther believed God, and it was counted to him for righteousness. Rom. 4:3-5, 16, 24; Gal. 3:9, 11, 14; John 7:39.

"Justified by faith, we have peace with God through our Lord Jesus Christ . . . and rejoice in hope of the glory of God." Rom. 5:1, 2, 11; Eph. 2:14-17; Col. 1:20; Phil. 4:4; 3:1; 2:17, 18.

Here is the third great Lutheran principle — *Faith Alone!*

And we sing, as my hope, so

> My faith is built on nothing less
> Than Jesus' blood and righteousness.
> I dare not trust the sweetest frame,
> But wholly lean on Jesus' name.
>
> I cling to what my Savior taught
> And trust it, whether felt or not.
>
> Thy Word first made me feel my sin,
>   It taught me to believe;
> Then, in believing, peace I found,
>   And now I live, I live!
>
> Believing, we rejoice
>   To see the curse remove;
> We bless the Lamb with cheerful voice
>   And sing His bleeding love.

Luther, too, was an apostle, not of men, neither by man, but by Jesus Christ, and God the Father, who raised Him from the dead. As it pleased God to reveal His Son in Paul, so it pleased God to reveal His Son in Luther. Gal. 1:1, 16.

Luther was born, not of blood, nor of the will of the flesh, nor of the will of man, but of God. John 1:13.

Columbus found a new world, Copernicus found a heaven, Luther found a new God, a God gracious in Christ. If God be for us, who can be against us? Rom. 8:31-39.

Now his happy heart turned his lips to sing his "tower experience," his spiritual autobiography, in his deathless hymn —

> Dear Christians, one and all rejoice,
> With exultation springing,
> And with united heart and voice
> And holy rapture singing.

He was holy and happy, good and gay, pious and joyous. His motto was —

> The Christian's heart still walks on roses,
> E'en when the Lord a cross imposes.

In this "tower experience" we have a clear television of the dramatic rebirth of Luther and at the same time of the birth of the Reformation and the whole world of Protestantism.

Old Archimedes cried, "Give me a place to stand, and I'll move the earth!" In Rom. 1:16-17 God gave Luther a place to stand, and he moved the world.

William Ewart Gladstone, "the Grand Old Man," judges: Justification "for Luther was the note and test of life or death. . . . There came upon Christendom, initiated by the bravery of Luther, a powerful impulse, which passed into a mighty struggle . . .; but it resulted in a new state of things."

Lawyer William Samuel Lilly, secretary of the Catholic Union of Great Britain, in his *Renaissance Types* writes: "Of the greatness, the titanic greatness, of the man there can be no question. The greatness of the revolution wrought by him is manifest to all. We may, with strict accuracy, ascribe to him the Protestant reformation and all that came of it. Evangelical Protestantism . . . is Luther's creation. . . . Luther's revolution was the salvation of the Papal Church."

With his new and true understanding of "the righteousness of God" Luther began his lectures on the Psalms on July 12.

How? We now know how. In 1884 they found his copy, full of notes, faulting other commentaries, striking new notes. With his understanding of Paul he opposed Augustine, Thomas Aquinas, Duns Scotus, William of Occam, the whole intellectual world.

"Unless you labor and pray to spread among the people a holy fear for the Gospel your time and labor is lost." As professor, as preacher, as vicar he stressed the Bible; in it he lived and moved and had his being. "What the pasture is to the herd, a house to man, a nest to the bird, a rock to the chamois, a stream to the fish, that the Bible is to the faithful souls."

Martin Pollich of Mellerstadt, M. D., Ph. D., D. D., according to Mathesius "one of the greatest lights of the world," the father and first rector of the university, visited the classroom of the new Doctor. What was his impression? "This brother has deep eyes and will have wonderful fancies. That monk will confound all the learned doctors, propound a new doctrine, and reform the whole Roman Church; for he studies the writings of the Prophets and Evangelists; he relies on the words of Jesus Christ, and no one can subvert that either with philosophy or with sophistry."

So reported by Brother Walter Pollich.

In his funeral sermon on Luther, Justus Jonas quotes him: "Take care of this young monk. He has an excellent, keen mind, the like of which I have not met in all my life; he will surely become an excellent man."

Another visitor was Master Balthasar Vach. What had he to say? He said very picturesquely, "That monk will set up the devil as abbot."

At least the new Doctor was no Professor Dryasdust.

Towards the end of 1513 Elector Frederick's chaplain, George Burkhardt of Spalt, Spalatinus, rates Doctor Martin "an excellent man and scholar, whose judgment I value very highly."

When the great scholar Reuchlin was in danger of his life from the bloodthirsty Hoogstraten and other Dominicans, Luther in a letter to Spalatin in February, 1514, boldly broke a lance for the great Hebraist, when many liberals feared to give an opinion for fear of the consequences. Reuchlin was defended in 1515 in the famous *Letters of Obscure Men,* which mercilessly scourged the ignorance and vices of the clergy. Europe roared. The refined saint Sir Thomas More praised them to the skies, and the elegant Erasmus burst something or other and almost died laughing. Luther, however, was disgusted with the vulgarity. Where the Humanists had sneers and jeers, he had tears.

On March 3 Spalatin wrote John Lang at Erfurt: "I think so much of him as a most learned and upright man, and, what is extremely rare, one of such keen judgment that I wish to be entirely his friend." So wrote Christopher Scheurl and others.

In May Staupitz ordered Luther to preach at the meeting of the Order at Gotha. He preached against the vice of slander so common among the monks, "the little saints."

Did they mob him? They honored him: they elected him vicar of their eleven cloisters.

Humanist Canon Conrad Mut, Mutianus Rufus, heard of the sensational sermon and asked about him. John Lang wrote the information, said he had not "put rouge on it," and owned his debt to the preacher.

In 1515 Luther lectured on Romans.

John Oldecop of Hildesheim wrote: "I was twenty-one years old then — April 16 — and liked to hear Martin's lectures on the Psalms and Paul's Letters. I also went to all his sermons. The students heard him gladly, because he gave all the Latin words so well in German." He "already had many hearers. He was fiery in the pulpit and denounced sin, as it is right, without fear or favor." On All Saints' Day the girls attended the students' banquet and behaved unseemly, and Luther thundered from the pulpit "so hard and sharp, that the parents after that kept their marriageable daughters at home. For that he received from the best burghers laud, honor, and praise."

Oldecop wrote this in his *Chronikon* in his old age, 1563, when a bitter enemy.

"Luther's Preface to the Epistle to the Romans" was Englished by W. W. Loudon 1575 (?) and often reprinted.

LUTHER PREACHING CHRIST CRUCIFIED
By *Lucas Cranach, the Predella of the Altar Piece
in St Mary's, the City Church*

John Wesley confessed, "I was (fundamentally) a Papist and knew it not." — *Journal* I, 418.

"I went to America to convert the Indians; but, oh, who shall convert me?"

Luther, in his Preface to Romans, "about a quarter before nine" in the evening, Sunday, May 22, 1738. — *Journal,* May 24, 1738.

"Who has wrote more ably on justification by faith alone than Luther?"

About 1900 Johannes Ficker found Luther's copy of his lectures on Romans, full of notes, in the State Library at Berlin and edited the wonderful find in 1908, and Pastor Eduard Ellwein turned it into German in 1927.

On October 26, 1516, he wrote his old friend and Greek teacher, John Lang at Erfurt: "I need a couple of private secretaries, as I do almost nothing the livelong day but write letters. . . . I am convent preacher, the director of the studies of the monks, the reader at meals, am asked to preach daily in the City Church, am district vicar (that is, eleven times prior), business manager of our fish farm at Leitzkau, lawyer in our case against the Herzbergers now pending at Torgau, lecturer on St. Paul, assistant lecturer on the Psalter.

Rarely have I time for my hours of prayer, in addition to my own temptations of the world, the flesh, and the devil. See what an idle fellow I am. . . . I begin tomorrow to lecture on Galatians, though I fear the plague will not allow me to finish the course. The plague takes off two or at most three in one day, and that not every day. . . . You would persuade me to flee to you; but shall I flee? I hope the world will not come to an end when Brother Martin dies. I shall send the brothers away if the plague gets worse; I am stationed here and may not flee because of my vow of obedience, until the same authority which now commands me to stay shall command me to go. Not that I do not fear the plague (for I am not the Apostle Paul, but only a lecturer on him), but I hope the Lord will deliver me from my fear."

Faithful, though fearful, at the post of duty, like the Roman soldier at Pompeii who saw the stream of fiery lava from Vesuvius coming on to overwhelm him and yet stood faithful unto death, because he had been put there and had not been called away.

Towards the end of 1516 he wrote a friend: "Pray for me, for I confess to you that day by day my life draws near to death, for I daily grow worse and more miserable."

During Lent, 1517, Luther preached on the Lord's Prayer, which John Schneider, Agricola, printed. "Through Luther's writings and the Holy Ghost I became born again and a believing Christian." After Luther's death he paid a very fine tribute to "that man of God."

It was put into Bohemian and Italian. At Venice the censor cried: "Blessed the hands that have written it! Blessed the eyes that see it! Blessed the hearts that believe it and thus pray to God!"

Beatus Rhenanus urged Ulrich Zwingli to sell it from house to house. And this brought the Swiss under the influence of Luther.

Desiderius Erasmus, monk and priest, was patronized by the kaiser, four kings, and four popes. To hear biographer Professor Drummond say it, he was also "the greatest scholar of all time." Yet an unknown monk in "a mudhole on the border of civilization" wrote Spalatin, "I do not hesitate to differ with Erasmus," and begged him to tell the literary idol of Europe he was all wrong on the righteousness of God!

On March 1, 1517, he wrote John Lang: "I am reading our

Erasmus, and my opinion of him becomes daily worse. . . . The opinion of him who attributes something to man's will is far different from the opinion of him who knows nothing but grace." The keenest pair of eyes in Europe at once caught the world-wide difference.

In April, 1517, came his first printed work, in German, *Explanation of the Seven Penitential Psalms*—6, 32, 38, 51, 102, 130, 143. Before the last pages left the press, a second printing was needed, and then many more.

Justus Jonas wrote: "I confess that I owe you my life for your Psalter. I pray and conjure you for Christ's sake to neglect no opportunity to write to us." Himself a master of German, he yet confessed: "Compared with him we creep and stammer: he walks in erect as into an open sea and has the ocean, both of words and matter, out of which we drip droplets and are happy with the little dippers; he can do all things alone what all of us together cannot do." He likened him to Elijah, who drove the horses and chariot of Israel. 2 Kings 2:12.

On September 4, 1517, Luther presided at a debate of 97 theses "Against the Scholastic Theology," and enthroned Christ and dethroned Aristotle — in the realm of religion.

He had the theses printed and sent out. Erfurt and Leipzig and even Luther's own colleagues were angered by his attack on Aristotle, but in time Amsdorf, Schurf, and even Carlstadt were won over.

Christopher Scheurl wrote a great change in theological studies was in sight, and soon it would be possible to become a theologian without either Aristotle or Plato.

Luther wrote John Lang: "Our theology and Augustine prosper and rule now at our university. Aristotle is gradually going down hill, the lectures on the *Sentences* are discredited in an astounding manner. No one can any longer reckon on hearers unless he will lecture on the Bible or Augustine or some other recognized Church Father."

Was Luther right to fight Aristotle? Petrarch, "the Father of Humanism," "the First Modern Man," at Bologna found "Philosophy so prostituted to the fancies of the vulgar that it aims only at hairsplitting on subtle distinctions and quibbles of words. . . .

Truth is utterly lost sight of, sound practice is neglected, and the reality of things is despised. . . . People concentrate their whole attention upon empty words."

This at Bologna, held the head of all universities.

The poet is not alone.

Pope Pius II told the University of Vienna, "All your studies are beggarly and empty quibbles."

The French Catholic Nisard pungently styles the learning of that day "an amalgam of the corrupted tradition of Aristotle with the no less corrupted tradition of Christianity."

The author of the *History of the Council of Trent* tells us: "If it had not been for Aristotle, the Church had wanted for many articles of faith."

Yes, Luther was right in hating Aristotle, "the damned pagan," with a perfect hatred.

As Luther dethroned Aristotle in the realm of revealed religion, so Lord Bacon learned from Luther to dethrone Aristotle in the realm of natural science.

The *London Quarterly Review* of January, 1855: "October 31 should be a festive one in our calendar, as it is the birthday of the glorious Reformation, the rebaptism, in the laver of evangelical freedom, of the Gospel of Christ. There has been no day like it for nineteen hundred years, but the day of Pentecost, with its divine consecration and its converting power." Professor Froude of Oxford and many more say the same in similar strains.

Archdeacon Frederick W. Farrar: "As a reformer who altered the entire course of history, Luther alone resembles St. Paul. What the reformer did when he nailed his theses to the door of the cathedral of Wittenberg, that St. Paul did when he wrote his epistle to the Galatians. It was the manifesto of emancipation: it marked an epoch in history." — *St. Paul*.

Hegel wrote: "As the masterpiece of universal art, the Athene of Athens and her temple hill owed their origin to the money of the allies of Athens and led to the ruin both of Athens and her allies, so the finishing of the Church of St. Peter and of Michelangelo's Last Judgment, in the papal chapel, marked the day of doom for the proud edifice of the Papacy."

POSTING THE NINETY-FIVE THESES
From Castelar's "La Revolucion Religiosa"

Chapter Five

THE NINETY-FIVE THESES

Giovanni de' Medici, son of Lorenzo the Magnificent of Florence, was made an abbot at seven and a cardinal at fourteen. When he entered Rome by the Porta del Popolo, his father warned him against the wicked cardinals in the "very focus of all that was evil," who would "drag you down into the abyss into which they themselves have fallen."

In 1513 he became Pope Leo X and swore to reform his court from top to bottom.

"God has given us the papacy, let us enjoy it!" "This could only mean sensual pleasures," adds his biographer. His table cost

$18,400 per month. He daily gaily gambled at cards for high stakes.

In 1516 he stole the principality of Urbino from the rightful heir, and this little war cost him 700,000 ducats.

In 1517 Cardinal Petruzzi and others tried to murder the "god on earth," but were found out. To save their necks, they put money in his purse; Riario, for instance, alone paid the little nest egg of 150,000 ducats. In order to have a majority, Leo simply made thirty-one cardinals, who showed their fine sense of the fitness of things by putting 500,000 ducats into the pockets of the pope — when he wasn't looking.

He made 500,000 ducats a year by selling offices. Pasquino has Leo say, "Bring me gifts, spectators! Bring me not verses! Divine Money rules the ethereal gods!"

A lampoon runs: "Leo X devoured three pontificates: the treasure of Julius II, the revenues of his own reign, and that of his successor."

The Vicar of Christ attended the *Mandroga* and Ariosto's *Suppositi,* indecent plays. In 1514 he and Isabella Gonzaga witnessed Bibiena's *Calendra*—"glaringly immoral," says the *Catholic Encyclopedia.* Some of the Holy Father's friends were syphilitic, but the Milanese Chronicler Giovanni Andre Prato from respect for the Office of the Keys wished to keep silence about the pope. The humanist physician and philosopher Girolamo Fracastore wrote *Syphilis* and dedicated it to Cardinal Bembo, and the syphilitic "god on earth" in the Vatican recited the poem, describing the dread disease and its cure with mercury and sulphur and gave the poet a money reward.

Pietro Bembo lived with Morosina for twenty-four years, yet the Holy Father made him his private secretary and a cardinal, prince of the Church.

Mario Salomini, professor of law, dedicated to Leo a treatise complaining about simony, which prevailed, the war carried on by the pope, and the worldliness of the pope's court, and he warns the pope cannot escape the judgment of God.

Canon Sigismondo of Siena wrote: "Many were of opinion that it was bad for the Church that her head should be absorbed in amusements, music, the chase, and buffoonery, instead of being occupied by the thought of the needs of his flock, and bewailing its misfortunes. The salt of the earth has lost its savor, and nothing remains for it but to be cast out and trodden on by men."

When the Holy Father killed a number of cardinals, the good canon cried, "Now popes and cardinals have become antichrists!"

Poet Baptista of Mantua, Mantovano, asked the Vicar of Christ to reform his court, infected by a deep corruption which spread poison throughout all countries.

Cardinal Pucci said at the Lateran Council in 1516: "Rome, the Roman prelates, and the bishops sent out daily from Rome, we together are the causes of so many errors and corruptions in the Church. If we do not regain our good name, which is almost wholly lost, everything will be ruined." The dissolute but able Jerome Aleander told him thousands in Germany were only waiting the word to cry out against Rome.

In the session of March 16, 1517, a speaker pointed to the Gospel as the only source of wisdom and reform, but the council did not reform, it went on to deform.

"To thee is given all power in heaven and in earth," said the council to Pope Leo X, who said, "We, with the approbation of the present holy council, do renew and approve that holy constitution — the *Unam Sanctam* of Pope Boniface VIII."

"It is necessary for salvation that all human creatures be subject to the Roman pope."

The learned Catholic Ignaz von Doellinger comments mournfully: "The last hopes of a reform of the Church were carried to the grave."

Pico della Mirandola said to the Lateran Council in 1517: "If Leo leaves crime any longer unpunished, if he refuses to heal the wounds, it is to be feared that God Himself will no longer apply a slow remedy, but will cut off and destroy the diseased members with fire and sword."

"In that very year this oracular prediction was fulfilled," adds the Catholic Ludwig von Pastor, who says the pope's court was called "a great classical bacchanalia and a monstrous orgy of paganism."

To this Leo, Marcellus said at the council, "Thou art another god on earth."

When the god died, his heart was covered with dark, livid spots, and the spleen was wasted. The Romans laid the fault, as usual, on the pope's doctors. A servant was flung into prison for giving him poisoned wine.

What had been said to Pope Boniface VIII was repeated to Leo X: "You slipped in like a fox, you ruled like a lion, you died like a dog."

Sannazzaro celebrated his patron —
> Without the Church's Sacraments Pope Leo died, I'm told;
> What wonder? How could he enjoy what he himself had sold?

Margrave Albrecht of Brandenburg, a prince of Hohenzollern, in 1513 had himself elected Archbishop of Magdeburg when twenty-three, though the legal age was thirty. He had to bribe the pope for a permit to break the law, and also pay the regular fees for the pall — a strip of lamb's wool three fingers wide with crosses on it.

It was against the law to hold more than one office, yet in the same year Albrecht made himself administrator of Halberstadt. He had to pay the pope for a permit to break this law also.

In 1514 Albrecht had himself elected Archbishop of Mainz, the Primate of all Germany, and also one of the seven electors to choose the German kaiser.

Three great bishoprics held by one man, and that man too young to hold any!

Kaiser Karl V was coolly told cardinals had been made of children in the cradle!

Elector Joachim I of Brandenburg thought his brother's election was "plainly by divine inspiration"; but he was only a plain layman and couldn't know any better; the pope could not see it that way, not at all. So Joachim went to see the pope to make the crooked straight. Leo wanted 15,000 ducats to call it square; he went down to 12,000, "because there were twelve Apostles." Joachim quickly countered with seven, "because there were only seven deadly sins." The honors of this witty wordy warfare were about even, and so they split the difference on 10,000 ducats, which Albrecht was to pay out of his own pocket.

Alfred Baudrillart, rector of the Catholic Institute of Paris, says

Albrecht "employed the chief artists of his time, and rewarded them in princely style. He collected the most celebrated musicians from all parts, gave splendid entertainments, and made a dazzling display of pomp. But the religious convictions of this archbishop had little depth; his moral conduct was not worthy of respect."

"Not worthy of respect" — well, hardly! He kept a harem for himself, his chief mistress being Ursula Niedinger; they say he even robbed one of his mistresses, Elsa, of her jewels, and then flung her into prison. What he enjoyed himself he would not refuse to others, and so his priests kept concubines; but they had to buy a license from him, and so the archbishop made some pin-money on the side. Think it over!

This is the saintly clergyman whom the polished Erasmus styled "the finest ornament of Germany in the present century." If he was "the finest," what were the others? Kaiser Karl said Albrecht was neither Catholic nor Lutheran, but pagan. And yet Lawyer William Samuel Lilly, secretary of the Catholic Union of Great Britain, tells us, "Leo X and Archbishop Albert, whatever their faults, are by no means bad specimens of the great ecclesiastical dignitaries of those times." What were the really bad ones?

The princely vices kept the young sport broke — how pay the Holy Father?

Easy! He borrowed 30,000 gulden from the Fuggers, the great international bankers of Augsburg.

How pay? Easy! The god on earth offered his dear son to proclaim a plenary indulgence in his territory for eight years to build the church of Sts. Peter and Paul to give a worthy resting place to the bones of these great apostles. The Holy Father and the dear son went fifty-fifty. The Holy Father got his fifty, and the dear son's fifty paid his debt to his Holy Father. Fugger's agents were on the spot to collect the proceeds when the chest was opened.

For three gulden you could buy a cow, for thirty-six cents a pair of shoes, for one cent a bushel of wheat; when during a famine wheat cost fourteen cents a bushel, Luther thought he had a right to complain of the high cost of living. So Albrecht bought his office for about $300,000.

John Tetzel was a Dominican monk, but a little thing like that did not keep him from having two children; and a little thing like

TETZEL
Reproduced from
Castelar's
"La Revolucion Religiosa"

that did not keep Albrecht from hiring him to sell the indulgences, for he was a successful drummer.

While working for Leo and Albrecht, Tetzel was also working for his own pocket all the time, and he looked out first for Number One. He and his helpers got over 300 florins a month, at least 3,600 a year, and the net yield in the archdiocese of Magdeburg was only 5,149 in various years and this profit was divided equally between the pope and the archbishop. Pretty high overhead expenses. The sale in St. Bartholomew's in Frankfurt brought in about 48 florins, and Tetzel's expenses were about 45 florins! Great financier, this Tetzel. These facts have only recently come to light. Too bad Luther did not know of them; his language would have been still more picturesque.

From the proceeds of his huckstering Tetzel could support his sister so that she could sport four horses, and he left his heirs 2,000 florins. It certainly was a going concern, coining German sins into Roman ducats. Here at last was the philosophers' stone — the alchemist was turning base metal into pure gold.

Wherever Tetzel went, he was given an ovation. The civic

authorities, trades unions, and school children would receive him with processions. Before him was carried the pope's Bull of Indulgence on a splendid cushion of satin or cloth of gold. A cross with the pope's coat of arms was carried in the rear. "In short, God Himself could not have been more magnanimously received."

In the church he harangued the poor people on the blessed benefits to be got from buying his wares. "Do you not hear your dear parents crying out, 'Have mercy upon us? We are in sore pain, and you can set us free for a mere pittance. We have borne you, we have trained and educated you, we have left you all our property, and you are so hardhearted and cruel, that you leave us to roast in the flames when you could so easily release us!'"

Could the simple-minded and goodhearted Germans refuse such a piteous appeal? They could not, and they spent their hard-earned money freely.

Mayor John Hess of Goerlitz writes in his *Annals* that Tetzel boasted he could do more than the Mother of God in the way of forgiving and retaining sins. Soon as the coin in the chest doth ring, the soul will into heaven spring. He would tear off the heads of opponents and thrust them thus bloody into hell.

In 1482 the Paris theologians had condemned this pecuniary poetry —
    Soon as the coin in the chest doth ring,
    Souls out of purgatory spring.

Kings, archbishops, and princes were to give twenty-five Rhenish gold gulden; abbots, counts, and barons, ten; people with incomes of five hundred gulden were to give six; the next class, one; poorer ones, one half, or one quarter, or even less. The poor? The poor could beg till they had the price. Upon payment a receipt was given, quite businesslike; in fact, the thing was called "The Holy Business." There was a regular businesslike price list — *Taxa cancellariae apostolicae* — perjury and robbing a church cost nine ducats, murder eight ducats, etc.

"Note well, that dispensations or graces of this sort are not given to poor people."

Cardinal Borgia said, "God does not want the death of the sinner, but that the sinner should live — and pay."

What is an indulgence? The surplus good works of the saints

are added to the merit of Christ; of this treasury the pope holds the key and sells as much as you pay for to forgive the guilt and punishment of the living and to free souls from the pains of purgatory. No matter what were the fine-spun theories in the beginning, this is what it came to.

As early as about 1100 the famous Abelard accused many bishops of selling indulgences "under the appearance of loving mercy, but in truth for sordid love of lucre," and Berthold of Regensburg, who died in 1272, complains of the then recent "penny preachers, who replace repentance with indulgence money and thus destroy a part of the souls in their pastoral care."

Prof. Johann von Wesel, of the Erfurt University, about 1450, doubted the virtue of indulgences — for which he died in prison. Aeneas Sylvius, who became Pope Pius II, said the Roman court gives nothing without money; even the gifts of the Holy Spirit are sold; forgiveness of sins is granted only upon payment of the clinking coin. Pope Sixtus IV on Nov. 27, 1477, taught money paid by the living would shorten the pangs of those in purgatory. The priest and monk Erasmus wrote on February 16, 1521: "Everyone knows that the Church was afflicted with tyranny and with ceremonies and with laws made only for gain."

W. S. Lilly of Cambridge University, secretary of the Catholic Union of Great Britain, in his *Renaissance Types:*

Luther's condemnation of indulgences "had the sympathy of Erasmus, as of all good and wise men. . . . There can be no question at all that indulgences, as then preached 'with intolerable impudence' [Erasmus], were practically what Cardinal Aegidius did not hesitate to call them: 'an incentive to sin and a danger to souls.'

"What he thought he was buying was forgiveness of his past sins, and at the same time liberty to commit more. To the crowds who flocked to the indulgence fairs the message practically was that St. Peter, for hard cash, would open and guarantee heaven."

The Catholic Professor Pastor, in the *History of the Popes,* says the indulgence was "degraded into a merely financial transaction. The need of money instead of the good of souls became only too often the end of the indulgence. . . . Neither religious nor secular clergy shrank from the direct sale of spiritual gifts and gave absolution for money to those who did not even profess to have contrition. . . . Eck reported that 'permissory letters' were given as the actual reward of crime. . . . Cardinal Canisio was of opinion that the facilities for absolution encouraged sinners and were inducement to sin. . . . There is no doubt that his — Tetzel's — doctrine was virtually that of the drastic proverb: 'As soon as money in the coffer rings, the soul from purgatory's fire springs.'" (Vol. VII, pp. 338—349.)

Columbus thought, "He who has money has the power to transport souls into Paradise."

Cardinal Ximenes forbade the swindle in Spain.

Elector Frederick built a castle and, joining it, a church, which was graced by altar paintings from Albrecht Duerer and Lucas Cranach. Begun in 1493, it was dedicated in 1499, on November 1, All Saints' Day, and its right name was All Saints' Church. And rightly so, for on his trip to the Holy Land in 1493 and elsewhere the pious prince had by 1505 gathered 5,005 relics of the saints and placed them in the church. In 1516 Staupitz at Antwerp and Burkhard Schenk at Venice were on the lookout for more. By 1518 they had grown to 17,433; by 1520 to 19,013. Eighty-three clerics were needed for the 9,901 yearly masses.

What could you see? Man, what couldn't you see? You could see most wonderful things. You could see a piece of the burning bush of Moses; 204 particles and a whole corpse of the Holy Innocents of Bethlehem; some of the hair, shirt, skirt, girdle, veil, and milk of the Virgin Mary; the girdle of St. Paul; a link of Peter's chain and a piece of his staff; some hay and straw on which the Christ Child had lain; parts of his crib, cradle, and diapers; nine thorns of His crown; a piece of the scourge; nails which pierced His hands and feet; a piece of the sponge with which He was offered drink; 35 particles of His cross; etc. Wonderful! Still more wonderful, if you venerated all these relics, you would get an indulgence for your sins in purgatory for 127,799 years and 116 days!

The face of Europe was pock-marked by such places of superstition.

On October 31, 1516, Luther preached against the abuse of these indulgences and thereby greatly offended the elector and began his "thirty years' war," 1516—1546. From the same pulpit of the

Castle Church he again, on another festival, in February, 1517, did the same thing. "When it is evening, the pilgrims to this or that shrine, or to the celebration of this or that saint's day, return home with full indulgence; that is, full of beer and wine, full of unchastity and other horrid vices. . . . Indulgence is impurity and permission to sin and license to avoid the cross of Christ."

Remember it is an honored professor of theology at a Catholic university who is preaching this in a Catholic church to a Catholic congregation.

When the elector would make Staupitz a bishop for bringing home the relics in 1516, he consulted Luther. The monk wrote Spalatin, curtly objecting to tempting him "to carouse and practice the vices of Sodom and Rome." Staupitz was not made a bishop. When Staupitz fell into disfavor the next year, the same Luther pleaded for the same Staupitz at the same court. In spiritual matters the prince is "seven times blind, as is your friend Pfeffinger (the elector's treasurer). I do not say this privily as a slanderer, nor do I wish that you should in any way conceal it. When the opportunity comes, I am ready to say it to both of them."

Also, the monk reminded the elector of a promised gown, and he wanted the gown and not promises. Also, he warned the elector not to place a heavier tax on the people. "God ordains it so that at times a great mind may be directed by a lesser one, so that no one may trust himself, but only God, our Lord."

The penniless peasant monk talks to princes in the accents of a king, and the prince neither murmurs nor mutters!

Elector Frederick had spent a fortune of 200,000 florins collecting his choice relics, and the good Saxons could get very good indulgences at his favorite Court Church right in Wittenberg, and — and — he wanted to keep the good Saxon money in good old Saxony and not go out of his land to help his rival Hohenzollern pay his personal debts, and so he forbade Tetzel to enter Saxony, just as Duke George forbade him to enter Leipzig — "to cheat the poor man of his money and of his soul."

Tetzel came to Jueterbogk, near the border of Saxony. What can keep people from rushing to a bargain counter?

Among those who "ran like crazy" to buy the new grace in April, 1517, were some of Pastor Luther's church members, whom he had sharply reproved for their immoral life. When he refused them the Sacrament, they defiantly flourished their bought indulgences and accused him to Tetzel, who built a bonfire to show he had a right to burn Luther as a heretic.

Thus Pastor Luther was brought face to face with the horrible destruction of souls wrought by this "holy business."

He protested to some "magnates of the Church." Some laughed, none acted.

About October, Luther had Albrecht's "Instructions" to the peddlers, in which the indulgence was praised outright as man's reconciliation with God; and for those in purgatory it could be bought without repentance and confession!

Verily, the house of prayer had again become a house of merchandise, a den of thieves, where souls were murdered for their money. (Matt. 21:13; Mark 11:17; Luke 19:46.) Luther, like Christ, drove these thieves out of the Church of God. "The zeal of Thine house hath eaten Me up." (John 2:13-17.)

It was up to Luther to "bell the cat."

On October 31, 1517, Luther took John Schneider, Agricola, went to John Grueneberg, picked up the printed Latin Ninety-Five Theses, and posted them on the north door of the Castle Church, the University's bulletin board. They called on all the world to a debate on the worth of indulgences. It was a routine matter for the usual Friday debate.*

This was the world's greatest Halloween. The Man with the Hammer was the world's greatest knocker.

Luther sent the Theses to Albrecht with a letter. "The poor creatures believe that if they buy indulgences, they are sure of salvation, that souls fly out of purgatory as soon as they throw their money into the box, and that the grace is so great that there is no sin which cannot be absolved thereby. . . . In the instructions for the use of the agents published in your name it is said that one of the principal benefits to be had from indulgences is the inestimable gift of God whereby man is reconciled to Him and all the punishments of purgatory blotted out, and to those who buy pardons contrition is unnecessary." If he did not stop the scandal,

---

* The Theses may be had of Concordia Publishing House.

THE CASTLE CHURCH

someone might attack the archbishop, which would hurt his good name.

Luther also wrote his ordinary, Jerome Scultetus, Schulze, of Brandenburg in Berlin, the inspector of the Church and University of Wittenberg.

The first thesis reads: "When our Lord and Master Jesus Christ says, 'Repent,' etc., He wants the whole life of the Christians to be a repentance."

Luther plants himself upon Scripture. Leopold von Ranke calls this the kernel of the Reformation.

The Theses were reprinted in various cities — "which made the mare go," Agricola wrote. Myconius tells us they were spread "as if angels had been the messengers. No man will believe what talk they made." Like Lord Byron, Luther woke up one morning and found himself famous.

"Dr. Jerome Schurf took me sharply to task. 'You would write against the pope? What do you hope to effect by it? They will not suffer it.' And I replied, 'What if they must suffer it?'"

On November 11 he wrote: "If the work is of God, who will hinder it? If it is not of God, who will further it?"

INTERIOR VIEW
OF THE CASTLE CHURCH
BEFORE 1760

In like language he replied to his fearful prior, Ulrich Adam, who came specially to beg him not to disgrace the order by being burned as a heretic.

At the university only Carlstadt stood by him.

Prince Adolf von Anhalt, the Bishop of Merseburg, expressed his joy to the Saxon counselor Pflugk that the poor people, who were to buy the new grace, were warned against Tetzel's fraud.

Dean Albert Krantz of Hamburg said: "You speak the truth, good brother, but you'll not do anything; back to your cell and pray, 'God have mercy upon me!'" At Steinlausig Prior Fleck told his Franciscans, *"There* is a man who will do it!" And he wrote Luther: "Venerable Doctor, proceed! Press forward! These papal abuses always displeased me too," etc. Germany's greatest artist of all times, Albrecht Duerer of Nuernberg, sent his approval in the form of woodcuts and copper plates.

Kaiser Maximilian told Frederick's counselor, Degenhard Pfeffinger, Luther's Theses were not to be despised, and the elector had better take care of him, for he might someday be useful against the prelates.

In February, 1518, Luther sent his *Resolutions* on the Theses, more severe than the Theses, to his bishop, Schulze, Scultetus. "Good Catholic" verdicts the bishop, who also condemned Tetzel. Yet he sent Abbot Valentin von Lehnin to ask him to remain silent; but soon he let Luther print the *Resolutions*.

Tetzel saw the Theses in Berlin about November and bragged, "In three weeks that heretic will be thrown into the fire!"

Who was the first to use rough language?

He sent counter theses to enlighten Wittenberg. The students burned them in the market square to enlighten Wittenberg. Next day Luther told the students he did not wish in that way to enlighten Wittenberg.

Johann Mair von Eck, professor at Ingolstadt, denounced his former friend Luther as "a Bohemian heretic, insolent rioter, despiser of the pope."

"Bohemian" meant a Judas and a Benedict Arnold rolled into one. Who was the first to call names?

On March 8 Erasmus sent the Theses with words of praise to Dean Colet of St. Paul's, to Archbishop Warham, and later to Cardinal Wolsey. Thus began what Cardinal Gasquet calls "the Lutheran invasion of England."

On the 15th Luther preached, "Though they call me a heretic — for such truth is very bad for the money box — I shall not worry much about such ranting."

On May 30 Luther sent his *Resolutions on the Theses* to Staupitz to be forwarded to the pope. Worded in the usual monkish humility, yet they told the god on earth, "I cannot recant." "It is against the Holy Ghost to burn heretics."

A steel hand in a silk glove. Mild in manner, bold in matter.

Albrecht rid himself of Luther by reporting his case to Rome, before December 13, 1517.

When Confessor Prierias showed the heretic's heresies to the pope, he yawned, "Brother Martin is a very fine intellect, and these things are monks' squabbles." Again, he thought the Theses were written by a drunken German, who would change his mind when sober.

On February 3 the pope's bastard brother, Giulio, "the other pope," asked the vicar general of the Augustinians to "silence the man."

Did Volta order Staupitz to force "the man" to recant? On March 31, "the man" replied to Staupitz, "As I did not begin this work to become famous, I shall not drop it though I become infamous."

"Every decision of the pope in matters of faith and morals is infallible, because from God, and must be accepted by everybody on pain of temporal and eternal punishment. The pope's kingdom is that of the Son of Man; he is not only the ruler of the whole world, but he is virtually the whole world, the world soul, who could make and unmake emperors at will."

"Whosoever is not imbued with the doctrine of the Roman Church and the Roman pontiff as the infallible rule of faith, from which even Holy Scripture draws its strength and authority, is a heretic."

"If the pope were so wicked as to lead souls in crowds to the devil, still no one could depose the pope."

Whence these ravings?

From Silvester Mazolini da Prierio, Prierias for short.

Who's he?

Master of the Palace, theological expert, and confessor of His Holiness, Pope Leo X, god on earth.

The French Catholic Audin explains: Prierias "was under the fascination which the pope exercised over all minds. It is certain that his veneration for the papacy approaches to worship. . . . The views of Prierias in regard to the power of the keys were ultramontane, like those of all the schools of this period. . . ."

The official theological authority declared it was pure Catholic doctrine that the soul flies to heaven the moment the coin clinks in the chest. He even defended Tetzel's alleged statement that his indulgence would forgive a man even if he had violated the Holy Mother of God. As a good cook Tetzel had only added to wholesome food the stimulating spice.

Holy spice! The uncouth Dominican monk swore by all that's holy he hadn't said it: the polished papal prelate publicly protested it was quite properly said!

The polished papal prelate goes on to say, Had the pope only given Luther a fat bishopric, he would now gush praises of the indulgences. He suspects Luther's father was a dog, for biting was

73

the habit of dogs; he calls Luther a leper with a nose of iron, a head of brass, ignoramus, heretic, devil, etc. Of course he repeatedly threatens to burn him alive.

This is the man whom Audin rates "a polished and elegant man. His language was always calm, ornate, perhaps too carefully elaborated." "We know that Raphael has selected the head of Prierias for that one of the ancient sages in his 'School of Athens': the mind of Prierias was as fine as his head."

Erasmus laughed at some of the expressions and cracked his jokes at the expense of the Dominican.

In August Luther had Ghinucci's order to be in Rome in sixty days, also the *Dialogue of Prierias*. At first he trembled, then laughed at the drivel of the senile scribbler.

"It is this gentlest of gentlemen who is both my adversary and judge?"

"I hoped the pope would protect me, for I had so fortified my Theses with proofs from the Bible and papal decretals that I was sure he would condemn Tetzel and bless me. But when I expected a benediction from Rome, there came thunder and lightning instead, and I was treated like the sheep that had roiled the wolf's water. Tetzel went scotfree, and I must submit to be devoured."

Erasmus tells Cardinal Campegi that the attack "is not approved by anyone except such as are Luther's sworn enemies."

Oh, yes, Luther hit back, hit hard at this "hellish manifesto."

Prierias boasted he had written his work in three days. Even the pope wished his confessor had taken three months! In two days Luther had ready his scornful reply of about 15,000 words.

Anthony Trollope, one of the swiftest literary workers that ever lived, said it would have taken him fifteen hours without laying down his pen and using his native English to write that much. And Luther wrote in Latin, "extremely forcible and expressive Latin — suggestive of flower work in iron."

Luther's case was to come up at the meeting of the Augustinians at Heidelberg in April, 1518. Count Albrecht of Mansfeld warned Martin not to leave Wittenberg, for he would be hanged or drowned. The fearless monk jokingly wrote: "My wife and child are provided for; my fields, house, and all my property have been distributed; my reputation and good name have already been picked to pieces: so there is nothing left but the unsightly and broken little body."

On the 11th Luther sets out with Leonard Beier and the messenger Urban.

At Weissenfels the pastor recognizes and entertains him.

At Judenbach he runs across Pfeffinger, the elector's purse holder, the same that was so slow coming across with the goods Frederick had promised for Luther's gown. Now he makes the rich courtier shell out and foot the hotel bill of ten groschen for himself and his two companions, Leonard Beier and the messenger Urban.

"It was a comfort to me, among other things, to have the chance of making the rich man poorer by a few coins. For you know how I just like to incommode the rich, if I can in any way manage, especially if they are friends," he humorously writes Spalatin, who was to pay Luther's messenger, Urban. These few charming words reveal the sunny soul of Luther, though his sky was very threatening, and they show how thoughtful he was for others, though himself in the thick of troubles.

This Degenhard Pfeffinger had his soul insured in thirty-five brotherhoods, to pray his soul out of purgatory. He left them legacies on his death in 1519.

On the 15th Luther reaches Coburg. "Here also the elector's treasurer, whom I have not yet seen, because he is gone up to the Fort, must positively pay for us. I have done penance for going afoot and therefore need no indulgence. We nowhere found a wagon to give us a lift."

On the 18th he reaches Wuerzburg "at last." Prince-Bishop Lorenz von Bibra invites him to his castle, Marienburg, towering high above the city, and is so pleased with him that he wrote the elector to stand by the godly man, for injustice is done him. The bishop also offered at his own expense to have the monk taken to Heidelberg. Martin declined the kind offer with thanks, for here he had met Lang, and climbed into his wagon and on the 21st rode into Old Heidelberg.

"You have, by Jove! a stunning letter of introduction from your elector," said Jacob Simler; and so Pfalzgraf Wolfgang Wilhelm, who had studied at Wittenberg in 1515, invited Luther with

Staupitz and Lang to dinner and showed him the treasures of the "really royal castle" — of which we saw only the really royal ruins.

How did Staupitz regard the "Lutheran hue and cry"? He honored the suspected heretic by ordering him to conduct the public disputation at the promotion of Leonard Beier in the large cloister hall and to prepare the theses. They treated sin, original sin, grace, free will, faith, and chiefly man's inability by his own reason and strength to will the good. He added twelve philosophical theses, in which he used Pythagoras, Anaxagoras, Parmenides, and chiefly Plato to down Aristotle.

Luther defended his teaching "so cleverly, that he made no little fame for Your Love's University. And great praise was given him by many learned men," wrote Prince Wolfgang to the elector.

Erhard Schneph and Theobald Billicanus were won over, and John Brenz wrote: "Never can I thank you enough. Keep on, dear Father, to comfort the stricken and to raise up the sorrowful."

Young Martin Bucer of the rival Dominicans on May 1 wrote friend Beatus Rhenanus: "No matter how much our chief fighters strained themselves to unhorse Luther, they did not win a finger's breadth. Wonderful is his grace in responding, incomparable his patience in listening. His keen mind reminds one of the manner of the Apostle Paul. With his replies, terse as telling, taken from the store of Holy Scripture, he rouses all to admiration. The day following (April 26) I had a confidential talk with him and shared his frugal meal, but which was spiced with precious conversation. Whatever I might ask, he knew how to explain all most clearly. With Erasmus he agrees altogether, but surpasses him in saying freely and frankly at what the other only hints. Oh! that I could only write you still more! He it was that at Wittenberg ended the reign of Scholasticism and brought it about that Greek, Jerome, Augustine, and Paul are publicly taught there."

The first sketch of Luther, and how charming! And from a rival Dominican!

The Heidelberg meeting did not harm the heretic.

Luther went home, but in a wagon, such were the orders of Staupitz. "I came home in a chariot who had trudged forth on foot. I was well all the way, and my meat and drink agreed with me wonderfully, so that people say I am stouter than before."

Desiderius Erasmus, monk and priest, friend of four kings, four popes, and the kaiser, rated by his biographer Drummond "the greatest scholar of the world," warbles this lyric about Philip Melanchthon: "Immortal God, what hope is this youth, yes, this boy, who must be admired almost equally for his command of both literatures! What keenness of phantasy, what purity of language, what beauty of expression, what memory for unknown things, what mature reading!"

This boy wonder of eighteen in 1518 came to Wittenberg and at once found in Luther "his father in Christ."

"If there is anything on earth that I love, it is the studies of Martin and his pious writings, but above everything else, I love Martin himself."

"No writer ever came nearer St. Paul than Luther has done" — in the "Sermon on Good Works."

"Never was there a greater man on the face of the earth. I would rather die than separate myself from this man."

"Luther is too great, too wonderful for me to depict in words. If there be a man on earth whom I love with my whole heart, that man is Luther. One is an interpreter; another a logician; still another an orator, copious and beautiful in speech; but Luther is all in all — whatever he writes, whatever he utters, pierces to the soul, fixes itself like arrows in the heart — he is a miracle among men."

In December, 1518, Spalatin rejoiced, "The sacrosanct, true, and genuine theology . . . is taught at the University of Wittenberg — thank God — with such success, that Luther and Carlstadt have filled auditoriums and pupils not only very studious, but also making great progress. Melanchthon teaches Greek to about 400 hearers."

In the spring of 1519 came the Latin *Commentary on Galatians* — "my Kate von Bora" — Luther's highest double compliment.

Melanchthon rated it "Theseus' clue to the maze of Biblical science."

Spalatin wrote, "Doctor Martinus is working in the highest fame of his name."

"A Commentarie of Doctor Martin Luther upon the Epistle of Paule to the Galatians, first collected and gathered word for word out of his Preachynge and now out of Latin faithfully translated into Englishe for the unlearned. Lond. 1575. 4to." Translator unknown. Edwin, Bishop of London, with praises introduced the work which "certain godly learned men have most sincerely translated into our language, to the great benefit of all such who with humble hearts will diligently read the same. Some began it with such skill as they had. Others, godly affected, not suffering so good a matter in handling, to be marred, put to their helping hand, for the better framing and furthering of so worthy a work. They refuse to be named, seeking neither their own gain nor glory; but thinking it their happiness, if by any means they may relieve afflicted minds and do good to the Church of Jesus Christ, yielding all glory unto God, to whom all glory is due."

It was printed many times to bless many souls.

The Scot Peter Bayne, LL. D.: "Irony of this order is, so far as I know, unique in literature. . . . The defiant and leonine Luther, the Luther who, like the horse in Job, scents the battle from afar, and the snorting of whose nostrils is terrible, always triumphs over the meek and lamblike Luther. How much prettier had it been otherwise! Yes; and where then had been the Reformation?"

John Bunyan wrote his name among the immortals with *Pilgrim's Progress* and wrote in "Grace Abounding": "Methinks I must let fall before all men, I do prefer this book of Martin Luther upon the Galatians (except the Holy Bible) before all the books that ever I have seen, as most fit for a wounded conscience."

Sick unto death, Charles Wesley was converted by Luther's *Romans,* which tuned his heart to sing God's truth in hymns we love to sing today.

After four hundred years the Presbyterian James H. Brookes of St. Louis placed Luther's *Galatians* next to the Bible, as he told Prof. R. Bischoff. And Dr. Th. Graebner's edition is used in the Presbyterian Princeton Theological Seminary.

Spalatin asked Luther to comfort the sick elector. At the end of August, 1519, came *Tessaradecas,* "The Fourteen" — printed in 1520. Instead of the fourteen saints usually invoked in trouble, Luther offers fourteen original, soulful devotions. Erasmus sent them with praises to the bishop of Basel, and as late as 1524 told Baron Hieroslaus Laski, ambassador of the king of Poland: "Luther is a learned man; his teachings are beyond my power to judge; he certainly taught much well and attacked abuses strongly; I approve most his commentaries on the Psalms and the *Tessaradecas,* approved even by those that condemned the rest."

They came out in England.

"A right comfortable Treatise, containing fourtene Points of Consolation for them that labor and are laden; written to Prince Frederick, Duke of Saxonie, he being sore sicke, thereby to comfort him in time of his great distrese, Englished by W. G.(ace), Lond. 1578. 8vo."

Lazarus Spengler, the famous secretary of Nuernberg, in 1519 wrote: "A Defense of a Lover of Christian Truth, in which he Testifies to the Blessed Influence on his Life of Luther's Teaching."

"I have also often heard from many excellent and learned persons, lay and clerical, that they thanked God for having lived to hear Doctor Luther and his teaching. In Doctor Luther God has raised up a Daniel from among the people to open our blind eyes, to chase away by means of the Holy Scriptures the scruples and errors of troubled consciences, and to show us the right, straight way to Christ, the only Rock of our salvation."

Friedrich Mecum, Myconius, like Luther, tried all practices of popery, but, like Luther, found no peace of soul. He found it in Luther's works and became one of the first followers of "this God-sent man and last Elijah, the beginner, when as yet no one had dared dream of this matter."

Franciscan Eberlin von Guenzburg read Luther's writings in 1520 and then preached so Lutheran that Aleander reported him to Rome and he had to flee for his life from Freiburg in Breisgau.

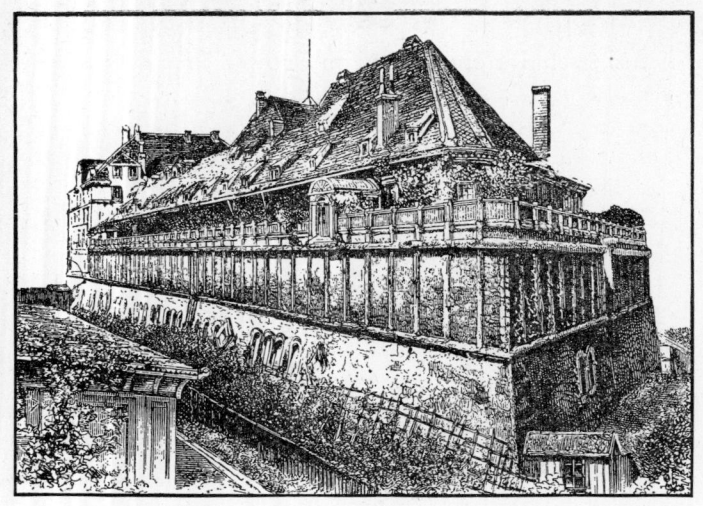

THE PLEISSENBURG AT LEIPZIG

Chapter Six

CONTROVERSIES ABOUT THE THESES

I. LUTHER AND CAJETAN

Old Kaiser Max, "the last of the knights," feeling his end coming on, called his last *Reichstag* to Augsburg in 1518 and spent much money to have his grandson Karl elected German kaiser, though only eighteen. In order to curry favor with the pope, the kaiser lettered him to ban Luther, who teaches damnably and heretically not only about indulgences, but also about the pope's ban, since it is to be feared he will infect not only the unlearned masses, but also mighty princes. The kaiser will not fail promptly to carry out the pope's judgment — burn the monk.

What a great power that single simple monk!

The pope on August 3 ordered Cajetan to arrest Luther at once.

General Gabriel della Volta of the Augustinians on the 25th ordered Provincial Gerhard Hecker "to capture the said Brother Martin Luther, have him bound in chains, fetters, and handcuffs, and detained under strict guard in prison at the instance of our Supreme Lord Leo X. . . . The thing is too important to admit delay; therefore we command you to spare no labor, to refuse no expense to get this heretic into the hands of the Supreme Pontiff."—Before Luther had a hearing!

On September 14 Staupitz wrote: "As far as I can see, you can only expect the cross, i. e., martyrdom. Therefore leave Wittenberg in time and come to me, that we may live and die together. The prince (Archbishop Matthew Lang) agrees to this."

Not so cheerful.

About September 25 Luther gets the elector's order to go to Augsburg for a hearing before Cajetan.

While he is tramping, let us look at the *Reichstag*. In 1461 the princes appealed against the sale of indulgences and called the clergy "public fornicators, keepers of concubines, pimps, and sinners in various other respects."

In 1479 the *Reichstag* said the papal appointees were better fitted to be drivers of mules than pastors of souls.

In 1510 the *Reichstag* presented a long list of grievances against the tyranny and extortion of the pope.

And now, when in 1518 Pope Leo X demanded a tax of 10 per cent for the holy war against the terrible Turk, the *Reichstag* replied Germany was bankrupt by the indulgence traffic, and, anyway, the real enemy of Christianity was not the Turk, but "the hound of hell," in Rome. This reply was prepared by a Wuerzburg priest and printed by Freher: "Divine things are despised, Christ is sold, the sheep are sheared. The pope gets more taxes from his own states than any Christian king from his, and still we buy palls, send loads of gold to Rome, promise presents, exchange gold for lead (papal bulls), permit indulgences all over. Who has brought in the nameless vices? Who has taught crimes that cannot be mentioned? Who has defiled human society? Who understands so well to deceive, cheat, perjure, forge wills, etc.? Is it not that dirty crowd that pours out of Rome over all the earth? . . . You would overcome the Turk. I praise the aim. But

KAISER
MAXIMILIAN I
After Duerer

I fear much you err in the name. In Italy you are to seek him, not in Asia.... This Cerberus you can quiet only with a stream of gold."

All the Vicar of Christ could do was to make a cardinal of that paragon of virtue, Elector-Archbishop Albrecht of Mainz, whom Kaiser Karl called neither a Catholic nor a Lutheran, but a pagan.

Kaiser Max could not get a crown for grandson Karl, and so he crowned Ulrich von Hutten poet laureate and died January 12, 1519.

Luther left Wittenberg — how?

"The fire was always before my eyes. Now you must die, I said to myself. What a disgrace I'll be to my dear parents!"

At Weimar Franciscan John Kestner cheered him. "I fear they'll burn you. If God upholds the cause, it will be upheld; if He does not, I cannot; and His will be the shame." Irreverent, were it not sublime. At Nuernberg they urged him to hurry back home.

To all gloomy forecasts he cheerily replied, "Even at Augsburg Christ reigns.... Let Christ live! Let Martin die!"

Link thought Luther's shabby gown would never do and gave him a better one.

On October 2 he broke down and had to hire a wagon for the last three miles.

All in, he put up at St. Anna of the Carmelites, whose prior, John Frosch, had studied at Wittenberg in 1516.

Everybody wished to see the new Herostratus, who had set fire to the Church, as the old one had fired the Ephesian dome. The learned patrician and imperial counselor Dr. Peutinger dined him on October ninth.

Luther was told to wait for a safe-conduct from Kaiser Max before daring to see Cajetan in the palace of the papal banker Jacob Fugger.

In the meantime, Cajetan's chamberlain, Urban de Serralonga, came to urge Luther in "the genuine Italian style" to agree to all Cajetan might say, return to the bosom of the Church by going through the motion of swearing off his heresy while still retaining his heresy, just as others had done.

It would surely be an easy thing to speak six little letters, *revoco,* I revoke. Luther would not revoke unless refuted. Ha! ha! would you start an argument? You've taken the indulgences altogether too seriously. Why not teach untruth, if untruth only brings in lots of money? Of course, one may not question the pope's power. That is so great that with a mere nod he can suspend articles of faith valid today. He had been too threatening to the pope and cardinals; what would he do, had he them in his power?

"Show them all due respect."

"Do you think the elector will go to war for you?"

"By no means."

"But where will you then stay?"

"Under heaven," dryly said the laconic Luther.

The oily, wily Italian could do nothing with the simple Saxon, laughed, and left.

On the 11th Luther wrote young Melanchthon: "I now go, if God so wills, to be sacrificed as an offering. I'll rather die than revoke."

The next day Link, Frosch, and three other monks went with Luther to the great Romanist.

83

CAJETAN

"I had been coached how to conduct myself toward the cardinal. First I threw myself down on my face. When he bade me rise, I rose to my knees. Only after another nod I stood upright. I excused myself for having waited for the safe-conduct and assured him I only wanted to hear the truth from him."

After a few friendly words he declared curtly: "Three things I demand on the order of His Holiness: 1. Repent and recant your errors. 2. Promise to teach them no longer. 3. Refrain from all things that could disturb the peace of the Church."

Luther asked his errors be named.

Cajetan named the 58th and 95th Theses, disproved by the decretal *Unigenitus* of Pope Clement VI of January 27, 1343, and Thesis 7 of the *Resolutions* — "Not the Sacrament, but faith justifies." This is new and false.

Luther replied in this point he could not give in.

"You must, whether you will or not, recant that today. Otherwise I'll condemn all you say on account of this one sentence."

The Italians laughed sneeringly, "after their manner."

Luther denied the authority of the pope's decretal, because it twists Holy Writ and only repeats the opinion of Thomas Aquinas.

"I therefore unconditionally prefer the Bible passages I quote in the Theses."

"The pope is above the council and the Holy Scriptures." Proof — Nicholas V condemned the Council of Constance. "You are also a Gersonist. All followers of Gerson are also condemned the same as Gerson himself."

Luther dared remind him that the University of Paris had just recently appealed to a general council.

Cajetan growled, "For that the Parisians will yet suffer."

When Luther quoted Scripture, the cardinal laughed out loud.

Again and again the cardinal imperiously demanded, "Recant, admit your error. That and nothing else is the will of the pope."

They made no headway, and Luther asked for twenty-four hours to think the matter over and left.

The next morning Link, Frosch, Ruehel, Feilitzsch, Peutinger, and Staupitz returned with Luther. The cardinal smiled, received the formal *Protestatio,* which Luther read — As long as he was not refuted, he could not be forced to recant. He was not conscious of having taught anything against Scripture, the Fathers, the decretals, and reason. He was willing to defend his Theses in a public debate. He was willing to answer the cardinal in writing and submit it to the judgment of the universities of Basel, Freiburg, Louvain, and even Paris.

After long discussions Cajetan let Luther put his position in writing.

He wrote Carlstadt: "I am certain that I would be the most accepted and beloved of all if I were to repeat this one word *'revoco* — I revoke.' But I do not want to become a heretic by contradicting a belief that made me a Christian. I shall rather die, suffer myself to be burnt, exiled, and cursed."

The next morning, the 14th, Ruehel and Feilitzsch returned with Luther, who had written his justification of the two points attacked by Cajetan.

Luther repeats his readiness to recant if proved wrong from the Scriptures, the highest authority, and finishes in a flood of feeling:

"These proofs which I have brought, and many others, compel me, take me captive, lead me to the teaching which I have stated. Therefore, most reverend Father in Christ, I humbly pray you to deal meekly with me, to have compassion on my conscience, and to give me the light of a better understanding. Plead for me with the pope that he may not cast out into darkness my soul which is seeking nothing but the light of truth, and is quite willing and ready to yield when better informed."

The cardinal, in Hutten's picture, "lean, dried up, and sapless like a dead reed, a typical begging friar," took Luther's paper with contemptuous words and gestures, but promised to send it to Rome and positively refused to discuss the case, Pope Clement VI having settled it. In a high and angry voice he called for recantation: "I started to speak nine or ten times, but every time he thundered at me and had the floor alone.

"At last I, too, began to shout and said, 'If it can be shown that the extravagant — the *Unigenitus* of Clement VI — declares the merits of Christ to be the treasure of indulgences, I shall recant, as you desire.'

"Good heavens, what gesticulations and rude laughter this remark caused!

"The cardinal eagerly seized the book and read from it with breathless rapidity till he came to the place where it says that Christ by His Passion acquired a treasure.

"Then I, 'O most reverend Father, consider this word *acquire*. If Christ by His merits *acquired* a treasure, then His merits *are* not the treasure, but that which the merits merited, namely, the Keys of the Church, forgiveness of sins, are the treasure. Therefore my conclusion was correct.'

"At this he was suddenly confused, but not wishing to appear so, he bravely skipped to other points, thinking it prudent not to notice what I had said. But I was hot and burst forth, indeed without much reverence, 'Do not think, most reverend Father, that we Germans do not know grammar; these are two different things, to *acquire* a treasure and to *be* a treasure.'"

Now the Cardinal tried to prove the bold monk wrong from the Bible, though he did not hold it infallible; but that did not work, and so he came back to his hobby, the *Unigenitus*.

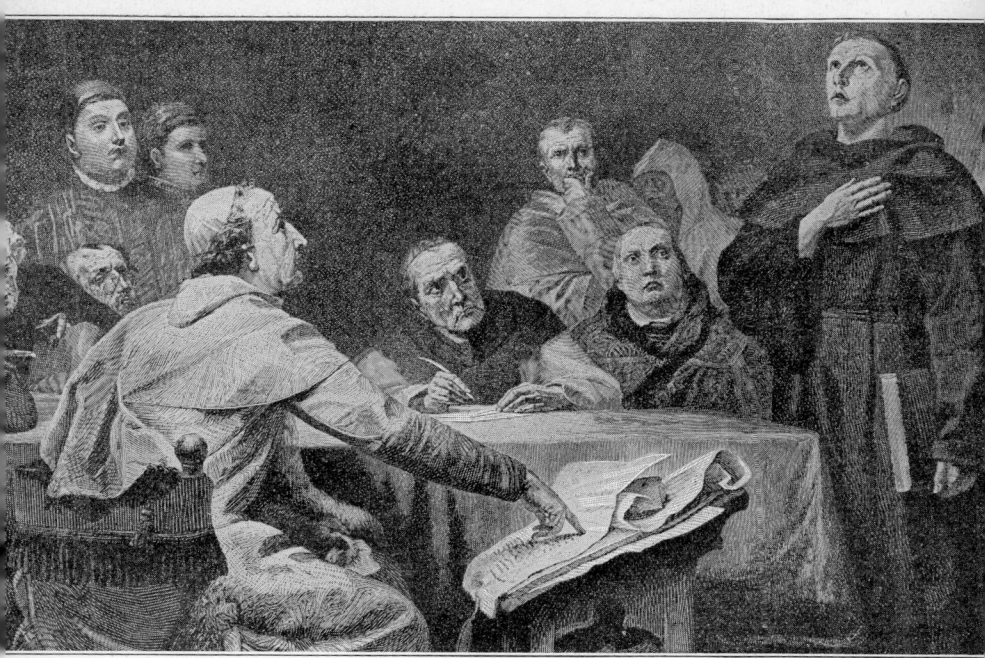

LUTHER AND CAJETAN
After Lindenschmidt

"Recant! I have been empowered by the pope to ban you and all your followers, and to put all places that receive you under the interdict."

When even that threat made no impression, Cajetan rose and cried, 'Go, and do not come before my eyes unless you will recant.'"

The laugh was on the legate. Tell it not in Gaeta, publish it not in the streets of Rome! The legate was one of the most learned theologians and skillful debaters of his time, and he was an authority on indulgences, having published a special treatise on the subject dedicated to a cardinal, afterward a pope. Now this learned lord and "light of the Church," as Pope Clement VII called him, backed by all the authority of the papacy, was made a laughing-stock by a poor German monk in a borrowed coat! Yes, it is to laugh!

The legate did not wish to see Luther, who had "deep eyes and wonderful speculations in his head." And yet he worked on Staupitz and Link to work on Luther to recant, and they did!

Luther might well have said, "God deliver me from my friends; I can take care of my enemies."

Staupitz ran all over Augsburg for a loan to get Luther out of Germany to a safe place beyond the reach of the pope's arm, say to Paris; but no one had the ready cash.

On the 16th he said to Luther, "I discharge thee from obedience to me, and commit thee to the mercy of Christ."

The rats forsake the sinking ship. The fatherly friend thereby washed his hands of Luther's acts and clearly foreshadowed his disgraceful death; later he forsook his friend and Saxony and the Augustinian Order and became the Abbot of St. Peter's Benedictine cloister at Salzburg.

Dr. Peutinger got wind of the pope's orders of August 23 to hale Luther to Rome and to curse and ban all favoring Luther, and on October 16 both Link and Staupitz silently stole away to Nuernberg.

On the same Saturday Luther in legal form made his famous *Appeal from the Pope Ill-Informed to the Pope to be Better Informed.* In other words, he asked for a change of venue, the present trial judges, Ghinucci and Prierias, being biased.

Luther had said no one knew just what indulgences were, and he was right, for the long-debated question had never been settled by the pope. And the learned Cajetan knew but too well there was no law to condemn Luther for heresy. If there is no such law, why not make such a law? Happy thought! Cajetan at once drafted such a law, and on November 9 the pope issued it as the bull *Cum postquam,* condemning the errors of certain monks on indulgences and other points. "Rome has spoken, the case is settled."

On Sunday, October 17, Luther wrote his "most beloved Father in Christ," "I would most gladly recant, if my conscience would permit me." And he makes the amazing offer, "I am quite ready and promise . . . to keep silent," if his enemies also keep silent. He asked leave to depart. No answer. On Monday he asked again. Again no answer. On Tuesday no answer. Suspicious silence. "The legate loved me so much that for love of me he would shed blood — my blood." Wednesday night Canon Eitelhart Langemantel pointed to a small door in the city wall, which opened for Luther. In shorts and socks, without spurs and sword, the strange horseman trotted off on his hard-trotting nag. After riding thirty-two miles at a stretch to Monheim the rider sank into the stable bedding like dead.

At Nuernberg Willibald Pirkheimer, Hutten's "First Citizen of Germany," dined him with great honors and had him meet Albrecht Duerer.

Here he received Spalatin's letter with a copy of the Holy Father's *breve* of August 13 ordering his prompt arrest. What a narrow escape! Arrest without a hearing!

Near Saalfeld Count Albrecht of Mansfeld laughed heartily at the riding of the monk and dined him.

On the 28th the heretic drew up a formal appeal to a German council — "Luther's greatest heresy," said the cardinals.

On October 31, the first anniversary of the posting of the Theses, he reached Kemberg and read mass — "So holy I still was then." In the afternoon he was home and wrote Spalatin: "I am so glad and peaceful that I wonder at the much ado so many great people are making about my struggles and sufferings."

Luther says: "Had the cardinal at Augsburg acted more moderately and received me as a suppliant, things would never have gone so far. For up to that time I knew but little of the errors of the pope. Had he kept quiet, I should have done the same." The pope's legate Campegi also said: "Cajetan has destroyed this cause by trying to use force in a matter that called for wise counsel and strategy."

England's most magnificent Cardinal Wolsey told Cardinal Campegi in 1528, and repeated it many times, "Beware lest, in like manner as the greater part of Germany, owing to the harshness and severity of a certain cardinal [Cajetan], has become estranged from the Apostolic See and faith, it should be said that another cardinal [Campegi] has given the same occasion to England with the same result."

By the way, this learned Cardinal Cajetan taught indulgences did not at all benefit those who could do enough for themselves. Cardinal Bellarmine thought this good and pious, but against the common teaching of Rome, as Cajetan admitted. Cardinal Bellarmine also admits the money greed of the indulgence peddlers.

THE DINNER TO DR. FROSCH

At some reception at Augsburg, Johann Frosch, the prior of the Carmelite cloister there, told the important and courted Elector Frederick of his plan to take the Doctor's degree at Wittenberg. "Oh! charmed to hear it! We shall make a Doctor of you, and I shall stand the dinner." Exit happy John Frog, and the elector busied himself with his important business.

When Luther came to Augsburg, he put up at the Carmelite cloister, and Prior Frosch, Wittenberg student of 1516, was all kindness and hospitality, and mentioned to his distinguished guest his plans and the elector's promise. "Come by all means; it will be all right if the prince has promised."

Luther, amid all his trials and troubles, places these details before Spalatin. "See, then, that what Frosch hopes for shall be honorably given him."

Dead silence from Spalatin. After eight days Luther again bombards Spalatin. Here is the illustrious Frosch actually present in Wittenberg and loudly proclaiming the elector promised him an honorary dinner!

"Obliquely waddling to the end in view," Luther learned the elector was "ignorant or dubious of the promise" made to Frosch.

Here was a pretty "How do ye do?"! Frosch, of course, was truthful, and Frederick, of course, was truthful. Frederick's honor must be kept sacred and Frosch's feelings must be spared. Frosch could not have his dinner at the palace, Frosch could not have his dinner at the University. Luther asked his great and good friends among the burghers of Wittenberg, but the honor of honoring Frosch seemed no honor to these solid and stolid Philistines in those dim November days. Where there is a will, there is a way. The promise of our Saxon prince must not be broken; Frosch, worthy of honor, must not be left unhonored. Rather than that, we must startle the monastic silences and let the cloisters of our own convent attest the Doctorial Majesty of Frosch. But we are truly poor; the company will be large; we cannot possibly manage without help. If the prince will send some venison, we can perhaps pull through.

Frosch got his degree of Doctor; on November 22 Frosch got

his dinner; Frosch's heart was glad, Fredericks' honor was saved, and the whole was due to Martin Luther.

This was not all. So far Frosch was glad to think he was a man whom a prince delighted to honor, and Luther kept himself behind the curtain. Now he would step forth and do a little honoring in his own name. Frosch had been kind to Luther at Augsburg, Luther would be kind to Frosch at Wittenberg. Accordingly, he arranged a little supper in his honor. Luther's keen eye had noticed the absence of Melanchthon at the formal dinner, and Frosch also had felt it, and in the afternoon Luther wrote a jolly note insisting on the presence of "Philip Melanchthon, Blackearth, Greek, Latin, Hebrew, German, but never Barbarian" to do honor to the new Doctor, the worthy Prior John Frog.

Yes, the edelweiss grows in the Alpine heights.

In the world's mighty drama only a little interlude, but how close it brings us to the human Luther. A gentleman and diplomat united in this Knight of the Golden Heart.

Speaking of Albrecht Duerer, Lazarus Spengler, and other celebrated lights of Nuernberg, Scheurl remarked: "Nearly all the conversation at table concerns a certain Martin. Him they celebrate, adore, champion. For him they are prepared to endure everything." And to Eck: "The clergy's love for the man is astonishing. They are flocking to him in droves. They subscribe to his opinions, they applaud him, they bless him."

II. LUTHER AND MILTITZ

Karl von Miltitz had been sent to Rome in 1515 by Frederick to get indulgences, relics, and, above all, the Golden Rose, which the pope granted from time to time to specially deserving papists. In 1518 Miltitz returned with the coveted prize to bribe the elector to betray Luther and send "the child of Satan and son of perdition" in chains to Rome. He had no less than seventy "Apostolic Letters" from the pope to princes and prelates to arrest Luther, or pass him through their lands to Rome.

Frederick coolly took the rose, and coolly left unchained "the child of Satan and son of perdition."

The noble Saxon chamberlain soon sensed a change in the sentiments of the people. Three out of four had it — Lutheranism — and an army of twenty-five thousand was not strong enough to lug Luther to Rome. Too late for force! Too late for ban and interdict! A change in the political weather demands a change in the papal political tactics.

Miltitz cited Tetzel to Altenburg. Tetzel begged to be excused from leaving Leipzig for fear of death at the hands of the people. We rub our eyes; are we in dreamland or in a German land? One short year after Luther's Theses, Tetzel, backed by the great archbishop of Germany and the pope at Rome, afraid to travel the short distance from Leipzig to Altenburg for fear of losing his life at the hands of good Catholic people! One short year after Luther's Theses, Tetzel had to quit the indulgence business, though the eight-year lease still had five years to run. Luther had killed "the Holy Business"; there were no more buyers. "Othello's occupation's gone." Surely, "the world do move," as black Brother Jasper of Richmond was wont to opine. And it was moving rapidly in those stirring days.

In the presence of a Fugger agent at Leipzig, Miltitz fiercely denounced Tetzel for his grafting and immorality. It is said the monk had two children.

The elector asked Luther to see Miltitz at Altenburg in January, 1519.

The gay young Saxon nobleman fiercely denounced the shameless indulgence hucksters; he spoke flatteringly of Luther's person and great influence; he regretted the harm Luther had done the pope and wept tears, real tears, as he said it. He remarked that within a hundred years there had not been a case that had so worried the crowd of loafing cardinals and Rome-worshiping Romanists and that they would rather give ten thousand ducats than let this affair go on. Miltitz dined, embraced, and kissed "the child of Satan and son of perdition," who had an uncomfortable feeling of a Judas kiss and of crocodile's tears. Miltitz did not insist that Luther recant and promised to get him a hearing before a learned German bishop, say, Lang of Salzburg or Greiffenklau of Trier. Luther promised to be silent provided his enemies were muzzled, and made a statement to the people to reverence the Roman Church.

We wonder at the length the peace-loving Luther was willing to go to have peace in the Church.

Miltitz was the guest of Degenhard Pfeffinger, who was quite sure Luther could have any dignity he wished if only he recanted. So Scheurl wrote on December 20, 1518.

In 1518 Wolfgang Capito thanked God for sending a new Daniel and had Froben reprint all the works of Luther.

On February 14, 1519, Johann Froben, the scholarly printer of Basel, wrote Luther he had "immediately reprinted Luther's complete works, as they were approved by all the learned. Six hundred copies have gone to France and Spain. They are bought in Paris, read, and approved at the Sorbonne. The bookdealer Francis Calvus of Pavia, a most learned man, devoted to the Muses, took a large number to Italy, to spread them all over in the cities. Nor does he do it so much for gain as to aid piety. "I have also sent copies to Brabant and England. I have only ten copies in stock. I have never had so much luck with a book. The abler one is, the more he is in love with you."

The same was done by Andreas Cratander, Adam Petri, and other printers of Basel; Petri even specialized in "Luther." Luther was the best seller, better than even the famous Erasmus. Many of the enthusiastic Humanists peddled the books themselves.

On the 18th the Basel Professor and Preacher Wolfgang Fabricius Capito wrote: "Switzerland and the Rhine country as far as the ocean are solid for Luther. . . . We have printed your collected works and sent them to Italy, France, Spain, and England, in this consulting the public welfare, which, we think, is advanced by having the truth spread as widely as possible."

On April 14, 1519, Erasmus wrote Elector Frederick: "Every one who knows the man — Luther — approves his life, since he is as far as possible from suspicion of avarice or ambition, and blameless morals find favor even among heathen." A month later he wrote in the same strain to Cardinal Wolsey: "The man's life is approved by the unanimous consent of all, and the fact that his character is so upright that even enemies find nothing to slander in it must considerably prejudice us in his favor."

Capito got Luther to write a complimentary letter to Erasmus, and with the grandeur of modest pride he says, "My name, too, has begun to emerge from obscurity" — quite quotable if it had been written by an ancient Roman.

On May 30, 1519, Erasmus wrote Luther: "Dearest brother in Christ, your letter showing the keenness of your mind and breathing a Christian spirit, was most pleasant to me. I cannot tell you what a commotion your books are raising here. . . . In England there are men who think well of your writings, and they the very greatest. . . . I have looked over your commentaries on the Psalms, which pleased me very much." The same day the timid Erasmus wrote Lang at Erfurt: "All good men love Luther's boldness."

III. LUTHER AND ECK

Luther promised his Bishop Scultetus to be silent if his enemies were silent; they were not. Luther promised Cajetan to be silent if his enemies were silent; they were not. Luther promised Miltitz to be silent if his enemies were silent; they were not. In his fight with Carlstadt, Eck attacked Luther and so forced him into the debate at Leipzig, the bitterly hostile rival of Wittenberg. At the same time the Leipzig Professor Jerome Dungersheim von Ochsenfart attacked him in a number of lengthy letters.

Hoogstraten in Koeln, the terrible inquisitor, who had almost burned the great Hebrew scholar Reuchlin, now called on Pope Leo to spill the blood of Luther. The Pomeranian Chancellor Olsnitzer reported from Rome they would do away with Luther by poison or dagger. "The Lord draws me, and I follow not unwillingly," Luther wrote Pirkheimer.

On March 13 he wrote Spalatin: "I do not know whether the pope is the Antichrist or an apostle of the Antichrist, so atrociously is Christ, that is, the truth, falsified and crucified by him in his decretals."

During Lent, 1519, Luther preached on the "Suffering Savior" — 24 separate editions from various cities have come down to us.

In March came the "Sermon on Good Works." "No writer ever came nearer St. Paul than Luther has done," said Melanchthon.

Duke Barnim of Pomerania, honorary rector of the university, and two hundred students escorted Luther to Leipzig, where he rolled in in a wagon and lodged with Melchior Lotther, the printer, on June 24.

JOHN ECK OF INGOLSTADT

The theological faculty stood sullenly aloof, and so Lawyer Pistoris on June 27 welcomed the debaters to the university, whence they went in stately procession to Thomas Church, where a specially composed mass in twelve voices was rendered by the trained singers and players of George Rhau; then in splendid parade, with banners and arms and drums, to Duke George's richly furnished Pleissenburg, where "a quarter of the citizens, 76 men in armor and with arms, flags, and drums" welcomed the comers. The young professor of rhetoric and poetry Peter Schade of Mosel, Mosellanus, with much clearing of throat and in a horribly cracky voice addressed them in Latin "On the Way and Manner of Debating, Especially in Theological Matters," spoke for two hours — and it was hot! The singers sang the grand old "Come, Holy Spirit" — and sang it three times, the whole assembly kneeling! A herald heralded a recess for dinner till two o'clock.

For four days Eck defended the free will of man, Carlstadt the free grace of God. So dreary and tedious was the debate during the oppressive heat in the low hall that the learned Leipzig lights slept so soundly they had to be wakened for their meals; perhaps that is too strong.

On July 4, at 7 A. M., Luther faced Eck. Over Luther's desk hung an embroidered St. Martin of Tours, over Eck's St. George the Dragon Killer — was Luther the dragon?

Many notables had come from far to hear Luther.

On the 5th Eck strongly hinted Luther was a Husite — Judas Iscariot and Benedict Arnold rolled into one. Luther retorted: Among the articles of John Hus and the Husites many are quite Christian and evangelic, which the universal Church cannot condemn, e. g., the statement: There is but *one* universal Church. No Christian was to be forced to believe as an article of faith what was not grounded on God's Word. Why, even authorities on Canon Law, like Archbishop Nicholas de Tudesco of Palermo, held the opinion of a single Christian was to count for more than pope and council when based on better grounds, and a council could err.

"That word fell like a stone into the hall." Luther had not only offended all Catholic feeling, but also all German national feeling. Duke George shouted his favorite curse, "The plague take it!" through the hall and caused a great stir. It seemed one could smell the smoke of the burning fagots to which the bold monk was heading. On the 6th Luther made the epochal declaration: "The Bible alone is infallible. Even councils can err and have erred."

On July 7 Luther again stuck to his guns that a council had no right to introduce new articles of faith, etc. Eck: "If you believe that a rightly assembled council errs and has erred, you are to me as a heathen man and a publican."

In the matter of purgatory Luther rejected the authority of the Council of Florence and of Second Maccabees; the Church had no right to put into the Bible what did not belong there.

In the matter of indulgences Eck sang small, and so no real debate was possible. Luther wrote: "Indulgences fell through completely, and he agreed to almost all I said, so that their use was turned to scorn and mockery."

On July 14 Luther ended by saying: "I see Dr. Eck goes into the Bible as deep as a spider into water; nay, he shuns it as the devil does the cross. With all due respect to the Fathers, I will rather hold by the Bible."

When Eck would be thundering his loudest, Luther would calmly be smelling of a spray of pinks!

In place of the usual gold ring, Luther wore one of silver with a tiny casket. What might be in it? Why, that is where the heretic carries the devil in order to consult him.

In winding up this historic debate, John Lang, the rector of the university, calls Luther a man of the greatest integrity — "Not less in life than doctrine you act the part of Augustine."

"Gentlemen, I am unable by any oratorical power of mine to do justice to the genius and virtues of men so eminent as these rival champions. Let me follow the example of the painter Timanthes. Having to paint the cruel sacrifice of Iphigenia, he delineated Calchas, the sad prophet of the Trojan War, Ulysses dissolved in tears, Menelaus oppressed with sorrow. But when he came to Agamemnon, he felt that the powers of his brush were exhausted and covered the face with a veil."

Classically and diplomatically the orator left it to his audience to decide whether the veiled Agamemnon stood for Eck or for Luther. Duke George thought he stood for Eck and sent him a stag, the usual sign of victory; Carlstadt received a hind for coming out second best; Luther got nothing, not having been in it officially!

While Eck was wined and dined ostentatiously, the Wittenbergers were ignored ostentatiously. Only the law professor Simon Pistoris and the physician Heinrich Stromer von Auerbach dared dine them.

The cellar of Auerbach is celebrated in Goethe's "Faust."

During these days Luther entered St. Paul's. When the massing Dominicans saw him, they grabbed the sacred vessels and rushed into the sacristy "as if the devil had chased them." He certainly was in the enemy's country.

In that same cloister lay the dying Tetzel, cursed by everybody — but Luther. He wrote a friendly, comforting letter "not to worry; the matter had not been begun on his account; the child has quite another father" — the pope.

Brother Martin, we like you for that brotherly letter.

Peter Schade, Mosellanus, professor of poetry, wrote thinking men gave the palm of victory to Luther. In a letter to Pirkheimer and in another to his pupil Julius Pflugk, he paints for us the first pen portrait of Luther.

Martin is only of medium size, haggard, from cares and studies so gaunt you can, when near, make out all the bones in his body. But he is in the prime of life. His voice rings high and clear. His learning and Bible knowledge are wonderful, so that he has almost everything in hand. Of Greek and Hebrew he has learned enough to form an independent judgment. He is never at a loss for matter; for an extraordinary wealth of ideas and words are at his command. In his life and manners he is courteous and friendly, no frown and pride about him, and can adapt himself to all occasions. In company he is pleasant, lively, always sure of himself, and of a cheering face, no matter what evil his enemies may be plotting, so that one must needs believe he does not undertake such important matters without the help of God."

Mosellanus also paints Luther's opponent.

Eck is a tall fellow, strongly and solidly built. His full, truly German voice sounding out of an enormous chest would do not only for a tragedian, but also for a town crier. But it is more harsh than distinct. The euphony of Latin, praised so highly by Fabius and Cicero, certainly does not get justice in his mode of speech. His mouth and eyes, in fact, his whole physiognomy, is such that you would take him for a butcher or rough *Landsknecht* rather than a theologian. As to his mind, he has a phenomenal memory. Had he an equally keen understanding, he would be the image of a perfect man. But he lacks quickness of apprehension and sharpness of judgment, qualities without which all other intellectual gifts are useless. . . . His gestures are almost theatrical, his manner arrogant; in short, he positively does not make the impression of a theologian, in fact, he is nothing more than an uncommonly bold, yes, shameless, sophist."

The Leipzig Debate advertised Luther throughout Europe, and the letters of Mosellanus brought still more of the educated to the side of the Wittenberger.

Writing *Against Luther's Foolish Chase,* Eck made insulting remarks about unlearned canons given to the Lutheran error, and was thus the first to use the term "Lutheran." In December John Oekolampad and Canon Adelmann put out the *Response of the*

Unlearned Lutheran Canons to J. Ecc. This, he says, hurt him more than anything else.

Lazarus Spengler wrote against Eck the *Defense of an Honorable Lover of the Divine Truth of Holy Writ,"* a warm and manly defense of Luther.

The Dressed Eck gave him a thorough dressing down, and the prize-fighting debater became a joke in Germany.

Crotus Rubeanus from Italy wrote Luther firsthand information of the efforts there on foot to crush him and hailed him as the "Father of the Fatherland, worthy of a golden statue and a yearly festival."

Pastor Jan Poduska and Vicar Wenzel Rozdalovsky of Prague sent him Bohemian knives and Hus' book *On the Church*.

Even older people came just to study under Luther. Among them was George Heyns, the former burgomaster of Brueck, father of Simon Heyns, pastor of the City Church, and of George Heyns, Chancellor Brueck. Though old and sickly, he made the long way from his home to hear from Luther "the consoling teaching about the Son of God."

The rush of students, also foreigners, caused a housing shortage.

The pope demanded the elector turn over "this son of perdition, this infected scrofulous sheep for punishment."

Luther would relieve the elector: "I shall leave your country." Frederick sent Spalatin: "He kept me from going to France at once."

On November 25 Luther was "disposing of everything and putting my affairs in order, so as to be ready and girt for travel." And the elector sent word to travel out of his country.

On December 1 Luther gave a farewell dinner, during which came a letter from the elector expressing surprise Luther was not yet gone. "My father and my mother forsake me, but the Lord will take me up," he quoted from Psalm 27:10. Before the end of the meal came another letter ordering him not to leave — yet.

On the 18th the elector wrote Cajetan he would not give up Luther.

What was Luther doing during these exciting times? He ordered Sir Thomas More's *Epigrams* and *Utopia*. Wonderful man, this Luther!

LUTHER BURNING THE PAPAL BULL

Chapter Seven

THREE MONUMENTAL WRITINGS

I. TO THE CHRISTIAN NOBILITY

The Pope's claim to temporal power is based on Emperor Constantine's donation of Central Italy to the bishop of Rome. Lorenzo Valla proved this donation to be a huge forgery. In February, 1520, Luther read Hutten's edition and cried out, "Good God! What iniquity on the part of the Romans! . . . That the forgery should have . . . taken the place of articles of faith! So agonized am I that I have almost quit doubting the pope is the very Antichrist, . . . so perfectly do all things which he lives, does, speaks, and orders suit the character."

"The time for silence is gone, and the time to speak has come."

(Eccl. 3:7.) Since the clergy have become quite careless, Luther speaks *To the Christian Nobility of the German Nation on the Bettering of the Christian Estate.*

Part One

The Romanists have drawn three walls round themselves, with which they have hitherto protected themselves, so that no one could reform them, whereby all Christendom has fallen terribly.

As the walls of Jericho fell at the sound of the ram's horn, so these walls of Rome fell at the sound of Luther's horn.

Part Two

Of the matters to be considered in the councils.

Here Luther lays bare the corruptions of the papal court with intimate knowledge and denounces the spiritual robbery in such fierce terms as Wiclif and Hus had never dreamt of. "I have said, and will say, nothing of the infernal dregs of private vices. I only speak of well-known public matters, and yet my words do not suffice."

Part Three

Luther is not a ranting rabble rouser; he is, indeed, the most destructive critic, but also the most constructive critic. He uncovers the sores only to give a cure for all — twenty-six for the bettering of the Church and six for the bettering of the State. These thirty-two planks he builds into his platform of progressive reform and writes himself down the greatest statesman of his day.

This work is an invective of intoxicating rhetoric reading like a dithyrambic. Demosthenes against Philip, Cicero against Catiline, Burke against Warren Hastings, Patrick Henry against George III, Zola against the persecutors of Dreyfus — all of them rolled into one do not equal this terrible indictment of Rome that scorches like livid lightning. Withal, he is as statesmanlike as Napoleon and Bismarck, changing the face of Europe. With this work Luther writes his name in the first rank of the world's greatest authors.

The work came out in August, and in eighteen days 4,000 copies were sold and a number of reprints were in press. Barth. Forzio turned it into Italian, and later it came out in English.

John Lang rated it "a classical, though a fierce and terrible booklet." Even grim Duke George growled to Rome: "It is not all untrue what is in the book, and it is not needless to come to the light of day. If no one dares talk of the evils in the Church, and everyone must remain mum, then at last the stones will speak."

Milton defended Luther's fierce language, showing he only got despite from Cajetan and Eck when writing with moderation. Farrar says nothing like this was written since Paul's letter to the Galatians; and Hausrath says: "As Paul's individuality comes out clearest in Second Corinthians, so Luther's genius in this heart-stirring writing." Preserved Smith calls it "new and original, fused by genius into a living organism. It is a work of world-wide importance, at once prophesying and molding the future, . . . Luther's greatest work." "Luther's greatest work" the historian Plank rates it, who is in doubt which to admire more, the greatness of the genius or the greatness of the courage. Leopold von Ranke holds them "world-historic pages."

Venetus again urged Staupitz to stop Luther; Link again urged Luther to stop; Cardinal Raphael Petrucci strongly warned Frederick to drop Luther, and the elector again became so restive that Luther on July 10 again said he would leave Saxony. Hutten offered to surround him with the swords of the German knights. Luther declined the sword of steel; he wrote Spalatin: "I will not fight the Gospel fight with force and carnage — I have told the man so black on white. By the Word has the world been conquered. By the Word has the Church been preserved. By the Word will her breaches be repaired. And Antichrist, as he began without hand, so will he perish without hand, by the Word alone."

Sense and chivalry.

II. THE BABYLONIAN CAPTIVITY

In his *Address* Luther had "sung high"; he promised an *encore* "still higher." He sang it in only two months in reply to attacks by the Leipzig Franciscan Augustin of Alfeld and the Dominican Isodoro Isolani, and called it *The Babylonian Captivity of the Church* — the picturesque title itself an inspiration of genius.

The pope's seven sacraments are seven rings chaining in a

sevenfold slavery the Christian from the cradle to the grave. Luther insists on the following truths:

1. The Lord's Supper is to be celebrated as Christ instituted it, not without the wine. The Husites are not the heretics, but the popes, who refuse the cup to the people.

Then, the priest does not "make God" by changing the bread into the Lord's body; the bread is nothing but bread, although with it the Lord gives us His body.

Furthermore, the Lord's Supper is not a sacrifice which we offer up to the Lord, in it Christ is not killed in an unbloody manner every time the priest says mass; this is sheer superstition. This witchcraft Luther utterly destroys.

2. Holy Baptism, which is good in itself, the Pope has practically thrust aside by overlaying it with countless vows, orders, satisfactions, pilgrimages, indulgences, special holy works to merit the grace of God, which is granted freely in Baptism. All needed vows we have made in Baptism, and all other vows are harmful.

3. Penance is really not a sacrament. We derive full comfort from the Absolution, the forgiveness of sins, and not from our sorrow and contrition. The repentant sinner is to be heartened in firm faith to trust the forgiveness of God. Faith is the thing, not the fine we pay.

4. Confirmation is not a sacrament. It is very good to teach the children, and, when ripe, to bless them with God's Word; but for this no bishop is needed.

5. Marriage is not a sacrament dependent on a priest. Jews and Gentiles are properly married without a priest. Marriage is not a means of grace, else did the pope sin grievously in forcing celibacy on his priests and inventing so many hindrances to marriage, which are only a part of Roman graft. "I, for my part, detest divorce, and even prefer bigamy to it; but whether it be lawful, I dare not define." Let us remember this was written as early as 1520.

6 Priestly consecration is not a sacrament; that is contrary to the universal priesthood of all believers and a fable invented to make of the priests everlasting slaves to the pope.

7. Extreme unction is not a sacrament; it is a medicine for the recovery of the sick, not a preparation for death.

The Dominican "F. J. Italus" had printed at Cremona *Luther's Recantation,* saying he had returned to the Roman Church. Luther says his *Babylonian Captivity* is his "recantation." Having heard rumors of his excommunication, he quotes —

> Why Herod, unrelenting foe,
> Does Christ the Lord's birth move thee so?
> He doth no earthly kingdom crave
> Who unto us Heaven's kingdom gave.

This work lays the ax to the doctrinal root of the papacy. Luther was well aware of this, but the single man went about the titanic work in a very cool and calm manner. He stalks through the Church and with a rod of iron smites these deadly superstitions as a potter's vessels, and only potsherds remain. He knocked away the underpinning, and papal dominion fell with a crash, and great was the fall thereof. The papacy was built on claims falsely based on Peter; Luther destroyed these claims by the truth really taken from Peter, the universal priesthood of all believers. 1 Pet. 2:9.

Every Christian is a priest of God — that is the spearthrust into the heart of the papacy; that is the blow freeing the layman from the slavery of the clergyman; that is the sword in the hand of Luther, who, like a king, touched the kneeling commoner and said, "Arise, Sir Knight"; that is the surgeon's lancet which cut the cancer from the vitals of Christianity; this is the formula that destroyed the deady spell of the papacy and created the modern world; Luther gave a place to stand to the whole modern civilization; with his "Alone by Faith!" Luther became the liberator.

This is the most radical writing of the most radical reformer. Erasmus thought everything else was pardonable, but this was the unpardonable sin.

Adrian of Utrecht, Kaiser Karl's teacher and governor of Spain, called the work "a devilish book; too crude for a theological student," Luther's freedom "a bondage of the devil."

We note with interest the judgment and the language of the future Pope Adrian VI, who before and after his election denied the pope is infallible.

From this book the papal legate Jerome Aleander drew his material for his three-hour speech against Luther at Worms in 1521.

King Henry VIII of England wrote *Assertion of the Seven Sacraments Against Luther* and won from the pope the title "Defender of the Faith."

Many more followed these high examples, the Sorbonne, Ambrosius Catharinus, Thomas Murner, Cardinal Sforza Pallavicini, *et al.*

The Swiss Glareanus sang the praises of this battle cry of freedom to Zwingli. A preacher of Basel sensed the situation and in a procession carried a Bible with the legend: "The Bible, that is the true relic; all others are dead men's bones."

Bugenhagen, the rector of Treptow in Pomerania, read it and angrily flung it to the ground, "No worse heretic has ever attacked the Church"; but he picked it up, studied the arguments, and said, "The whole world is blind; Luther alone sees the truth!" He became the pastor of the City Church at Wittenberg.

Many of his disciples said, "This is a hard saying; who can hear it?" From that time many of his disciples went back and walked no more with him. John 6:60-66.

III. THE LIBERTY OF A CHRISTIAN MAN

Pope Leo's nuncio Karl von Miltitz still tried to patch up the trouble and got Luther to write Leo about the end of November.

"In all things I will yield to anyone, but I neither can nor will forsake and deny the Word. . . .

"Your see, which is called the court of Rome, and which neither you nor any man can deny to be more corrupt than Sodom and Gomorrah and Babylon, and quite, as I believe, of a lost, desperate, and hopeless impiety, this I have verily abominated and have felt indignant that the people of Christ should be cheated under your name and the pretext of the Church of Rome; and so I have resisted and will resist, as long as the spirit of faith shall live in me. . . .

"I feel myself debtor to my brethren and am bound to take thought for them, that fewer of them may be ruined, or that their ruin may be less complete, by the plagues of Rome. For many years now nothing else has overflowed from Rome into the world — as you are not ignorant — than the laying waste of goods, of bodies, and of souls, and the worst example of all the worst things. The Church of Rome, formerly the most holy of all churches, has become the most lawless den of thieves, the most shameless of all brothels, the very kingdom of sin, death, and hell; so that not even Antichrist, if he were to come, could devise any addition to its wickedness. . . .

"At this day the name of the court of Rome stinks in the nostrils of the world. . . .

"I cannot bear with laws for the interpretation of the Word of God, since the Word of God, which teaches liberty, ought not to be bound. . . .

"Satan himself is in truth more the ruler in that Babylon than you are. . . .

"Behold, Leo, my father, with what purpose and on what principle it is that I have stormed against that seat of pestilence. . . .

"Beware of listening to those sirens who make you out to be not simply a man, but partly a god . . . having power over heaven, hell, and purgatory. . . .

"For since I know . . . you are laboring under such a condition of misery that you need even the least help from any the least brother, I do not seem to myself to be acting unsuitably if I forget your majesty till I shall have fulfilled the office of charity. I will not flatter in so serious and perilous a matter; and if in this you do not see that I am your friend and most thoroughly your subject, there is One to see and judge."

With this amazing letter he sent his booklet *On the Liberty of a Christian Man* to Leo.

"By this you may perceive in what pursuits I should prefer and be able to occupy myself to more profit, if I were allowed, or had been hitherto allowed, by your impious flatterers. It is a small matter if you look at the outside, but unless I mistake, it is a sum of the Christian life put together in small space, if you get its meaning.

"A Christian man is a free lord of all things and subject to none," is the clarion defiance of royal faith, 1 Corinthians.

"A Christian man is the free servant of all things and subject to all," is the willing subjection of loyal love.

These two truths are sharply separated, and then their relation is shown. Heaven is a gift through faith; faith proves its thanks by works of love.

"So we must be sure the soul can lack all things bar God's Word, and outside God's Word nothing can profit the soul. But if the soul has the Word of God, it lacks nothing more; but in the Word has all sufficiency, food, joy, peace, light, art, righteousness, truth, wisdom, freedom, and every good in plenty."

Unmoved by the rumbling thunder and the flickering lightning on the southern horizon, Luther serenely played this pastoral symphony, the pure and perfect expression of his inmost soul, which kept its poise amid the wreck of matter and the crash of worlds.

He sang a song, sweet and strong, a two-part song of faith and love in a perfect blend, faith which worketh by love, so clear and pure and distinct as to be heard with rapturous joy all over the world to the present day.

It is Luther's most pious piece, "the whole sum of Christian life."

Arthur Cushman McGiffert of Union Seminary classes it as "one of the world's great religious classics." Jesuit Hartmann von Grisar gives it high praise.

"A Treatise touching the Libertie of a Christian man, translated by James Bell, Lon. 1579. 1636. 4to." Another, without name and date, "published by John Bydell."

Luther says: "I wrote so much that . . . I weakened myself so that I could not sleep and Dr. Esch had to give me a sleeping powder, the effects of which I still feel in my head."

The effects of his three writings the whole world still feels in the head and heart, and the whole modern civilization is based on the principles laid down in these three great Reformation writings.

Principal Henry Wace of King's College, London, published these three great works under the title, *First Principles of the Reformation,* and says: "From them, and by means of them, the whole of the subsequent movement was worked out. It ought never to be forgotten that for the assertion of the principles themselves, we, like the rest of Europe, are indebted to the genius and the courage of Luther. It was one thing for Englishmen, several decades after 1520, to apply these principles; it was another thing to be the Horatius of that vital struggle. These grand facts speak for themselves, and need only to be understood in order to justify the unprecedented honors now being paid to the Reformer's memory.

"The result was a burst of new life wherever the Reformation was adopted, alike in national energies, in literature, in all social developments, and in natural science."

On November 25 Luther was at the wedding of Melanchthon and Kate Crapp, daughter of a Wittenberg alderman.

THE BULL

"Arise, O God, and plead Thine own cause! . . .

"Arise, Peter! Arise, Paul! Arise, all the company of saints and all the holy Church! A wild swine of the forest uproots the vineyard of the Lord."

Follow forty-one statements of Luther which are now condemned to be burned as heresy.

The 33d — "To burn heretics is against the Holy Ghost."

This is a world-historic bull. Why? It split Christendom into Roman and Protestant.

The god on earth signed it on June 15, 1520, while enjoying his favorite outdoor sport of pig sticking at his Villa Magliana.

Paride de Grassis, the pope's master of ceremonies, diaried how the Holy Father and the cardinals were living in sin.

Erasmus found the bull ferocious. John Eck, the chief author of the bull, in May, 1520, in a confidential letter said in Rome little is known of Luther's errors.

Three years later he said the most learned men could not see why some of the statements were condemned, being so harmless.

Also, the bull had nothing "evangelical and Pauline." The greatest mistake, the bull lacked a thorough disproof of Luther's statements out of the Bible, the Fathers, and the canons of the councils.

The Catholic *Hochland* of October, 1917, printed: "Today every Catholic can subscribe to the Ninety-Five Theses."

Early on December 10 the Wittenbergers saw posted on the door of the City Church Melanchthon's

NOTICE!

"Let everybody in whom zeal for the truth of the Gospel has been kindled be at nine o'clock near Holy Cross Chapel outside of the city walls," etc.

Luther threw into the fire a number of books, the pope's bull, and also the Canon Law, the world's highest law. "Because you have destroyed God's truth, God this day destroy you in this fire!" Psalm 21.

"Amen," said the hearers.

The thousand students, of course, pulled off students' stunts, and a good time was had by all.

Luther wrote Spalatin: "In the year 1520, on the tenth of December, at the ninth hour, were burned at Wittenberg, at the east gate, near the sacred cross, all the books of the pope: the decree, the decretals, the extravagant of Clement VI, and the latest bull of Leo X."

Could Thucydides or Tacitus be more calm and concise?

It reads like a record of a Babylonian king graven in granite, or like Julius Caesar giving an account of a battle in his iron language.

This "sacred drama" is the world's greatest bonfire, Luther's *Auto da fé*, act of faith. He burned his ships behind him; he drew the sword, and threw away the scabbard. Luther says he first trembled, and then prayed, and then rejoiced over this act more than over any other. Here was Christian courage, moral heroism. The pope burned Luther's writings, and Luther burned the pope's writings. And the pope was the vicar of Christ on earth and could command for the suppression of heresy the swords of all the kings of Christendom.

Christopher Scheurl wrote: "Everything resounds with your deeds; now either the Roman or the Saxon front must waver."

At Kaiser Karl's court the Venetian Andrea Rosso judged: "Indeed an enormous event; in view of Martin's great following its importance cannot be estimated too highly."

Poet-laureate Thomas Murner, D. D., and Ambrosius Catharinus sent out fierce denunciations, harmless fireworks.

King Henry's ambassador at Worms, Bishop Tunstal, wrote Cardinal Wolsey: "After Luther perceived that he should not be permitted to come to the Diet hither, as once it was accorded, and safe-conduct granted to him (which, at the instance of the pope's orator [Aleander] was revoked), despairing to be heard in his defense, did openly in the town of Wittenberg gather the people and the university together and burn the decretals, etc., as books erroneous, as he there declared; which his declaration he put in print in the Dutch [German] tongue and sent it all about the country; which declaration by some idle fellow hath been translated into Latin, which I send your Grace . . . call before you the printers and booksellers, and give them a strait charge that they bring none of his books into England, nor translate them into English," etc.

Later Henry agreed with Luther and said to this same Bishop Tunstal: "The lives of Christ and the pope are very opposite, and therefore to follow the pope is to forsake Christ."

No, Henry was not always a fool.

In May, 1520, Erasmus wrote Melanchthon: "It was decided that his [Luther's] books should be burned in England, but I stopped this by writing letters to Cardinal Wolsey. . . . Almost all good men favor Luther. . . . Commend me to Luther. . . . Luther's answer to the condemnation of Cologne and Louvain wonderfully pleased me."

To Rector Paltz of Erfurt: "Hitherto he has certainly profited the world."

To Pope Leo X, on September 13, 1520: "Luther wrote well on the Scriptures. It was above the mediocrity of my learning and talents" to write against him.

Again: "It is much easier to conquer Luther with bulls and with smoke than with arguments. . . . There are many things in Luther's books which are worthy of being known. . . . All who have written against him have composed nothing worth reading. . . . Among those who wish Luther dead I see no good man. The letters of Adrian of Utrecht are full of bitterness; he favors disciples worthy of himself, vain, deceitful, ambitious, and revengeful."

To Rector Rosemund of Louvain on October 18: "From the taste of Luther's works which I have had, I liked his gifts, by which I conjectured he might have been a chosen vessel for Christ had he wished to use his gifts for Christ's glory."

To Diercx, in 1520: "A prominent Dominican said, 'Would that I could fasten my teeth in Luther's throat; I should not fear to go to the Lord's Supper with his blood on my mouth.'"

Writing to Pirkheimer in September, 1520, he expresses his vehement sorrow that "a man from whom he had hoped so much good should have been driven wild by rabid clamors."

In 1530 he writes Bishop Sadoleto: "They should have let alone Luther and his theses about indulgences, and not have poured oil upon the flame."

The Catholic Lilly writes: "Erasmus always held, and never shrank from saying, that Luther had been hounded into revolt; that the Roman Curia had to thank their own blindness and blundering for converting 'a harmless necessary reformer into a needless and noxious rebel.'"

Yes, indeed, "a stupendous event."

For centuries the pope through the king had burned heretics. "To burn heretics is against the will of the Holy Ghost," rang Luther's tenor solo clear and high against the world. The pope condemned that protest as heresy at that day, and the pope condemns that protest as heresy to this day! To this day the pope says, if he had the power, he would burn heretics! "It is a heresy to say that a pope has ever been in error."

"To burn heretics is against the will of the Holy Ghost," is the charter of intellectual and moral freedom for mankind.

On January 3, 1521, the Pope, in the bull *Decet Romanum Pontificem,* excommunicated the "heretic" Luther personally. The bull was, however, so full of errors that the papal nuncio Aleander at Worms returned it to Rome for corrections. On May 6 the revised "holy curse" arrived at Worms.

In January, 1521, the imperial counselor, Jerome von Enndorf, published a pointed protest against the bull, which rode roughshod over the rights of the kaiser, which could not be tolerated.

As early as March 8, 1521, Archbishop Warham wrote Cardinal Wolsey: Oxford "is infected with Lutheranism, . . . a thing pleasant to the Lutherans beyond sea, and a great encouragement if the two universities . . . should embrace these heretical tenets. It would create a great scandal if all now suspected were brought up to London" (to be punished).

When Luther was banned by the pope, Hutten invited him for protection to the Ebernburg of Sickingen, the head of the German knights, who complained of being oppressed by the princes, secular and spiritual. Luther declined to mingle his religion with politics.

In all the world Luther stood alone, "as a field flower," but with his single pen he created the Fourth Estate, the power of the printing press, and with that the modern tribune mobilized the plain people. Never was a lordly patron of the press who prospered it so much as Luther, in the forefront of the greatest authors of the world. Whatever he wrote was a best seller. Glarean wrote Zwingli one dealer at the Frankfort Fair in 1520 sold 1,400 copies of Luther's works, which had never before happened with any other author. Every one speaks well of Luther.

READY TO FACE THE DIET
After Gustav Koenig

Chapter Eight

LUTHER AT WORMS

KARL ELECTED AND CROWNED

Pope Leo X had threatened to ban Frederick for protecting that "wild swine" Luther; now the Holy Father was running him as a candidate for the crown of the Holy Roman Empire of the German Nation! It has been said: "Politics makes strange bed fellows."

On June 21 papal legate Orsini through papal nuncio and chamberlain Karl von Miltitz informed Frederick if he favored the papal policy at the election, he could have a cardinal's hat and a "splendid archbishopric" for any one he would name — Luther! At Worms the elector told this to some princes.

"The Most Christian" King Francis I of France told Sir Thomas Boleyn "he would spend 3,000,000 of gold, but he would be emperor."

Old Max had offered to make Henry VIII of England the German kaiser, and now, though there was no ghost of a chance, Richard Pace was sent to get the crown for Henry, "which was of the Germany tongue"!

Pace reported the money of France and Spain was flowing on all sides and also asked for money to corrupt the honest German electors, though of the opinion the empire was "the dearest merchandise that ever was sold," and would prove "the worst that ever was bought to him that shall obtain it." Not a bad prophet.

Karl, Francis, and Frederick were nominated. Pace was sure Frederick could have had the crown for the asking. But he rose to decline the honor and made Karl kaiser of the Holy Roman Empire of the German Nation on June 28, 1519.

Every elector repeated after Albrecht of Mainz: "I swear on these Gospels here open before me my voice, vote, and my suffrage shall be given unbiased by any pact, price, pledge, or engagement under any pretense whatsoever. So help me God, and all His holy saints and angels!"

The crown of the Holy Roman Empire of the German Nation was put up on the auction block and knocked down to the highest bidder. No German would take it, and so it was knocked down to a foreigner, the nineteen-year-old king of Spain, for 12,000,000 gold florins, say $6,750,000.

The foreigner at Antwerp in September received Leo's legate, Girolamo Aleandro, librarian of the Vatican, and eloquent Latinist, who knew Greek and Hebrew, studied Chaldaic and Arabic, was versed in affairs, of great energy, about forty years old, one of the ablest men to serve the ends of the pope.

This wily Italian wheedled out of the lad an edict to burn the books of Luther, "the new Arius and Mohammed" — and they were burned in October at Louvain and at Liege. Ominous beginning!

Karl the Great, the first kaiser of the Holy Roman Empire of the

German Nation, was crowned at Aachen; at his grave Karl V was crowned on October 23.

The city of the Caesars was famed for some precious relics — cloth on which had lain the head of John the Baptist and the trousers of Joseph, in which the Christ Child had been wrapped; these were devoutly revered by the austere young Catholic Caesar.

Would Luther go to Worms if called by the kaiser?

"I will do what in me lies to be carried there sick, if I cannot go well. . . . He lives and reigns who preserved the three young men in the furnace of the Babylonian king. If He is unwilling to keep me, my life is a small thing compared with Christ's, who was wickedly slain to the disgrace of all and harm of many. . . . I will not flee, much less recant. So may the Lord Jesus strengthen me!" Not brutal bravado, but Christian courage to suffer martyrdom.

On January 4 Staupitz wrote Link: "Martin has undertaken a hard task and acts with great courage enlightened by God. I stammer and am a child needing milk."

THE SENTIMENT AT WORMS

On January 21, 1521, King Henry's ambassador Tunstal wrote Wolsey: "The Germans everywhere are so addicted to Luther, that, rather than he shall be oppressed by the pope's authority (who hath already condemned his opinions), the people will spend a hundred thousand of their lives. They have informed the emperor that he is a good and virtuous man, besides his learning.

"At the exequy of the cardinal of Croy, in the presence of the electors, the emperor, the pope's ambassadors, and the cardinals, a friar preacher made a sermon, and in the beginning said the pope was *Vicarius Christi in spiritualibus,* and the cardinals and bishops were *apostoli* etc. But how his tongue turned in his head I cannot tell; but after[,] he concluded that the emperor, when they do amiss, should reform their abuses, even to depose them. . . . In his said sermon he exhorted the emperor and all the princes to go into Italy, which is of the Empire, and to reform such abuses as be there; whereunto I understand many of the princes be inclined, because every man thinketh to gain thereby. . . . Luther offereth, if the emperor will go to Rome to reform the Church, to bring him 100,000 men, whereunto the emperor, as a virtuous prince, will not hearken. The said Luther hath many great clerks that hold with him."

Aleander on February 8 wrote Cardinal Guilio Medici, cousin of Pope Leo and "the other pope," the acting pope, he could rely only on the "red hats," the cardinals of Mainz, Salzburg, and Sitten, and their followers, "otherwise many wish Luther well," many more wish Rome ill. "All German princes bother the kaiser with fierce complaints against us. It rains daily Lutheran writings in German and Latin. Nothing else is bought here except Luther's books, even in the imperial court. . . . A little while ago at Augsburg they were selling Luther's picture with a halo; it was offered without the halo for sale here, and all the copies were disposed of in a trice before I could get one. Not the good old Catholic Germany."

That halo shows that, as Aleander says, "the people thought Luther sinless and infallible and having miraculous powers."

"Now the whole of Germany is in full revolt; nine tenths raise the war cry 'Luther,' while the watchword of the other tenth, who are indifferent to Luther, is 'Death to the Roman Curia!'" Only the kaiser sided with Rome; were he to yield in the least, all Germany would fall away from the papacy. And even the kaiser feared to use force on account of Elector Frederick and from a desire to use Luther to bring the pope to time. To Cardinal Pucci he reports that two knights discussed Luther's books with great admiration in the kaiser's room till he expressed his displeasure.

To Eck on February 17: "It is with great danger that I stay in Germany. . . . Not only men, but stocks and stones shout Luther's name. It is not remarkable that laymen should do so, but in this campaign the priests are the leaders, not so much to favor Luther, that pernicious monster, as to spout forth from his mouth their long accumulated venom against the city of Rome and the priesthood."

Aleander calls Luther "the Antichrist," but too much of an ignoramus to be the author of the books going under his name. Elector Frederick is "the infamous Saxon," a fat hog, with the eyes of a dog, which rarely look anyone straight in the face, a basilisk and a fox, who supports Luther only because of the fame and prosperity he brings to the university and town of Wittenberg. Aleander owns he used flattery, threats, bribery, and falsehoods quite freely for the good of the pope's cause. Also he earnestly urged the pope to redress the crying abuses in the Church by an intelligent study of the Scriptures, "after the example of the Germans."

On Ash Wednesday, February 13, Aleander rhetorically belabored the *Reichstag* for three hours to condemn Luther unheard. He got his ammunition from the "wild swine's" *Babylonian Captivity of the Church.*

Elector Frederick opposed the step so that he almost came to blows with Elector Joachim I of Brandenburg.

French Franciscan Jean Glapion, Kaiser Karl's confessor, at Worms told Saxon Chancellor Gregory Brueck he rejoiced over Luther's writings, finding in them a noble new plant in Luther's heart, with useful fruits that might have come to the Church. But when he read the *Babylonian Captivity* in October, 1520, he felt as if some one had scourged him from head to foot.

To Elector Frederick he said: "Luther has the merit of being the first to call powerfully for a reformation of the Church, disfigured by many abuses, and thereby strengthened and heartened many timid people, who from the bottom of their hearts wished for the same. I mean well, for I myself desire nothing more than the reformation of the Church. The Bible is soft wax to be pulled and twisted into any shape."

He did not praise Aleander's burning of Luther's books. Luther's Theses against the indulgences were to be praised, and there were not many scholars that did not agree with him. He thought the pope wrong in saying the kaiser had no business with Luther's case. He told the kaiser God would punish him and all princes did they not cleanse the Church from its enormous errors. God sent this Luther as a scourge for their sins. Ambrosius Catharinus was no match for Luther, he was writing into the air. Luther had almost brought the goods into port and should not now spoil it by refusing to retract the *Babylonian Captivity.*

Kaiser Karl himself was well pleased with Luther's writings till the *Babylonian Captivity.* He wished with all his heart so learned a man might be led back into the bosom of the Catholic Church.

To Sickingen and Hutten up in the Ebernburg Glapion said: "Not even mortal enemies can deny Martin was the first to open for all Christians the right door to the secret of the right understanding of Holy Writ." So Hutten wrote Erasmus.

The Venetian secretary wrote home, even if the Saxon elector would wish to expel or otherwise punish Luther, the German people would not permit it. The good Catholic Duke William of Bavaria said had Luther not gone beyond his first demands, he would have been not favored but worshiped by all Germany.

On March 13, the elegant Erasmus wrote: "I do not object if they wish Luther roasted or boiled; the loss of one man is small. ... No one would believe how deeply Luther has crept into the minds of many nations, nor how widely his books have been translated into every tongue and scattered everywhere.... I do not plead Luther's cause, nor I do care how he is punished."

On Maundy Thursday, March 28, the pope, in the bull *In Coena Domini* condemned Luther in so many words as an excommunicate heretic, and this was repeated from the pulpit every Maundy Thursday till 1770.

As usual, money was the least, and so Karl borrowed 130,000 florins from the Augsburg Welsers. Security? "Welser's Land," now Venezuela.

"Honorable, dear, and pious" — who's that?

The "wild swine," whom the Vicar of Christ had banned. Then who dares address him so lovingly? Kaiser Karl V of the Holy Roman Empire of the German Nation!

And what did he want?

"To obtain information about certain doctrines coming from you and certain books written by you."

"Honorable, dear, and pious!" snorted the disgusted Aleander, "this title they give to an open heretic against God and man. It's enough to drive a stone crazy, let alone a man." Politics certainly does make strange letters, and who can blame the righteous wrath of the worthy and virtuous legate? The Holy Father at Rome also received a jolt in his luxurious pleasures and went his legate one better: "Luther would not be received even in hell" — *ergo* he should not be received at Worms. In a burst of confidence we must admit quite frankly that we can pick no flaw in Leo's logic. The kaiser's agent at Rome, John Manuel, sent this bit of information on March 20, and at the same time advised his master to show favor to Luther, whom the pope greatly feared. The pope feared Luther, and the pope's legate feared Luther.

While Worms on the Rhine was seething like a witches' cauldron, Luther on the Elbe sent a little fuel to add to the flames. On March 7 he sent signed copies of his portrait to Spalatin to spread among his followers. Then he kept on calmly preaching and teaching as usual and for good measure keeping three presses going with his writings. He would be like Nehemiah, with one hand wield the sword against his Arabs, with the other wield the trowel to build the walls of Jerusalem. But he was "amid the swords, bulls, and war trumpets of the papists," and they would give him no peace. "Hercules had to deal with one hydra (with nine heads), I must fight ten of them." "I am doing the work of seven men," and yet so many precious hours were stolen by the endless visitors — Elector Joachim of Brandenburg, Duke Boguslav of Pomerania, and others.

LUTHER'S JOURNEY TO WORMS

On Tuesday after Easter, April 2, Kaspar Sturm of Oppenheim, the kaiser's herald, called Teutschland, a notorious Luther fan, with the banner of the German Reich over his arm, rode out of Wittenberg. There followed a covered wagon, the property of Christian Doering, the goldsmith and optician, drawn by three horses, furnished by the city council. In it rode the banned Luther with his cloister companion Petzensteiner; with Student Peter Swaven, a Pomeranian nobleman; with Amsdorf, who would as Squire Jerome go with the new Hus to be burned, for he had no safe-conduct, which touching faithfulness Luther never forgot. The university gave twenty gulden for traveling expenses.

On to Worms, where the greenish-golden Rhine is singing the melodies it sang to Caesar and Drusus; where it separated Worms and Krimhild's rose garden; where the Nibelungen queens scolded each other before Dagobert's dome; where began the strife between Kaiser Henry IV and Pope Gregory VII; where soon shall be staged the most dramatic and historic strife between a simple man and the world.

BURNING OF SAVONAROLA

Luther was sent for by the "Rom. Imp. Majesty," and so Leipzig presented him with "3 half Stobichen Rheinfall for 24 Gr. and 3 half Stobichen Rhenish wine for 12 Gr., total 36 Gr."

On April 6 Rector Rubeanus Crotus of the university with forty horsemen rode out two miles beyond Erfurt to greet him like a prince, escort him to the Augustinian cloister, and then to a great banquet in his honor.

"On the request of many excellent scholars" he had to preach in the crowded church on the Gospel of the day, John 20:19-23, "How to become godly and be saved." Eobanus Hessus likened him to Demosthenes or St. Paul, through whose powerful words hearts melted like snow in spring as he showed the way to the treasures of heaven, which had been closed for hundreds of years.

From Erfurt the herald reported to the kaiser: "Luther comes after all. All over all the world, old and young, boys and girls, stream out in a triumphal procession to Dr. Luther, without my being able to hinder them."

"The kaiser's men were thunderstruck," Aleander reports and blames the herald for the rousing receptions received by Luther.

At Naumburg Mayor Gresser dined the damned heretic, and a priest presented a portrait of Savonarola, who had been burned by Pope Aleander VI. Finding Luther unafraid of the omen, the priest bade him plant his foot firmly on God's truth.

At Eisenach he preached and fell so sick they despaired of his life. They bled him, and Oswald gave him "a precious water," which put him to sleep.

On Sunday, April 14, he stayed at Wolf Parente's "Hotel Ostrich" at the Corn Market at Frankfurt. He joyously played the lute, which gave Cochlaeus a chance to sneer at "a new Orpheus but in tonsure and cowl."

Matron Froeschin sent him two measures of Malmsey and hailed him as the herald of a dawning new era, breaking the pope's privileges, and of whom members of her family had prophesied.

"When we came to Weimar, there came the report at Worms Doctor Martinus was already condemned and my books burned. And so it was.... Now the herald asked me, 'Herr Doktor, will you go on?' I answered, 'Yes, though they have banned me and make it known in all cities, I will still go on and hold to the kaiser's safe-conduct.'"

The Weimarers warned him he would be burned like Hus. "And if they'll build a fire between Wittenberg and Worms reaching to heaven, I'll appear in God's name, since I have been called, and tread in Behemoth's mouth between his great teeth and confess Christ."

"When I was near Worms, Spalatin sent warning not to come and run into danger. But I answered, 'I am coming, dear Spalatin, even if Satan tries to hinder me by a worse sickness than that from which I am now suffering; for I have been ill all the way from Eisenach and am yet so ill as I have never been before. I know that the mandate of Karl has been published to scare me. Truly, Christ lives, and I shall enter Worms in the face of the gates of hell and the princes of the air.'"

At Oppenheim Bucer, Sickingen's chaplain, in Hutten's name

invited Luther to the Ebernburg, where Glapion, the kaiser's chapplain, had some important things to say privately.

"If the kaiser's confessor has anything to say to me, he may do so in Worms."

Had the trick worked, the safe-conduct would have expired, and Luther could have been done to death and not been able to appear at all at the *Reichstag*. The kaiser had given Sickingen a military command and Hutten a yearly pension of 400 gulden.

Spalatin wrote, the elector says he cannot protect Luther, already condemned, and advises him not to come!

"I'll go on to Worms, and if there were as many devils there as tiles on the roofs. Though Hus was burned, the truth was not burned."

A few days before his death he said, "I was fearless, afraid of nothing; God can make one so reckless. I don't know if I could be so joyful now."

Ulrich von Hutten remarked, "Fears death! There is no one in all Germany who knows so little of the fear of death as Luther; he despises it."

The best picture of this is Albrecht Duerer's striking "Knight, Death, and the Devil."

On April 16 at ten in the morning trumpets sounded from the spire of the Dome, and all Worms jumped up from lunch and crowded the streets. Enter the imperial herald Sturm and his servant. Behind them the covered wagon with Luther and his companions. Behind them the mounted young Erfurt professor Justus Jonas. Behind him about a hundred horsemen who had ridden out early in the morning to meet Martin Luther and were overjoyed to see him so cheerful. Surrounding all were about 2,000 Wormsers, escorting the new visitor to his room at the Knights of St. John in Kaemmerer Street, which he shared with his protectors, Herr Bernhard von Hirschfeld and Herr Hans Schott von Oberwindt. Housing shortage.

And Aleander had begged the kaiser to have the monk sneaked in secretly! He reports to Rome: "When Luther left the wagon, a priest embraced him, touched his gown three times, and, on leaving, boasted having handled a relic of the greatest saint. I suspect

KNIGHT, DEATH, AND THE DEVIL
By *Albrecht Duerer*

they'll soon say he performs miracles. This Luther, on getting down from the wagon, looked around with his demonic eyes and said, 'God will be with me!' Then he entered a room, where many lords looked him up, with whom he also dined, and after dinner all the world ran to see him."

Not even at the public entry of the new kaiser had there been such multitudes. The *Pfalzgraf* "roared like ten bulls" for Luther's cause. Erasmus wrote Jonas on May 10: "Luther has such favor from all men as I believe no mortal ever had before for centuries."

Charles Beard says never did a conquering general have such a triumph in ancient Rome as Luther from Wittenberg to Worms.

"When my enemies heard I was coming, they did not want my safe-conduct to be kept. But the Count Palatine on the Rhine opposed it and so sharply encountered the elector of Brandenburg, Markgraf Joachim the Elder, that they both reached for their daggers. But when they told the kaiser a heretic's safe-conduct need not be kept, he gave the noble answer, 'What one has promised, one must keep!'"

The next morning the sick Hans von Minkwitz wished to see Luther. Even on that day he went to comfort him and gave him the Lord's Supper. Just like him — cool, calm, and collected amid an earthquake; always the self-sacrificing pastor.

LUTHER'S FIRST APPEARANCE

On Wednesday, April 17, at 4 P.M., the imperial marshal, Ulrich von Pappenheim, and the imperial herald, Kaspar von Sturm, came to escort the notorious heretic to the bishop's palace, where Karl and Ferdinand stayed and the *Reichstag* met. They simply could not get through the dense crowds come to view the new Arius, and had to pick their way through back yards and houses.

After a wait of two long hours the heretic was led into the small hall. There, enthroned, sat Kaiser Karl V of the Holy Roman Empire of the German Nation. He was the son of the dissolute Philip the Fair, son of Kaiser Max, and Johanna the Monomaniac, daughter of Ferdinand and Isabella, friends of Columbus. He was a pale stripling of twenty-one, with pale-blue eyes, a hooked nose, poor teeth, and a heavy protruding jaw. Every educated person could speak Latin, but he could not speak Latin; the king of Spain could not speak Spanish; the lord of a large part of Italy could not speak Italian; the lord of the Netherlands could not speak Dutch; the German kaiser could not speak German; he could only speak French, and the business of the German Reich had to be done in French. Such was the mighty monarch on whose dominions in Europe and America the sun never set. Even now Magellan was circling the globe and discovering the Philippine Islands; even now Cortez was winning Mexico; even now, right here at Worms, was an Indian from America (discovered by Columbus, but first pointed out to him by the German Martin Behaim on his globe). Below him sat his brother, Ferdinand, archduke of Austria, later kaiser. On the right the spiritual electors, on the left the secular electors.

D. Butzbach reports 80 princes, 130 counts, 15 ambassadors, and crowds of knights and nobles.

LUTHER'S ENTRANCE INTO WORMS

This most brilliant gathering, the most fateful *Reichstag,* was faced by the lone Luther. Two worlds faced each other.

Johann von der Ecken, an official of Elector Cardinal Richard von Greiffenklau, roomed with Aleander, who calls him "the excellent Dr. Ecken, who at Trier had so very thoroughly burned Martin's books."

This bitter enemy was the spokesman of the young kaiser.

"Will you retract these books, or some of them?"

"I humbly beg Your Imperial Majesty to give me time to think, that I may answer without violence to the Word of God or peril to my soul."

Kaiser Karl had called Luther "to obtain information," had not said a single word about recantation; now he refused information and demanded recantation. In view of this historical, documentary fact this speech of the unworldly monk before the worldly magnates was a finished masterpiece. It was not *finesse,* adroitness, slippery diplomacy; it was sheer, downright, manly honesty. Had he wished to recant, he could have recanted at home. He had not made the

LUTHER BEFORE THE GERMAN REICHSTAG   BROWN BROTHERS

journey simply to plead "Guilty" or "Not guilty"; he had come to explain and defend his teaching in public.

Aleander reports: "Some think him a fool, some a demoniac; some a saint and filled with the Holy Ghost."

"After the first impression the kaiser said with great disdain, '*He* will never make a heretic of *me*,' and more than once remarked he would never believe *that* monk had written those books."

"In the meantime many of the nobility came into my lodgings and said, 'Herr Doktor, how are you? They say they want to burn you; but that must not be. Sooner they all must perish together!' And that would have happened."

Canon George Cuspinian of Wuerzburg drew a pen-and-ink picture of Luther, which he sent to his cousin John Cuspinian, the kaiser's councilor at Vienna, to which Luther added a note:

"Not a single dot will I retract, if Christ grants me grace."

"If Christ grants me grace" — no bully bravado there, but Christian courage.

The same night he was overheard making his famous prayer to God for help in God's cause. The night was spent in consultation.

On the 18th Luther again had to wait from 4 to 6, when the torches were lighted and the session began in the large hall, which was crowded; some had come at 10 to get standing room. Luther stood among the crowding, standing nobles.

Again von der Ecken asked, "Do you wish to defend all your books or to retract some of them?"

In a clear, brave voice Luther answered in German, as written by himself afterwards.

LUTHER'S SPEECH AT WORMS

He divided his books into three classes.

"In some I have treated piety, faith, and morals so simply and evangelically that my adversaries themselves are forced to confess that these books are useful, innocent, and worthy to be read by Christians. . . . Even the bull, though fierce and cruel, states that some things in my books are harmless, although it condemns them by a judgment simply monstrous. If, therefore, I should undertake to recant these, would it not happen that I alone of all men should damn the truth which all, friends and enemies alike, confess?

"The second class of my works assails the papacy as that which both by precept and example has laid waste all Christendom, body and soul. No one can deny or hide this fact, since general complaints witness that the consciences of all believers are snared, harassed, and tormented by the laws of the pope and the teachings of men. . . . If, therefore, I should withdraw these books, I would strengthen tyranny and open windows and doors to their impiety, which would then flourish and thrive more freely than it ever dared before. . . . Good God! In that case I were the tool of iniquity and tyranny.

"In the third kind of books I have written against some private individuals who tried to defend the Roman tyranny and tear down my pious doctrine. In these I confess I was more bitter than be-

LUTHER MONUMENT AT WORMS
By Rietschel

coming a minister of religion. For I do not pose as a saint, nor do I discuss my life, but the teaching of Christ. Yet neither is it right for me to revoke what I have said in these, for then tyranny and impiety would rage and reign against the people of God more violently than ever by reason of my giving in.

"As I am human and not God, I wish to enter no other defense of my teaching than the one put forth by the Lord Jesus when He was questioned before Annas and smitten by a servant: He then said, 'If I have spoken evil, bear witness of the evil.' If the Lord Himself, who knew that He could not err, did not scorn to hear testimony against His teaching from a miserable servant, how much more should I, the dregs of men, who can do nothing but err, seek and hope that some one should bear witness against my teaching. I therefore beg by God's mercy that if Your Majesty or Your Illustrious Lordships, from the highest to the lowest, can do it, you should bear witness and convict me of error and conquer me by proofs drawn from the Gospels or the Prophets, for I am most ready to be taught, and when convinced, will be the first to throw my books into the fire. . . .

"With these words I commend myself to Your Majesty and Your Lordships, humbly begging that you will not let my enemies make me hateful to you without cause."

Asked to repeat his speech in Latin, he did as bid, "although on account of the crush he was very hot."

Von der Ecken was told to demand a very short, clear-cut answer. "Luther, you have not answered to the point. Expect no debate. Answer uprightly and honestly, unequivocally and unreservedly: Will you retract your books and the errors in them, or not?"

With reckless daring Luther at bay defiantly fired back: "Since Your Majesty and Your Lordships ask of me a plain answer, I shall give you such without horns [reservations] and teeth [points]: Unless convinced by Scripture and reason [logical deductions from Scripture] — for I believe neither the pope nor the councils alone, since it is evident they have at times erred and contradicted one another — I am overcome in conscience by the Scriptures quoted and bound in the word of God. Therefore I can and will retract nothing, for it is neither safe nor wholesome to act against conscience. Here I stand; I cannot do otherwise. God help me. Amen."

Some deny Luther said these last words; none deny he acted these words. He stood! And what Phillips Brooks calls the finest monument in modern Europe stands in Worms to celebrate the historical fact that he stood, stood alone against pope and kaiser, against death and hell.

"To the fire with him!" was the farewell yell of the Spaniards. The Germans raised their arms and spread their fingers — the sign of victory!

Sixt Oelhafen about 9 hurriedly reported to Nuernberg: "Coming to his quarters, in my presence he stretched out his hands and with a merry face cried, 'I'm through! I'm through! Had I a thousand heads, I had rather have them all chopped off than recant."

Even the stolid Frederick was stirred enough to say proudly to Spalatin: "Well did Doctor Martin speak before the kaiser and all princes and estates in Latin and in German; he is much too bold for me!"

COMMENTS

J. A. Froude of Oxford comments: "No more notable spectacle had been witnessed in this planet for many a century — not, perhaps, since a greater than Luther stood before the Roman procurator." — Christ before Pilate.

William Stearns Davis judges: "Since the hour when Jesus Christ cried, 'It is finished' on the cross and by His sacrifice redeemed this world, mankind has seen few or no hours greater, more potent for the far hereafter, than that scene in the hall before princes and emperor."

Friedrich Nietzsche and Hans Preuss declare Luther saved Christianity.

Thomas Mann is rated by *Time* the greatest living German writer. This Jew writes: "I frankly confess that I do not love him . . . the venerable lout of Wittenberg. . . . No one can deny that Luther was a tremendously great man. . . . He actually saved Christianity. . . . Luther's revolution preserved Christianity. . . . He advanced the cause of European democracy; for 'every man his own priest,' that is democracy. . . . All that comes from Luther. He was a liberating hero."

THE EDICT OF WORMS

"This blessed day the kaiser with his blessed hands signed the blessed mandate, more terrible than any ever before," reported Aleander, the legate of the Roman pope, who wrote the most important state paper of the German kaiser.

"Luther dares bring in errors and heresies whereby the whole German nation and later other nations would come into an inhuman split and a miserable decline of good customs, peace, and the Christian faith. He destroys all obedience and government and writes nothing but what incites to riot, split, war, murder, robbery, and the complete fall from the Christian faith. He teaches a free, self-willed, lawless life. Not as a human being, but as the devil in human form with a monk's cowl he has collected the condemned heresies of many heretics, hidden for long, adding some of his own invention, into one stinking cesspool and pretends to preach the faith in order to destroy the true, real faith, and under the name and show of evangelical teaching crush all evangelical peace and love, also all good order and the most beautiful estate of Christendom. So everyone must see it is only fair and wholesome to proceed with all means of force against him as one possessed by the evil spirit and declare said Martin Luther a member cut off from God's Church, a hardened schismatic, and a manifest heretic. All and sundry are forbidden to house, shelter, feed, water, or harbor Luther and either by words or works, secretly or openly, to aid and abet him in any wise, but when possible to take him and deliver him to us [— to be burned, of course]. For one's trouble in this holy work a suitable reward will be given."

Everybody in the whole German Empire is to arrest every one of Luther's favorers and take their goods for his own use. He promised his confessor to hang the first one caught with a book or picture of Luther. He signed the ferocious edict in the Dome after mass on Trinity Sunday, May 26, but dated back to May 8.

He signed it laughing — he was only 21. "Woe to thee, O land, when thy king is a child!" Eccl. 10:16.

And then the laughing lad sailed down the Rhine to play with the Dutch girls and made Jeanne van der Gheest the mother of what he lovingly called "my bastard Margaret." When near 50, he made the Nuernberg patrician Barbara Blomberg the mother of Don Juan d'Austria, the hero of Lepanto. His only child born in wedlock was the notorious Philip II. Elliott-Binns calls Karl "a chronic adulterer."

But he spent large sums for masses for his soul in purgatory, and he devoutly kissed the pictures of the saints in his prayer book, and he fasted often, and he made a holy war on the Lutheran heretics.

Though the mighty kaiser himself graced the burning of Luther's books at Ghent on July 25, 1521, did that stop the spread of Luther's teaching?

In that very same July Cardinal Albrecht of Mainz wrote the pope: "Since the bull of Your Holiness and the edict of the emperor, the number of Lutherans is increased. There are very few laymen to be found who simply and honestly side with the clergy; while a great number of the priests favor Luther and a majority are ashamed to support the Roman Church."

THE WARTBURG IN THE DAYS OF LUTHER

Chapter Nine

LUTHER AT THE WARTBURG

Luther! What was become of Luther?

On leaving Worms he preached at Moehra, the home of the Luther sib. Near the Castle of Altenstein horsemen suddenly galloped up with raised weapons and cried "Halt!"

"I am torn out of the wagon and put on a horse" — with his Hebrew and New Testaments. "The horsemen ride criss-cross through the woods, to throw pursuers off the track, till it gets dark. During the night I come to the Wartburg near Eisenach."

The horsemen were Captain Hans von Berlepsch of the Wartburg and Captain Burkhard Hunt von Wenkheim of Castle Altenstein.

The monk had to doff his cowl and don doublet and hose, a red leather slouch hat, a gold chain, a sword, grow a thick crop of black hair and a full beard — behold the belted knight Junker Joerg, Sir Knight George!

Did he think of St. Killian, who came from Ireland about 600 to plant the Gospel in these parts? Or of the Venerable Bede, who labored for the conversion of the Germans? Or of the English women Thekla of Wimborne and Walburgis, who labored in this region? Did he dream about the strife of the Minnesingers, Wolfram von Eschenbach and Walther von der Vogelweide, and Klingsohr of Siebenbuergen ending the contest in 1207? Did he dream of Tannhaeuser and the Venusberg when he looked at the bare ridge of the Hoersel? Did he dream of St. Elizabeth of Hungary, betrothed when four to Louis of Thueringen when eleven?

He watched the gambols of the lambs, the flight of the doves, the colliers' fires by day and their smoke by night, and thought of the pillar of fire and of smoke in the wilderness; the smell of new-mown hay and of thyme was in his nostrils, and the music of the birds in his ears; at night the bats came out, and he heard the ravens and the owls.

"When I sat up at the Wartburg in my Patmos . . . I had two armed servants to attend me . . . and two pages of gentle blood, who brought me meals twice a day" — at 10 and at 5.

The poor monk felt oppressed by the kind care shown him. "It is my nature to be afraid of burdening people when perhaps I do not, but such a scruple becomes an honorable man." Highstrung, high-toned, high-minded, this "German beast and boor"!

"As a Junker I often went down to hunt, gather strawberries, and visited with the Franciscans at Eisenach." In August the amateur Nimrod wrote Spalatin: "I spent two days hunting, a worthy occupation for idle people. Here amid the nets and dogs I have entertained my theological thoughts, and though I felt some pleasure in seeing these things, yet the similitude and parable which are hidden beneath it gave me sorrow and pain. For what does the picture represent but that the devil, through his ungodly masters and dogs, the bishops and theologians, doth secretly chase and catch the innocent little things? The picture of the simple and believing souls did so vividly appear to my soul. To this was added that a 'wee rabbit,' which I had tried myself to keep alive and had hid in the sleeve of my coat, was scented by the dogs during my short absence, and they, through the coat, bit and crushed its right foot and choked it to death. Thus pope and Satan rage to ruin even the saved souls, without paying any attention to my exertions. I am sick of this chase; I consider that chase more enjoyable in which, with spears and arrows, bears, wolves, wild boars, foxes and the like, which represent ungodly teachers, are taken. This is to be my literary jest to you so that you game-eaters at court may know that you also will be game in Paradise, which Christ, the best Hunter, can scarcely catch and preserve."

Yes, a poet's eye sees poetry everywhere. Luther was no vulgar pothunter. He had the true sporting blood in his veins for really big game — the pope and Satan, foemen worthy of his steel. At the same time see the damned outlaw hugging poor Bunny! In that human Gibraltar there is a heart as tender as that of Francis of Assisi freeing a trapped hare, as tender and as poetical as that of Bobby Burns plowing up a mouse —

> Wee, sleekit, cowrin', tim'rous beastie.

Luther could not pass the time in such pastime, and he found his pastime in hard work. In about nine months he finished three interrupted works and about ten new ones.

"I am very idle, and still, at the same time, very busy, learning Hebrew and Greek and writing without end. The warden treats me far better than I deserve. The trouble with which I suffered at Worms has not left me, but got worse, for I am more constipated than I ever was and despair of a remedy."

The monk wrote *On Monastic Vows* and dedicated it to his father. In it he undermined the foundations of all monkery and held it one of his most important books; it had an enormous sale and wide influence in his day. In our day an eminent Catholic thought it worth his while to "refute" it point by point — after four centuries!

The new teaching needed preaching, and Luther the teacher became Luther the preacher, *the* preacher. He printed twenty-four sermons of his famous *Church Postil* — "my very best book."

This book began a new era, that of the Protestant pulpit, the first swallow to herald the coming summer of Gospel sermons. After four hundred years it is still the most widespread and wide-read postil of Christendom.

Good sermons are good, very good; still better a good translation of God's own Word.

"Would that the Bible alone might be on the tongue and in the hands, the eyes, the ears, and the hearts of all men! Would to God all explanations might perish and every Christian for himself read the bare text of Scripture and the pure Word of God!"

Luther had a good wishbone, also a good backbone. About New Year, 1522, he wrote Amsdorf: "I am going to translate the Bible, although I know the work is beyond my strength. Now I see what it means to translate and why no one that tried it has yet set his name to it."

In less than eleven weeks the New Testament was done, a titanic performance, though he had brought with him parts he had translated for his lectures.

Archbishop Albrecht of Mainz was still in need of money. Luther had queered Tetzel's confidence game of indulgences, and so a new scheme had to be gotten up to cop the coin by swindling the simple, superstitious people.

In 1519 Albrecht, the friend of Erasmus and Hutten, procured a papal bull granting indulgences to all seeking such grace at his relics at Halle. The printed catalog advertised hair of the Virgin Mary, and yarn spun by her, and six bottles of milk from her breast the basin in which Pilate had washed his hands; earth from Damascus from which God had created Adam, and from Hebron, where Adam had repented; manna from heaven fallen in the wilderness; a portion of Isaac's body; twenty-five pieces of Moses' burning bush; the finger Thomas thrust into the side of Christ; the arm of Luke that wrote his Gospel; the finger of John the Baptist that pointed to Christ as the Lamb of God, etc., etc. — "8,933 portions and forty-two whole bodies: makes an indulgence of 39,000,000,-245,120 years, 220 days." Holy humbug of the ecclesiastical Barnum!

The damned and banned monk wrote: "You seek to reinstate at Halle the idol which kills soul and body, which robs the poor

LUTHER PREACHING IN THE WARTBURG
After Vogel

Christian of his soul and money.... If in fourteen days I do not receive a distinct answer from you, I shall publish my little volume on the idol of Halle...."

What happened? The proud Hohenzollern prince, and archbishop, and elector, and cardinal, meekly answered: "Dear Doctor, I have received your letter dated the Sunday after the feast of St. Catherine and have read it with friendly feelings. What you say astonishes me; as the abuses which you point out have been stopped. Henceforward I shall conduct myself, with the help of God, as a good prince and priest. I own that I have great need of the help and grace of God, poor, weak sinner that I am, who sins daily. I know that without the grace of God, I who am but dung can do no good.

"Such is my answer, for I feel inclined to show you how much I love you. I submit willingly to a brotherly reprimand, and I hope the Lord will grant me grace to live in the practice of His holy commandments. Halle, 21st of October — "Albert (*with my own hand*)."

This from the most proud and powerful prince of Germany to a damned and banned heretic in hiding! Do you know the like? Neither do we.

Looking at Luther at the Wartburg, the Catholic Audin writes: "We fancy that we dream: and we would that this dream would last longer, for we cling to that wondrous being. There is in the letters which he writes from his 'Patmos' a mass of internal paintings which captivate by the finish of the details almost like a picture by Karl du Jardin."

"The pages had bought me a sack of hazelnuts, which I ate at times, and kept them in a chest. As I slept a little, there was such a racket as if a score of barrels were thrown down the stairs. . . . I get up, go to the stairs to see what's up. Then said I, 'Is that you [Satan], so be it.' And commended myself to the Lord Christ and again laid me down in bed."

Froude comments: "Think as you please about the cause of the noise, but remember that Luther had not the least doubt that he was alone in the room with the actual devil, who, if he could not overcome his soul, could at least twist his neck in a moment — and think what courage there must have been in a man who could deliberately sleep in such a presence!"

A good story goes one night Luther saw the devil and boldly hurled his oaken inkpot at him. The earliest form of it is by Fynes Moryson, who registered at Wittenberg on June 12, 1591, and saw "an aspersion of ink cast by the Divell when he tempted Luther, upon the wall of St. Augustine's college." Peter the Great also saw the spot at Wittenberg. Others saw it in the Coburg. Archdeacon Julius Charles Hare, chaplain of Queen Victoria, tells us: "At the Wartburg — in 1811 — I saw the traces of Luther's ink on the wall and there I first learned the art of hurling inkstands at the head of the devil." He studied the works of Luther and wrote an effective *Vindication of Luther Against His Recent English Assailants.* When Carlyle went to Germany to study the battlefields of Frederick the Great, he turned aside to visit the Wartburg and remarked about the famous inkspot: "A most small sneer has been grounded on it by some . . .; but the man's heart that dare rise defiant, face to face, against Hell itself, can give no higher proof of fearlessness. The thing he will quail before exists not on this earth or under it. Fearless enough!"

He saw the room in which Luther had translated the New Testament, "to me the most venerable of all rooms I ever entered. I kissed his old oak table," he wrote his mother, and on his return to London he told Baron Bunsen, "I think that little room in which Luther stood fighting God's battle against the whole world is the most sacred place on the earth." In his *Prinzenraub* he writes: "One feels . . . as if here, in fact, of all places that the sun now looks upon, were the holiest for a modern man. To me, at least, in my poor thoughts, there seemed something of authentically divine in this locality, as if immortal remembrances and sacred influences and monitions were hovering over it, speaking sad and grand and valiant things to the hearts of men."

Talking about devils, Prof. David Masson of University College wrote *Three Devils — Luther's, Milton's, Goethe's.* He awarded the palm to Luther's, 1. as a literary performance; 2. as a biographical phenomenon; 3. as an experimental and poetical masterpiece.

The story must be true. Seeing is believing. Didn't we see it with our own eyes in 1927? And what's more, with our second-sight we see it wherever we see Luther's writings. And every pitch was a strike! We fully agree with the poet —

> At Wartburg still the ink they show
> Which Luther at the devil threw.
> In these last days we've learned to know
> He fought more wisely than he knew.
>
> For this far more than flaming tongue
> Filled popes and devils with affright;
> The inkstand by the printer flung
> Has put the prince of hell to flight.
>
> Now silent lies great Luther's tongue,
> And palsied is the hero's hand;
> But that black thunderbolt it flung
> Still rolls and smites from land to land.

LUTHER IN THE "BLACK BEAR"
AT JENA, MARCH, 1522
After Thumann

Chapter Ten

LUTHER AND THE FANATICS

"Gabriel Zwilling, a young Augustinian monk . . . led his particular disciples on an image-breaking campaign . . . bishops and priests, officially the spiritual guides of the laity, either consenting to the desecrations or keeping silence." So writes the Catholic Clayton.

Professor Carlstadt so preached against the mass that on December 3 priests were stoned and an altar in the Franciscan convent destroyed by about forty students.

When rumors of these riots reached Sir Knight George, he took one servant and secretly rode through the danger zone of Duke George's lands. On December 3 he dined at the inn of Hans Wagner on the Bruehl in Leipzig. He rode to the house of Von Amsdorf, where Melanchthon also lived at the time. After talking over the situation and advising his friends for five days, he rode off as secretly as he had come; again he dined at Wagner's.

Returned to the Wartburg, he wrote a *Warning to All Christians to Keep from Uproar and Sedition*. Riots are a work of the devil; Christians labor only by word of mouth. No matter how right a man may be, he puts himself in the wrong by using force. "They that read aright and understand my teaching do not raise riots." This was in 1521 — note the date!

Things would likely have quieted down very quickly had it not been for the coming of the "Heavenly Prophets" from Zwickau, near Bohemia. The people were influenced by the Husites, Waldenses, and other radical and fanatical, dreamy visionaries and enthusiasts of the Middle Ages. Nick Storch, a weaver, had direct talks with the angel Gabriel. He was backed by Tom Muenzer, the pastor of the main church. Mark Stuebner, a former pupil of Melanchthon, was one of the chief converts. Directly inspired by the Holy Ghost, they despised the Bible and all book learning; they rejected Infant Baptism and the Lord's Supper; all forms of divine worship were useless, etc. Storch surrounded himself with twelve apostles and seventy-two disciples and began to prophesy, just like Christ! Riots resulted. Pastor Nicholas Hausmann, a staunch friend of Luther's, debated with them, and the ringleaders were driven out of town.

Nick Storch, Mark Stuebner, and Tom Drechsel came to Wittenberg and stirred the dying embers of riot into wild flames. Principal George Mohr gave the boys a permanent vacation, and the school was turned into a bakery. Professor Carlstadt told the students to quit their books and learn a trade or farm; and many of the 1,500 students did so. The professor himself hied himself to Orlamuende at one time and stood barefooted on a dung heap and pitched manure — best thing he ever did in his life. Vestments were torn, statues demolished, paintings destroyed, crucifixes broken and burned, confession was abolished, and people rushed to the Lord's Supper without due preparation.

Melanchthon was helpless and wailed they were as sheep without their shepherd and loudly called for the return of their Elijah.

Elector Frederick the Wise was unwise; he would resign, take his staff, and leave the country as a poor beggar rather than "do anything against God."

The ship was drifting to the rocks. Who could do anything? On February 28 the town council sent a horseman to George to return and end the anarchy and bring order out of chaos. The elector forbade George to return, but George returned and on March 5 lettered him why he returned. How? The Rev. Gordon Rupp of London judges it should be put into every anthology of great prose.

On March 3 John Kessler and John Reutiner, Swiss students, came to "The Black Bear" at Jena and saw a queer combination, a belted knight with one hand on the hilt of his sword and in the other — a Hebrew Bible! He invited them to his table, chatted with them, paid for their supper, and bade them good night.

Kessler writes the knight walked very erect, leaned backward rather than forward, his face lifted up to heaven, under black eyebrows deep-black eyes that twinkled and flashed like stars, so that you could hardly look into them.

On the 8th they arrived at Wittenberg, and — lo and behold! — found their genial Knight Hospitaler, Dr. Luther, at Jerome Schurf's.

The French Catholic Audin comments: "This is the most brilliant page of Luther's history, and for all the world we would not tear it out; for the Reformer becomes great before us when fearless he bursts from his exile to restore the statues which Carlstadt had broken down, to purify the Church of All Saints, polluted by so many profanities, and shut the mouths of the prophets. Luther is splendid in his wrath. Let Protestants with pride point out to us their father at Worms with his eyes directed, like that of a judge, upon the emperor."

"He said, 'I shall die sooner than delay — die for the salvation of my neighbor.' Such words well-became Luther." — *Luther* I, 5, 9.

On Sunday, March 9, Luther filled the pulpit in the City Church, to which he had been called by the city fathers, and preached eight sermons from Sunday to Sunday.

Carlstadt was never so much as named, much less blamed; yet

he was completely subdued. Zwilling was reformed and given a parish. Capito had run over from Halle to hear these sermons, now broke with Albrecht of Mainz and became a preacher of the Gospel. The "Heavenly Prophets" of Zwickau were routed; they left, cursing Luther.

Glad to have back their "Elijah," the city council sent him "a cup o' kindness" for the inner man and a new cowl for the outer man; also a present to Luther's father. Schurf wrote the elector it was plain as day the Spirit of God worked in Luther, "and I have no doubt he is come to Wittenberg at this time by a special act of God, and he by God's help leads us poor misled people back upon the way of truth by a plain showing up of our error."

Student Albert Burer wrote Beatus Rhenanus: "Martin Luther returned to restore order. . . . He is a man in whose face one may read benevolence, charity, and cheerfulness; his voice is mild and mellow; his delivery very graceful. Whoever has heard him once will wish to hear him again."

Luther said, "Peace, be still!" and there was a great calm. The master's voice was heard. Here was one of the greatest victories of oratory; if ever eloquence was a virtue, it was in this octave of sermons that quelled the religious riots of the fanatic Wittenbergers.

Bishop John Dantiscus of Culm and Ermland visited Luther and remarked his eyes had a keen look and a certain terrible lightning, and his features were like his books.

Audin writes: "Luther kept his audience captive for nearly two hours: the crowd was dumb, fascinated by the monk's preaching, so strong, so clear, so winning." P. 12.

"Luther again held forth, this time scourging the prophets with his eloquence. They were not present, but one of their disciples, on leaving, exclaimed in his enthusiasm, that he had been listening to an angel." P. 13.

"Luther erred in being diffident of his powers, for his success was great. His voice was clear and sonorous; his attitude graceful and free. He had said to Staupitz he would not imitate his predecessors, and he kept his word. For the first time a Christian preacher was seen to abandon the Schoolmen, and draw his texts and illustrations from the writings of inspiration." Pp. 36—37.

"What a singular power was that of the Augustinian, who set in commotion Italy and its men of letters, the pope and his thunders, the emperor and his councilors, the diet and its electors, Cranach and his disciples, Hans Lufft the printer and his workmen, France, the Netherlands, Spain, nearly all the world known at that period! 'I believe,' wrote the envoy from Frankfurt, 'that they like to crucify the friar; if that were to happen, I fear he would rise on the third day.' The envoy at that time alluded to the torture of mind and body which Aleandro gave himself in order to triumph over Luther." P. 294.

"Luther knew the secret of the gifts which God bestowed upon him. His language consorted with his external appearance. Sometimes it floated in a lyrical excess, or savored of intoxication to use an expression of Erasmus; sometimes it was coquettish like a female, employing allegory as a veil, to excite curiosity; by turns simple as a parable, impassioned as an ode; daring as an eagle in its flight, or like a white-plumed dove, as Menzel says; and sometimes so indifferent to human art, so disdainful to every check, so extravagant in its conduct, that his language seemed not that of a priest, but rather of another Hans Sachs. Even the Catholics were seduced and attributed it to the influence of evil spirits, as did Prateolus, that deceptive charm which, according to his disciples, breathed of the Holy Ghost: a wonderful organization, destined to command wherever there was trouble. Place him in the time of the Gracchi, and he would have carried with him the senate and the people; in that of the Crusades, and he would have repeated had he believed, the miracle of St. Bernard; in a public assembly like the National, and he would have been something greater than Mirabeau if he had faith; in the seventeenth century in our Catholic pulpits, and he would have been a second Bossuet and Bridaine." P. 410.

From one kind of fanatics Luther turned to another kind.

THE THREE PEASANTS
By Albrecht Duerer

Chapter Eleven

LUTHER AND THE PEASANTS' WAR

"The Reformation of Kaiser Sigismund," written about the time of the Council of Constance about 1438, was to help the oppressed peasants, and the ideas spread.

The peasants were staggering under a crushing load. In some places the legal rate of interest had been screwed up to 80 per cent, mainly by Jews.

Jesuit Hartmann von Grisar tells of "the intense discontent of the lower classes with their position. . . . Savage outbreaks of rebellion against the old traditional order of things were of frequent occurrence. In many localities the peasants were in arms against their princes and masters for the improvement of their conditions. ... Nicholas de Clémanges' (?) *Ruin of the Church* contained accusations against the popes and the government of the Church couched in rude and violent language."

Alvarez Pelayo, the Spanish Franciscan, in his *Complaint of the Church*, "makes the indignant assertion that those who bear the dignity of the primacy are God's worst persecutors." — *Luther* I, 54—55.

Under Kaiser Maximilian I about 1500—1510 there was another effort at reform, but it failed, and anarchy spread, and at death Max sighed, "Poor Germany!"

His grandson and successor, Kaiser Karl V, on February 8, 1520, heard from Elector-Cardinal-Archbishop Albrecht of Mainz: "We foresee so great a conflagration of the whole of Germany that we do not think the like will have been heard of in the past."

As early as 1517 Luther warned Elector Frederick not to put still heavier taxes on the poor.

In 1520 he wrote *To His Most Serene and Mighty Imperial Majesty and the Christian Nobility of the German Nation.* On 28 pages he rains sledge-hammer blows on the corruptions of the state and then on 54 pages offers a 27-point program of reform — "his greatest work," some say. Had it been heeded, there had been no Peasants' War.

In the same year he sent an amazing letter to Pope Leo X presenting his *Liberty of a Christian Man* — praised by Grisar and other Catholics. Had it been heeded, nothing more had been needed.

About December 15, 1521, he wrote from the Wartburg *A Faithful Warning to All Christians to Keep from Riot and Rebellion.* "It looks as if a riot is coming in which priests, monks, bishops, with the whole clerical order will be slain. Riot never brings reform; it has no sense and usually harms the innocent. Use the Gospel, speak, write, preach!"

In his majestic letter from Borna on Ash Wednesday, March 22, 1522, he warns the elector against using force should the kaiser "want to arrest or kill me."

In March, 1523, came *On Secular Government: How Far to be Obeyed.* "God crazed the princes that they think they may order their subjects as they please and master their consciences and according to their crazy brains lead the Holy Ghost to school. . . . They can do nothing but grind and abuse, pile taxes on taxes. . . . I fear there will be a tumult. . . . You drove and hunted men like wild beasts. . . . I already see Germany swimming in blood."

The first insurgents did not even mention religion in their *Twenty-Two Articles.* Later Preacher Schapeler and Sebastian Lotzer put up the "divine right" in *The Twelve Articles* adopted by three large peasant unions on March 6, 1525. They promised to be taught from the Bible and appealed to Luther.

In April Luther wrote the *Exhortation to Peace on the Twelve Articles of the Peasants in Suabia.* He does not pull his punches. In blistering words he blames the princes for the whole trouble (on the princes), mainly the spiritual. Governments are not to abuse their subjects, but to serve them. Repent and obey the Word of God. For God's sake, be fair and make needed concessions.

At call he could pour out contempt upon princes. Ps. 107:40.

Then he speaks lovingly to his "dear friends," the peasants, admitting their plight. But two wrongs do not make a right. He heartily and earnestly warns against force and riot; no matter how just their demands, riot is wrong. He protested against their abuse of the Gospel to enforce their demands, which were, all but one, political, social, and economic. These demands must be judged in the light of reason and according to natural law. He fought against mixing religion and politics, against turning the reformation into a revolution. "What kind of Christians are they that become robbers, thieves, and rogues for the sake of the Gospel?!" In the end he says both sides are in the wrong and calls on them to settle the matter in peace by impartial judges.

Luther knew his Bible and applied it to prince and to peasant. "Let every soul be subject unto the higher powers. For there is no power but of God. The powers that be are ordained of God. Whosoever therefore resisteth the power, resisteth the ordinance of God; and they that resist shall receive to themselves damnation." Rom. 13:1-5.

Thomas Muenzer, "elect of God," "inspired by the Holy Ghost," preached to kill the wicked, princes and priests, and set up the Kingdom of God. "Kill them like mad dogs. They will beg, plead, pray, cry like children. Have no mercy. At 'em! at 'em! at 'em! while the fire is hot. Let not your swords grow cold from blood!"

Without waiting word from Luther, to whom they had appealed, the peasants began the bloodshed. The deceived serfs at Weinsberg fell on Count Ludwig von Helfenstein, the son-in-law of Kaiser Max. As they led him away, he fell; the witch Hoffmann tore him to pieces with her hands. Jack Rohsbacher would show how to treat the daughter of a kaiser — he threw her down and kneeled on her breast; another peasant threw his sword at her and wounded her babe; she was carted off on a load of dung.

Goetz von Berlichingen compared himself and other knights to a pack of wolves devouring the sheep.

In the one cloister of Erbach there were eighty-eight hogsheads of wine, nearly all of it emptied by the peasants, writes the Catholic Cochlaeus. Seven cities were dismantled, a thousand religious houses razed, three hundred churches burned, and immense treasures of painting, sculpture, stained glass, and engravings destroyed. In mad fury atrocities of every kind were committed. Germany was hell with the lid off.

Luther risked his reputation and life going among the fanatical peasants and preaching to quell the riot till called to the bedside of dying Frederick.

In this most terrible crisis, when the whole work of his reformation was at stake, the one Strong Man wrote *Against the Murdering and Robbing Hordes of the Peasants,* in which he called on the government to offer fair concessions. If they were rejected, the revolt was to be put down by force of arms. In order to save the poor innocent ones from being forced into the riot, the government was to "stab, slay, kill" the rioters like mad dogs. Certainly fierce and ferocious language! "Think you this is hard? Think riot is intolerable."

What did the patient Lincoln do when they had fired on Fort Sumter? What did Sherman do "marching through Georgia from

Atlanta to the sea"? What did we do with our A-bomb? "War is hell."

The new elector, John of Saxony, Duke George of Saxony, and Philip of Hesse on May 15 defeated 8,000 rioters at Frankenhausen. Muenzer had crawled into a bed; he was hauled out; he turned Catholic and took the Roman Communion; he was beheaded at Muehlhausen. About 150,000 peasants perished, and a large part of Germany was a waste.

After the defeat of the peasants the princes far outdid them in acts of violence and blood.

At Wuerzburg many were beheaded for the sole crime of being Lutherans. At Bamberg nine wealthy peaceable burghers were executed, and the reason given was they were Lutherans. Provost Aichili hounded the Lutherans in Schwaben and Franken; he hanged forty Lutheran preachers on trees along the road. Duke George of Saxony killed many of his people for being Lutherans.

Luther protested against those "mad, raging, insane tyrants and bloodhounds. They use the sword to satisfy their passions, so I leave them to their master, the devil."

As was to be expected, Pope Clement VII lettered Philip of Hesse blaming the tragedy on "the wicked Lutherans," and Duke George also lettered his son-in-law, blaming "the Lutheran Gospel."

The *Landgraf* retorted, in helping suppress the war, "I have punished no Lutheran with the sword, but riotous people who did not behave after Luther's teaching. The Gospel, which now must be called Luther's teaching, brings no Peasants' War, but all peace and obedience. In those parts clinging to the Gospel, which is called Lutheran, there is less riot than in those which persecute the Gospel and in some there is none."

That is true; the only ones to keep their peasants peaceable with words and without force were Luther's elector of Saxony and Philip of Hesse.

Williston Walker writes: "Its strongest manifestations were in regions into which the reform movement had but slightly penetrated." — *History of the Christian Church*, p. 353.

The French Catholic historian Jean Marie Vincent Audin writes: "Nothing was heard at this time but the wailings of despair: every place resembled Dante's hell. Long before Luther, the peasantry had striven to cast off the double yoke of their tyrants" — in 1491, 1492, 1502.

"If the peasants had triumphed, Germany would have become chaos; literature, arts, poetry, morals, dogmas, and authority would have perished in the same storm." — *Luther,* 2. ed. 1854.

The Catholic Jules Michelet, Member of the Institute of France: "Their insurrection had nothing to do with Lutheranism. It was Muenzer who excited the peasants to revolt. . . . In no part of his life, perhaps, did Luther assume a position more elevated or more commanding."

Rector Alfred Baudrillart of the Catholic Institute of Paris: Luther had no more to do with this Peasant War than with all the former ones. "Luther did not have to create anything. . . . The princes, moved by ambition and avarice, the knights, and the revolutionaries of town and country formed an army quite ready to engage in warfare, and he had not even to organize its staff of officers." — *The Catholic Church, the Renaissance, and Protestantism,* page 94.

The Catholic Joseph Clayton, an Oxford man and member of the Historical Institute: "Luther cannot justly be held responsible for the revolt of the peasants against intolerable conditions. . . . Definitely he was on the side of law and order." — *Luther,* pp. 119, 120, 126.

The Catholic Sebastian Merkle, professor of history at Wuerzburg, admits the rebellious peasants twisted Luther's teaching about Christian liberty and abused it for their social selfishness.

The Catholic historian von Bucholtz: "The Peasant Revolt plainly lay outside of all connection with the views of Luther. The fanaticism dissolving dogma and the endangering of the secular government through force from below was against the innermost feelings of Luther."

The West Side Home News, New York City: "The Council of Trent, whose rulings were aimed, too late, to correct the abuses which Luther intrepidly denounced.

"As a Catholic I am grateful to Luther. In the light of history, a Luther was needed, and needed badly. . . .

"What the German peasant could grasp was the fact that he was woefully hungry, badly housed, and doomed to a life of virtual slavery, while mitred abbots, the supposed inheritors of the Savior's poverty and humility, rode abroad in princely pomp and lived on the fat of the land.

"His dull brain could not fail to realize that abbot and baron, bishop and prince, priest and proprietor, were closely allied in the work of ruling his soul and his body. . . .

"When Luther nailed his Theses to the door at Wittenberg, he nailed the coffin of the last vestige of feudalism. . . .

"Modern Catholicism owes a debt to Luther. He checked the recklessness that was hurrying the ancient religion to rank atheism. . . . I cannot withhold the tribute of an Irishman for Martin Luther, fighter."

LUTHER AND THE ANABAPTISTS

Some fanatics had direct talks with the Holy Ghost, despised the "dead" Bible, scoffed at Infant Baptism, insisted believers be again baptized, and were called "Again-baptizers," Anabaptists.

As early as December, 1532, Luther warned the preachers and the council of Muenster, a rich city of about 15,000 people; but he was fiercely denounced. Melanchthon also tried his hand, also without success.

In 1534 came Jan Bockhold, a tailor of Leyden, commonly known as Jan of Leyden, and Jan Matthisson, a baker of Haarlem. Bernard Knipperdolling housed them and was made burgomaster. The baker proclaimed himself the inspired prophet of God, and all "unbelievers," all who were not Anabaptists, were robbed of their all and driven in a rainstorm through deep snow out of town, mothers with half-clad babes on their arms.

On pain of death all gold, silver, jewelry was to be put into the courthouse. All books and works of art and musical instruments were destroyed. Everybody had to work for the government and eat a Spartan meal in common as one family — tyrannical communism.

Tailor Bockhold proclaimed himself king of the new kingdom of Israel; named twelve elders for the twelve tribes of Israel; introduced polygamy by taking sixteen wives; girls of ten and twelve were violated; wild orgies were held.

"Four prophets, two true and two false ones; the true are David and John of Leyden; the false, Luther and the pope; but Luther is worse than the pope."

Luther commented on the "Tidings Respecting the Affairs of Muenster."

When Hubert Ruescher questioned the inspired prophecies of Matthisson, Jan of Leyden thrust his pike twice through the body of Ruescher, and the prophet Matthisson sent a bullet into his back. The people sang hymns to God and went home.

Tailor Bockhold deposed the Twelve Elders and proclaimed himself King of the World, having the throne and scepter of his father David. At a love feast for 11,000, one had brought a captive soldier as his guest. The king saw he "had on no wedding garment," and with his own royal hand chopped off his head before all the banqueters. Executions were the order of the day; on June 3 alone fifty-two were done to death.

Famine stalked through the streets. One of the king's wives, Elizabeth Wandscherer, doubted it was God's will the people should starve while the king gorged himself with luxuries. The king led her to the public square, made her kneel, and with his own hand chopped off her head, while all the other wives had to sing, "All glory be to God on high!" Those tottering for weakness from starving had to dance with the king!

On June 24, 1535, the city was betrayed to the besiegers; thousands were killed on both sides; only after the fourth day could Bishop-Count Franz von Waldeck enter. The poor fanatics were tortured for a whole year and then done to death with unspeakable cruelties. The bodies of Knipperdolling and Krechting were placed upright in iron cages and hung on the tower of St. Lambert's Church "to serve as a warning to all restless spirits."

The Prophet of Meyerbeer is based on this prophet of Muenster.

Need we state that for all these outrages the Catholics blamed Luther?

Melanchthon   Luther   Bugenhagen   Cruciger
TRANSLATING THE BIBLE
After Labouchere

Chapter Twelve

THREE PRECIOUS BOOKS

I. LUTHER'S BIBLE

When the knight of the Wartburg had again become the friar of Wittenberg, he wrote Spalatin: "Now we are at work polishing everything, Philip and I. By the grace of God it will be a fine piece of work."

It is — the German New Testament. The artistic Luther took a world of pains even with trifles; for he agreed with the titanic Michelangelo: "Trifles make perfection, but perfection is no trifle." He wrote an introduction to the whole and one for each book; he explained things in the margin; he selected pictures from Master Lucas Cranach, some of them after Duerer's famous Apocalypse series. Melanchthon furnished a description of the Holy Land, but no map of Palestine could be had. The first "Teachers' Bible" came from the press of Melchior Lotther on September 21, 1522, three presses going at once. The 5,000 copies were sold in three months, though a copy cost 1½ gulden — "the price of a horse."

Cochlaeus, "the Scourge of Luther," complained: "Luther's New Testament is spread in such great numbers that tailors and shoemakers, yes, women and other simple idiots, as many as had received the new Lutheran Gospel, read it with the greatest desire as the spring of all truth. Some carried it in their bosom and learned it by heart. Hence in the course of a few months they presumed to so much skill and experience that they did not shun to dispute of faith and the Gospel not alone with the Catholic laymen, but even with Masters and Doctors of theology."

Why did he complain? He wrote to King James V of Scotland against Canon Alexander Alane, Alesius: "The New Testament translated into the language of the people is in truth the food of death, the fuel of sin, the veil of malice, the pretext of false liberty, the protection of disobedience, the corruption of discipline, the depravity of morals, the end of concord, the death of honesty, the wellspring of vices, the disease of virtues, the instigation of rebellion, the milk of pride, the nourishment of contempt, the death of peace, the destruction of charity, the enemy of unity, the murder of truth."

John Faber, Fabri, chaplain of Ferdinand and then bishop of Vienna, greeted Luther: "Your New Testament is more harmful than the books of the idols at Ephesus — Acts 19:19 — yes, it has done more damage than the hail of Egypt."

"Imitation is the sincerest flattery," said C. C. Colton; but misappropriation is the sincerest super-flattery. Jerome Emser sneered at Luther's "artistic and sweet-sounding" work and then based on it his own work under his own name on August 1, 1527. It even looked like Luther's work: Luther's illustrations had been bought from Lucas Cranach for forty dollars.

Luther wrote Duke Henry of Mecklenburg: "In Emser's New Testament I like the text very well, as it is altogether my text and stolen from me word for word, but his poisonous additions, glosses, and annotations" — well, that is something else again.

Emser warns the lay people against reading even his *opus*.

Grim Duke George of Saxony grumbled through his beard: "If that fellow would only put the whole Bible into German and then go to — wherever he pleases!"

"That fellow" gladly obliged his ducal enemy.

What pains he took! He studied zoology in order to give the right names to the animals named in the Bible. He had a butcher slaughter several sheep and teach him to name the parts, so that he could translate correctly. He asked Court Preacher Spalatin to name and describe the gems in Rev. 21:19 and, if possible, to send specimens from the elector's collection. Melanchthon had to correspond with learned men everywhere for information concerning the coins in the New Testament. He listened to the mothers talking to their children, at play in the streets, to the plain people in the shops and market; and as he heard them speak, so he wrote. He studied to get at the real sense of the Hebrew and the Greek authors and then wrote it down in the real, racy, plain, and popular German.

Luther did not rest on his laurels. He would make a good thing still better. He had Melanchthon, Cruciger, Jonas, Bugenhagen, Aurogallus, and Roerer meet with him regularly and work hard.

"In rendering Moses I make him so German that no one would know he was a Jew."

"Sometimes we have sought two, three, four weeks for a single word, and then sometimes we did not find it."

"We are now sweating over the Prophets. Good God! What a big job to make the Hebrew authors speak German! How they balk and will not give up their Hebrew tongue and speak in the barbaric German! Just as if you would force a nightingale to imitate a cuckoo!"

"In Job we are working so that in four days we barely finished three lines. My dear man, now that it is done into German and ready, everybody can read and criticize it; now one runs his eyes over three, four leaves without stumbling, and is never aware, walking as over a dressed plank, how we had to sweat and worry to get such rocks and blocks out of the way in order to walk along so smoothly. It's mighty easy to plow when the field's been cleared; but to fell the forest and grub out the stumps and get the field in order, nobody wants to tackle that job."

The work was abreast of the scientific scholarship of the time; it was based on the Hebrew text published by Gerson Ben Mosheh at Brescia in 1494, and on the Greek text of Erasmus of 1519.

Eighty-four times the Bible and parts were printed under Luther's eyes at Wittenberg, despite the fact that two hundred and fifty-three forbidden reprints were made in other cities. Ever since the Bible has been the best seller.

Luther took a proper pride in his work. "I do not wish to praise myself, but the work speaks for itself. The German Bible is so good and precious that it surpasses all the Greek and Latin versions, and more is found in it than in all the commentaries, for we clear the blocks and rocks out of the way that others may read without hindrance."

True, every word of it. And we like the flush of honest pride mantling his manly cheek; we detest and despise the hypocritical pride lurking in mock humility. If your book is not the best of its kind, why the impertinence of publishing it?

They worked from 1525 to 1534 and then bettered the work from 1539 to 1542.

Luther called his cloister club his "Sanhedrin." It certainly was more important than the Round Table of King Arthur or the Tobacco College of the king of Prussia. It was the model for the Jerusalem Chamber of the Revisers of King James' Version. We like to think of it as the Honorable Order of the German Heptasophs, The Seven Wise Men of Wittenberg.

The Dominican John Dietenberger of Mainz did with Luther's complete Bible what Emser had done with Luther's New Testament. What a tribute!

The notorious John Eck tried his hand at it. What luck? "The worst of all Bible translations in the German language." Says who? Says his biographer Wiedemann. And the Catholic soldier Montluc cried in a despairing rage: "We had beaten our enemies over and over again; we are now winning by force of arms; but they triumphed by means of their diabolical writings."

About the year 400 Jerome had translated the Bible into Latin, and in 1343 this faulty translation was done into very clumsy German, and this was copied repeatedly. Of course, such manuscripts were so costly that only the very wealthy could own a copy. Since 1466 the Bible was printed fourteen times, but Mathesius called it "un-German and dark." Worst of all, the Roman Church had forbidden Bible reading in 1229 in France, in 1234 in Spain, in 1408 in England, in 1486 in Germany.

The German Gutenberg invented the printing press at Mainz about 1450, and the German Luther was the first man to make full use of the press to appeal to public opinion. He was the shining pioneer of the Fourth Estate. He is credited with the creation of the German book trade. In 1518 only 150 works were published in German; in 1524 there were 990 — an increase of more than 500 per cent in five years.

We omit a myriad of Protestant tributes and offer only a very few of the many Catholic praises.

Kaspar Ulenberg of St. Columba at Koeln, who died in 1617, confides to us the interesting bit of information Luther was really begotten of the devil before his mother was married to Hans Luther and carried with him a devil in a locket. Kaiser Max at Augsburg saw a devil hid in Luther's cowl.

Why should the good man be surprised? Devils are devils, and devils do devilish things; but Luther's devil certainly was an odd fellow. All other devils try their devilish best to keep people from reading the Bible, but this one does his devilish best to get people to read the Bible!

Wonder what all the black devils thought of the white sheep in their family.

This bitter enemy himself worked on Dietenberger's German Bible, and so we look for no good word from him about Luther's Bible; yet we read a long surprising tribute, from which we give only a few sentences.

"The meaning of the Hebrew and Greek text he clothed in pure and ornate German, on the development of which he throughout spent much labor. In writing, teaching, and explaining in the German language . . . no one could be compared with him. . . . In this translation of the Bible he took pains above all things through a certain beauty and charm of speech to spur all to read and to win the hearts of men."

The French Catholic Audin has pages of praise, from which we cull a few words. "A colossal work, which would daunt any other but himself . . . a task the accomplishment of which has invested his reputation as a scholar with so bright a halo. . . . Sometimes, in these short prefaces . . . we are pleased to meet with the cultivator of art and poetry. In these short sketches, which are models of style, the genius of the translator is tinged with the colors of the original. There are pages which flow spontaneously from his pen, so full of inspiration that you might fancy you heard the prophet himself."

The Catholic Friedrich von Schlegel: "It is known that all thorough philologists regard Luther's translation as the norm and ground text of classic expression, and not only Klopstock, but many more authors of the first rank have formed their style by this norm and drawn out of this spring. . . . What the Catholic faults in Luther's translation pertains indeed to only a few single passages."

The English Catholic Clayton: "Nothing can detract from the greatness of Luther's literary achievement. . . . These existing translations were dull and lifeless, literal translations from the Vulgate, unilluminated by a spark of genius. . . . It remains an amazing performance, carried out by a single man in a few short months without external aid."

The Catholic Prince Metternich of Austria read Luther's German Bible, but thought the pope was right in forbidding the Bible to the common people.

Jesuit Hartmann von Grisar has a long laud, from which we give a few words: "The excellence of Luther's translation of the Bible from the point of view of the text is unquestionable. For what the author, above all, aimed at, viz., a popular rendering of the text which should harmonize with the peculiarities of the German language, that he certainly achieved."

The Rt. Rev. Mons. Patrick O'Hare, D. D., LL. D., in 1916 wrote 367 virulent pages of *The Facts of Luther,* in which he is forced to admit: "He had a large, full, and flexible vocabulary, which he used with force in his translation, where is displayed the whole wealth, power, and beauty of the German language. He wished to make his Bible really a German book and understood by all alike.

... He gave them German, simple, idiomatic, racy, colloquial, classical; and as his Bible sold for a trifle, it was purchased by many, read widely, and exercised a decided influence in giving the whole country a common tongue. We cannot deny that his translation surpasses those which had been published before him in the perfection of language. . . . His work is praised as the first classic of German literature."

Ignaz von Doellinger, the greatest Catholic scholar of his day, admits: "Luther alone it was who impressed the imperishable seal of his spirit upon the German language and the German spirit, and even those among the Germans who abominate him from the bottom of their soul as the mighty heretic and misleader of the nation cannot do otherwise: they must speak with his words, must think with his thoughts."

We close with Jew Thomas Mann who is rated by *Time* the greatest living master of German. "I frankly confess that I do not love him . . . the venerable Lout of Wittenberg. . . . I would have gotten along much better with Leo X, the amiable Humanist. . . . No one can deny that Luther was a tremendously great man. He actually saved Christianity. . . . In the German Luther, Christianity took itself childlikely and rustically seriously at a time when it did not take itself seriously at all elsewhere: Luther's revolution preserved Christianity. No aspersions against Luther's greatness! It was his momentous translation of the Bible that really first created the German language; and it was also he who, through the breaking of the scholastic fetters and the renovation of the conscience, tremendously promoted the freedom of research, of criticism, and of philosophic speculation. By the establishment of the direct relationship of man to his God he advanced the cause of European democracy; for 'every man his own priest,' that is democracy. . . . All of that comes from Luther. He was a liberating hero."

In the British and Foreign Bible Society in London in the place of honor hangs Ward's painting of "Luther Finding the Bible."

II. LUTHER'S HYMNBOOK

On returning from the Wartburg, Luther found the radical and erratic Zwilling and Carlstadt had turned everything topsy-turvy, and so he reformed the Order of Service in the churches; he did so in a liberal spirit, with a gentle and conservative hand. "I condemn no ceremonies but those opposed to the Gospel. . . . In short, I hate nobody worse than him who upsets free and harmless ceremonies and turns liberty into necessity." There is conservative and progressive statesmanship! From this sound principle he wittily and wisely wrote the Berlin Propst George Buchholtzer, who was troubled by the rich ritual introduced by the ceremonious Elector Joachim II of Brandenburg:

"In God's name make your processions with a silver or gold cross and with cowl and mantle of velvet, satin, or linen. And if your master, the elector, does not find one hood or cassock enough, put on three, as Aaron, the high priest, wore three richly adorned garments, from which the priestly robes under the papacy got their name. And if His Electoral Grace does not find one circuit or procession enough, with its ringing and singing, make seven, as Joshua marched about Jericho with the Children of Israel, shouting and blowing trumpets. And if your lord, the margrave, would enjoy it, let His Electoral Grace leap and dance in front of the procession with harps, kettledrums, cymbals, and bells, as David did before the ark when it was brought into the city of Jerusalem."

Do you want anything more broad-minded? Yet some manage to call him narrow-minded!

Gregory the Great, who died in 604, introduced instrumental music and choir singing into the Church, but it was a holy monopoly of the clergy; the people were condemned to silence, and since the singing was in Latin, they could not even understand it. During the Babylonian Captivity of the Church the congregation had to hang their harps on the willows, and they could not sing the Lord's song in a strange land (Psalm 137). All contrary to Col. 3:16.

Now that all believers were held a royal priesthood, 1 Pet. 2:9, all believers were to take part in the worship of God in His holy temple and not leave all to professional papal priests as heretofore.

While Luther was studying the Bible, the spirit of the Psalmist and of the Prophets had fallen upon him. "I am minded, after the example of the Prophets and Fathers of the Church, to make German psalms for the people, that is, spiritual hymns, so that the Word of God may be kept among the people through the song."

This practical need was the rod that smote the rock of Luther's poetic soul, and out gushed a stream of hymns. Poetically silent for over forty years, he blossomed out over night the greatest poet of his age — a most surprising phenomenon in literary history.

He translated the Bible that God might speak directly to His children; now he made hymns that they might speak directly to their Father in melodies such as earth had never heard. By the Bible he had opened the ears of the deaf, by hymns he would now loose the tongues of the dumb.

In 1524 appeared the world's first Protestant hymnbook — eight hymns, four by Luther. In the same year a second edition came out with twenty-five hymns, eighteen by Luther; another edition with thirty-two hymns, twenty-five by Luther; they had their own tunes printed in; later on twelve more hymns by Luther were added. From this tiny spring at Wittenberg has gushed out the mighty stream of Protestant hymnology.

The first hymnal of Protestant Englishmen was the *Goostly Psalmes and Spiritualle Songes,* forty-one hymns of Luther and others translated by Miles Coverdale, Bishop of Exeter, in the original meter, and sung to the original Lutheran melodies. Henry VIII and Bloody Mary forbade the book, "to the great loss of English hymnology," as Herford laments.

Jacobi, under George I, 1722—25, Englished most of Luther's hymns.

The first hymnary of the Scotch Protestants was *The Gude and Godlie Ballates,* translated from Luther and others, in the original meter, and sung to the original Lutheran tunes. It was the work of the three Wedderburns, of whom John at least had gone to Wittenberg in 1539 and associated with Luther. The earliest known edition is that of 1567; likely there were earlier ones. Luther was very friendly to Scots for the work of early Scottish missionaries to Germany after the devastation of the Huns.

The Lord's Prayer in verse in Knox's *Psalter* is a singularly faithful, yet spirited translation of Luther's version.

Besides Wedderburn, Hamilton, Fyffe, M'Alpine, Alesius, and others came to Wittenberg, learned the truth, and then spread the truth. And so to Wittenberg, says Prof. A. F. Mitchell, "our native country owes a debt of gratitude which its historians have hitherto been slow to acknowledge."

In Luther's hymns there is such a manly tone as is found nowhere else. "A Mighty Fortress" is simply known as Luther's Psalm. It is Luther, it is Protestantism, it is the Gospel. Frederick the Great called it God Almighty's Grenadier March; Heine styled it the Marseillaise of the Reformation; Carlyle translated it and found "something in it like the sound of an Alpine avalanche, or the first murmur of an earthquake." We like to think of the great Duerer's famous "Knight, Death, and the Devil" as the counterpart in painting of Luther's "Mighty Fortress"; both the poem and the painting express Paul's challenge, "If God be for us, who can be against us?" (Rom. 8:31—39.)

Grove's *Dictionary of Music* says: "Luther is the establisher of congregational singing. The choral originated by Luther cannot be surpassed for dignity and simple devotional earnestness. The choral melodies of the Lutheran Church have exerted a powerful influence on classical music. In the seventeenth century, Germany possessed the finest school of organists in Europe, not likely to be surpassed in modern times."

Julian's *Dictionary of Hymnology* says: "The church hymn, as a popular religious lyric in praise of God to be sung by the congregation in public worship, is the work of Luther. The treasures of Lutheran hymnody have enriched the churches of Sweden, Norway, Denmark, Scotland, England, America."

Leonard Woolsey Bacon says: "To an extent quite without parallel in the history of music, the power of Luther's tunes, as well as of his words, is manifest after three centuries, over the masters of the art, as well as over the common people. Peculiarly is this true of the great song *'Ein' feste Burg.'* ... The composers of the sixteenth and seventeenth centuries practiced their elaborate artifices upon it. The supreme genius of Sebastian Bach made it the subject of study. And in our own times it has been used with conspicuous success in Mendelssohn's *Reformation Symphony,* in an overture by Raff, in the noble *Festouverture* of Nicolai, and in Wagner's *Kaisermarsch,* and is introduced with recurring emphasis in Meyerbeer's masterpiece of the *Huguenots.*"

Waldo S. Pratt of Hartford Seminary "wonders today at the crystalline brilliance of his [Luther's] verbal expression, at his facility and felicity, at his fusion of homely earnestness with richness of sentiment. In all these regards he is not only the molder of a language, but also the founder of a noble literature."

"Luther was a genuine pioneer in Protestant hymnody. He naturally became the model for the early hymnists of Germany, and it can be shown that his example had much to do with the spirit and style of hymnody in other countries.... All this affluence and beauty of verse are in signal contrast with the flat and monotonous practices into which English psalmody settled a decade or two later. It is a lasting pity that English usage derived nothing from the German at this point."

The Jesuit Cardinal Bellarmine says bitterly: "The fine songs of Luther have seduced more souls from the [Roman] Church than the archheretic with his teaching."

The Jesuit Conzenius is credited with like words.

No doubt these are strong statements, but they stress the importance and influence of Luther's hymns.

Walter Buszin writes: "A Catholic Jewish musicologist at an Eastern university refers his classes to Luther's sane attitude on music and points to the richness of the Lutheran musical heritage and advises to read Luther to acquire a wholesome philosophy of life, music, and religion." — "The Musical Heritage of the Lutheran Church," p. 14.

III. LUTHER'S CATECHISM

While Luther was up in the Wartburg, Carlstadt reformed the Wittenberg city school to death. Luther returned and brought it back to life and in 1524 sent a *Letter to the Aldermen and Cities of Germany to Erect and Maintain Christian Schools,* of which Ranke says: "This work has the same significance for the development of learning as the *Address to the German Nobility* for the temporal estate in general." Professor Painter calls it "the most important educational treatise ever written."

Children should go to school an hour or two every day, learning a trade at home the rest of the time. Girls should be sent to school as well as boys. Public libraries with good books in each town are called for.

Up-to-date America in the twentieth century is trying to catch up with the ideas Luther published four hundred years ago; he certainly was a Progressive. United States Commissioner of Education Claxton, on October 29, 1916, at New York said Luther is the father of the Gary system of work-and-play education.

Luther made a visitation, or survey, of a part of Saxony and found the priests very ignorant; some did not know even the Ten Commandments and the Lord's Prayer, and some were very immoral. And the people? Of course, they were sunk in ignorance and superstition.

What was to be done? Leave it to Luther! In 1529 he published a pair of heavenly twins, the Small Catechism and the Large Catechism, each one the best of its kind. As it often happens, the little brother became more famous than the big brother.

Erasmus said the papists "had brought it to be a matter of so much wit to be a Christian that ordinary heads were not able to reach it." In Luther's Catechism ordinary heads can reach it, can even pray it. Luther wrote the elector that thanks to this simple instruction the youth of Saxony now understood the Bible better than monks and nuns under the papacy. "It is a right Bible for the laity." So it has been in all these centuries, in Europe and in America; often imitated, never equaled.

Justus Jonas said you could buy it for six pennies, but you could not pay for it with six thousand worlds. Mathesius thought if Luther had done nothing else, the world could never pay him enough. It found its way to Venice, and a Catholic cleric cried, "Blessed are the hands that have written this holy book!"

Listen to what the great historian Leopold von Ranke says of this gem of purest ray serene: "It is as childlike as deep-minded, as plain as unfathomable, simple and sublime. Happy he that feeds his soul with it, that clings to it! He has an unfailing comfort in every moment, behind a thin shell the kernel of truth, which satisfies the wisest of the wise." We say, Amen!

Professor McGiffert says: "The versatility of the Reformer in adapting himself with such success to the needs of the young and immature is no less than extraordinary. Such a little book as this it is that reveals most clearly the genius of the man"; he calls it "the gem of the Reformation."

Others knew a good thing when they saw it, and Scotland's first Catechism was a translation of Luther's; Archbishop Cranmer gave it to the English; Norway, Denmark, Sweden, and others took it to heart. "From Greenland's icy mountains" the Eskimos prayed it through the labors of Hans Egede, "from India's coral strand" the Hindus prayed it through the labors of Ziegenbalg, and it was the first book translated into the language of the North American Indian by the Swede Campanius.

As a fruit of Luther's efforts old schools were bettered and new ones begun. Luther is the father of popular education, of the public school for every boy and every girl.

And Luther insisted upon higher education, upon the study of the ancient languages in which the Bible was written.

He complained hitherto men had studied twenty, forty years and learned neither Latin nor German, that the high schools had turned out asses and blockheads. Pope Pius II bears him out in this complaint.

The Catholic Joseph Clayton, F. R. Hist. S.: "These two catechisms, admirably effective for the instruction of ministers and laity ... became part of the library of Lutheran theology. Luther's intimate knowledge of the people for whom he wrote, his capacity to persuade and convince the indifferent, are manifest in these catechisms. . . . Luther's purpose was to establish a lively and reasonable Christian faith among the people growing up in doubt and perplexity — the old order being apparently overthrown, a new order not plainly set up — and to check the flood of paganism that threatened to submerge all Christian belief and the very existence of all moral law. When Luther wrote he rarely wrote in vain. The catechisms did achieve very largely the purpose of their author. Thousands lost to the Catholic Church were saved from utter unbelief by these documents." — *Luther,* pp. 146—147.

Ignaz von Doellinger, the most learned Catholic of his day, pays this tribute: "Luther gave what no other single man gave to a people: the Bible, the Catechism, and the Hymnbook."

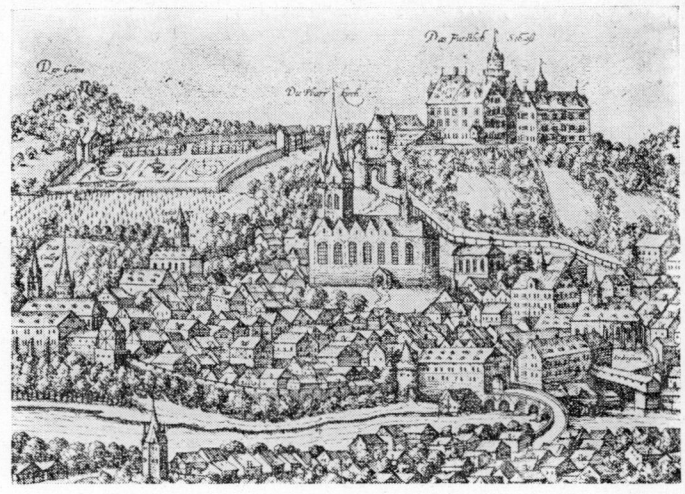

MARBURG

Chapter Thirteen

MORE BATTLES

I. LUTHER AND KING HENRY VIII

"Pops sentenc against Martin Luther, published at London: — The xii th daye of Maye in the yeare of our Lord 1521 and in the thirteenth yeare of the raigne of our Soueraigne, Lord Kinge Henry the eighte of that name the Lord Thomas Wolcey by the grace of god Legate de Latere Cardinall of seinct Cecely and Arch Bishop of Yorke came vnto Saint Paules churche of London with the most parte of the Byshops of the Realme, where hee was receiued with procession and sensid by Mr. Richard Pace then beeinge Deane of said churche. After which ceremonies done there were 4 Doctors that bare a Canope of cloth of gold ouer him goinge to the highe Alter where hee made his obligacion which done hee proceeded forth as aboue said to the crosse in Paules churche yeard where was ordeined a scaffold for the same cause, and hee sittinge vnder his cloth of estate which was ordeined for him his 2 crosses on euerie side of him, on his right hand sittinge on the pace where hee set his feete the Popes Embassador and nexte to him the Arch-Byshop of Canterbury on his left hand the Emperors Embassador and next to him the Byshop of Duresme and all the other Byshops with other noble prelates sate on twoe formes oute righte forthe, and then the Byshop of Rochester made a sermon by the consentinge of the whole clergie of England by the commandment of the Pope againste one MARTINUS ELEUTHERIUS, and all his workes because, hee erred sore and spake againste the hollie faithe and denounced them accursed which kept anie of his bookes and there manie burned in the said churcheyard of his said bookes duringe the sermon which ended my Lord Cardinall went home to dinner with all the other Prelates."

This account in the British Museum of the state affair shows Luther must have been held a man of great power so early. This was not enough. There came *A Defense of the Seven Sacraments, Against Martin Luther, by the most invincible King of England and France, Lord of Ireland, Henry, the Eighth of that Name.* London. July, 1521.

The work of the royal quill was dedicated to Pope Leo X, and His Holiness was so tickled that he entitled the loyal champion "Defender of the Faith" — still borne proudly by Britain's kings and granted to every reader an indulgence for ten years and ten periods of forty days. In order that Germans, too, might have this boon, Duke George of Saxony had the royal *opus* done in German.

Cardinal Campegi wrote Cardinal Wolsey of being "overcome with joy at reading the King's golden book, inspired more by an angelic and celestial than by a human spirit." The royal scribe was also happy — "Itt is to Hys Graces grete contentacion and comforte to have understoude att large ... how lovingly the Popis Holynesse haith acceptidde hys bokes wretyn agaynst Luther."

O joy! "Behold, how good and how pleasant it is for brethren to dwell together in unity!" Ps. 133:1.

In this heavenly harmony a note of discord was struck by Chancellor Sir Thomas More, "the greatest wit of England." He said the king erred in granting the primacy of the pope a *divine* institution — just like the heretic Luther against Eck at Leipzig in 1519.

The king's great argument is: "If indulgences are impostures, then all the popes are impostors; and it is easier to believe that one little friar is a diseased sheep than that all the popes of old were perfidious shepherds."

Perfectly simple! The gravest matters are decided, not by weighing arguments, but by counting noses! Only by this royal rule Christ was wrong, and Athanasius, and Columbus, and Galileo, and many more.

The monk held marriage so sacred that he would in a case of confessional casuistry rather permit two wives than grant a divorce. This opens the floodgates of the holy wrath of the virtuous monarch and calls forth the most edifying rhetoric in the treatise in defense of the sacrament of marriage.

"The insipid water of concupiscence is turned by the hidden grace of God unto wine of the finest flavor. Whom God has joined together, let no man put asunder. O wonderful word such as no man could have uttered save the Word which was made flesh! . . . Who does not tremble when he considers how he should deal with his wife, for not only is he bound to love her, but so to live with her that he may return her to God pure and without stain, when God, who gave, shall demand his own again."

This fine preaching is spoiled by the preacher. This married man seduced Bessie Blount and Mary Boleyn, and divorced his wife, and three months after Anne Boleyn's coronation took a mistress, and chopped off Anne's head, and had two mistresses in 1534 and another in 1535, and divorced his perfectly innocent "Flanders mare," the Lady Anne of Cleves, and married Catherine Howard, and chopped off her head, and married Catherine Parr.

This is the immaculate saint that said of Luther: "What a wolf of hell is he! What a poisonous viper! What a limb of Satan! How rotten is his mind!" and advocated the famous and favorite short argument with heretics: "If Luther cannot be constrained to silence, he should for once be made useful to the world by the terrible example of his death."

Luther paid the royal rowdy in his own coin. Luther's words had "hands and feet," a punch and a kick.

"They want war: they shall have war."

Since "that king of lies, King Heinz, by God's ungrace king of

England," had acted so unlike a king, he was not to be treated like a king. "For since with malice aforethought that damnable and rotten worm has lied against my King in heaven, it is right for me to bespatter this English monarch with his own filth, and trample his blasphemous crown under feet. Living, I shall be the enemy of the papacy; burned, I shall be its destruction." The king ought to be whipped for his ignorance of Aristotle, and Luther was the man who would like to do it.

"My doctrines, I am convinced, are of heaven.... My doctrines will remain."

They remain the doctrines of the whole Protestant world.

Paolo Sarpi, the greatest Venetian, said: "So great a name as that of the English Henry mixed up in the dispute and, beaten, served to give *éclat,* to render it more curious, and to conciliate general favor towards Luther."

Blackwood's Magazine of December, 1835, says: "There is something sublime in the miner's son dragging popes and kings into his wrestling ring and handling them with as much roughness and as little ceremony as he would a hobnailed clown from a country market place."

What a fighter!

The Rev. E. S. Buchanan in 1928 Englished Luther's Reply "one of his most brilliant and closely reasoned answers to his detractors."

The English monarch gathered himself together and sent John Clarke to Nuernberg to complain about Luther to the government. The government was sorry to hear of any rudeness; that was all. Henry sent a herald directly to Saxony. Elector Frederick and his brother John said if Luther had been impolite, they were sorry, to be sure. They also pointedly pointed His Royal Highness to an expression in his own book, according to which he "did not think it very becoming in him to engage in controversy with such a man or to quarrel with a fool or to be so foolish as to be vexed at the insane raving of a madman." And that was that.

The burly British bully now mobilized his filth battery to cannonade the heretic with muck.

Thomas Murner of Strassburg, priest, LL. D., Poet Laureate, perpetrated 32 booklets against "the highly learned doctor Martin luter." One was *Whether the King of England is a liar,* for which the king gave him 100 pounds.

"The cleverest, wittiest, and coarsest" enemy showed his wit and scholarship in *The Great Lutheran Fool.*

The saintly Bishop Fisher fired three bombs at Luther: "Now Luther is become a big fox.... What do I say? ... A fox? He is a mad dog, a ravening wolf, a cruel bear, or rather all of these animals in one; for the monster includes many beasts within him." The saintly soul could not see how such good books could come from such a heretic. It is strange, passing strange.

Anthony Wood rates Sir Thomas More "one of the greatest prodigies of wit and learning that England ever before his time had produced." This "blessed" saint printed such filth against Luther that it cannot be printed today. Even his friend Erasmus was disgusted with the gutterals — and Erasmus was not squeamish.

King Christian II of Denmark reported King Henry now favored the Gospel and got Luther to write him a very humble letter on September 1, 1525, for the sake of the cause. The king, however, spurned the plea and printed Luther's letter and a Response on December 2, 1526, again in 1527; a translation in 1526 and again in 1527.

"A copy of the letters wherein the most redoubted and mighty Prince, our soverayne lorde Kyng Henry VIII . . . made answer unto a certain letter of Martyn Luther, sent unto him by the sayme and also a copy the foresayd Luther's letter in such order as hereafter followeth. Imprinted at London in Flete street by Richard Pynson." (No date.)

II. LUTHER AND ERASMUS

"The kaiser invites me to him in Spain, King Ferdinand to Vienna, Margaret to Brabant, the English king to England, Sigmund to Poland, Francis to France, and all with rich salaries," wrote Erasmus.

Why not? "Among men of letters Erasmus is the greatest who has ever lived," writes H. C. Vedder of the Baptist Crozer Theological Seminary, and biographer Dr. Drummond says the same.

The monk and priest saw the evils in the Church and had sneers where Luther had tears. He wrote Mosellanus on August 8, 1522: The Kaiser, Henry VIII, and certain cardinals "all want me to attack Luther. I do not approve Luther's cause but have many reasons for preferring any other task to this." The effete aesthete would be neutral on the Olympian heights.

It is curious to read the champion's admission to King Henry, fearing stoning in Germany did he write against Luther, and to hear no one in Basel was willing to print anything even by Erasmus against the popular hero of Europe.

Luther got wind of what was afoot and wrote Erasmus very sternly if he would not side with the Gospel, he should at least remain silent and not publicly oppose him. But popes and princes paying pensions prodded the prodigy to save Peter's sinking ship, and he spurned Luther's plea for peace and in 1524 felt forced to prove he had no free will by writing *On Free Will,* suggested by King Henry.

"The Vindicator of Theology" borrowed much of Bishop Fisher's works. Like a bulldog he jumped at Luther's throat.

The French Catholic Audin judges: "He impaired his work, already so feeble, by commonplace compliments to his opponent; his exordium is a hymn to Luther. . . . His peroration is a new canticle in honor of his rival."

He wrote Bishop John Fisher of Rochester on September 4, 1524: "How I triumph I know not; I certainly sustain a threefold contest with those Roman pagans who are jealous of me; with certain theologians and monks who are turning every stone to destroy me; and with some rabid Lutherans who roar at me because I alone, they say, retard their triumph. . . . The Lutheran faction is increasing every day and now extends to Savoy, Lorraine, Spain, and even Milan. Burgundy, next door to us, is thrown into confusion."

Kaiser Karl V of the Holy Roman Empire of the German Nation on December 13, 1527, wrote his Paladin: "Thanks to you alone, Christianity has arrived at results to which the emperors, the popes, the princes, and all the efforts of learned men have been unable to attain."

"The Defender of the Faith" and Chancellor Blessed Sir Thomas More were also charmed.

The gentle Melanchthon wrote the gentle Erasmus on September 30: "You have thrown on passages some grains of black salt" — insults. He replied on December 10, 1524: "I hope mankind will be the better for the acrid medicines with which he has dosed them. Perhaps we needed a surgeon who would use knife and cautery. . . . His genius is vehement. We recognize in him that Achilles of men who knows not what it is to yield. . . . Success like Luther's might spoil the most modest of men."

Luther did not feel like replying to "so unlearned a work of so learned a man." But they told him, "Silence gives consent." "Joachim [Camerarius of Nuernberg] persuaded my Kate, and on her pleading I did it" — *On the Unfree Will,* in December, 1525.

He generously gives full credit to Erasmus for all he had done for science and the world, but blames him for being uncertain and wavering, slippery as an eel, and then shows from the New Testament our salvation does not depend on man's free will, but on God's free grace.

What did he turn out? "A book which changed the course of history." R. H. Murray, Litt. D., of Dublin, in his *Erasmus and Luther.* Who's the enthusiast?

Erasmus wrote the Dominican Faber: "You see how fiercely Luther strikes at me, moderate though I was. . . . Ten editions of his reply have been published already. The great men of the Church are afraid to touch him, and you want poor me to do it again, me who am too weak to make myself feared and too little of a saint in my life not to dread what may be said of me. . . . He yet expects me to thank him for his gentle handling."

Even now Luther wrote Erasmus, trying to come to an understanding with him; but again the Humanist rejected the plea for peace. Why?

Pension-paying patrons, popes, and princes prodded the priestly prodigy into another attack. Audin tells us: "He accordingly shut himself up in his cell, and there . . . he labored for ten whole days in provoking his style, as one would a lion to make him roar; but all to no purpose; in spite of all his efforts his work was a mere effort, without fancy, energy, or fluency — *The Hyperaspistes.*"

Melanchthon ridiculed it.

Luther likened it to the hissing of a viper, but did not deign to dignify it with a reply, but treated it with silent contempt.

William Farel likened Erasmus to Balaam, who cursed the people of God for gold.

McGiffert of Union Seminary holds Luther's reply "an example of dignified polemic. Luther was a genuine evangelical. And if Erasmus was not a thoroughgoing rationalist . . . his spirit was akin to that of the rationalists of all ages."

Ephraim Emerton of Harvard says in this question Erasmus showed all the "timidity of a Scholastic," and refers it finally to the judgment of the great authorities of the Church. Luther comes out here in reality as a champion of the boldest liberty of human judgment.

Good Catholics themselves were sorely disappointed with their champion. Erasmus himself tells us a good Catholic at Constance hung up a picture of Erasmus in order to spit on it whenever the spirit moved him to do so.

A Spaniard attacked Erasmus in the *Antapologia*.

Looking into this work, Pope Clement VII remarked: "The Holy See has never set the seal of its approbation on the spirit of Erasmus, but it has spared him in order that he might not separate himself from the Church and embrace the cause of Lutheranism to the detriment of our interest."

Dominican Cardinal Lancelotto Politi, Ambrosius Catharinus, who fought Savonarola, Cajetan, Carranza, de Soto, Spina, and Luther, smelled Pelagianism in the *Free Will* and fiercely fell on Erasmus.

Alberto Pio, Prince of Carpi, who stood high at Rome, to Erasmus on May 1, 1526, suspected all theology coming from the author of *The Praise of Folly,* "that infected soil whence sprang spontaneously such great trees bearing poisonous fruit."

Hesius wrote Blosius: "It would have been better for Christianity if Erasmus had never touched theology. Many people think he would have done less evil in openly siding with Luther than by walking on two feet and seeming to range himself now with one party, and now with the other." Cardinal Sadoleti and many others said the same.

Peter Canisius, the first German Jesuit, rated Erasmus' "philosophy of Christ" "the theology of Pyrrhus."

The good Catholic Alexander Pope terms him "the glory of the priesthood and the shame."

Lay theologian Imbart de la Tour "will look in vain in Erasmus' work for that which was the power of Luther . . . the richness of soul and of accent found in Luther."

The Catholic Christopher Hollis finds "Luther was a religious man, who believed in an untrue religion: Erasmus was an irreligious man. . . . Intellectually Erasmus was not the forerunner of Luther. . . . The *Hyperaspistes* . . . can only be described as a piece of masterly mudslinging."

Franz Xaver Kiefl, professor of dogmatics at Wuerzburg and later Praelat of the Dome, passes a like judgment.

Stunica found no fewer than 6,000 heresies. No wonder Pope Paul IV placed all the works of Erasmus on the Index of Prohibited Books.

Martin Luther on *The Bondage of the Will;* to the venerable Mister Erasmus of Rotterdam, 1525, faithfully translated from the original Latin by Rev. H. Cole, London.

E. T. Vaughan Englished it with preface and notes. Lond. 1823. 8vo.

III. LUTHER AND ZWINGLI

Landgraf Philip of Hesse and Ulrich Zwingli of Zurich would form a league from Venice to Denmark against the growing power of Kaiser Karl V. For that the difference in doctrine had to be cleared out of the way. So Philip invited the main opponents to a "friendly, non-disputatious conversation" to his castle at Marburg, though it should cost him 6,000 gulden. Luther held it "a theological means for a political purpose," yet he went — for the sake of peace.

A PRIVATE TALK

Friday, October 1, at six in the morning, Luther had a private talk with Oecolampadius, and Melanchthon with Zwingli. At night the Landgraf talked union so earnestly to Melanchthon that tears started to his eyes.

THE DEBATE

Saturday morning at six Luther was invited to take the floor. He began quite graciously, often calling his opponents "My most beloved Sirs." He had chalked on the table, or the velvet table cover, the Greek word for "is" or the words "This is My body," and now said these words are plain as they stand and must be believed as they read. The body and blood are really present with the bread and wine and really received by all communicants. He asked for "clear proofs from Scripture," not arguments from reason and mathematics.

Oecolampadius said, "The flesh profiteth nothing," John 6:63, and so denied the bodily eating and held to nothing but a spiritual eating.

Luther had always taught the spiritual eating of John 6 to be necessary; in fact, without it the bodily eating was useless. But Christ did not say *His* flesh profiteth nothing, and John 6 does not belong here. The question is whether the words of institution teach a bodily eating of the really present body and blood. It matters not *what* is commanded, but *who* it is that commands. He would eat anything the Lord commanded. The servant does not question the will of the Lord. It is needful to close the eyes. I stick to my text.

Zwingli repeated the same arguments from John 6. Then he made the damaging admission no text teaches expressly that the bread is a figure of the body. Then "is" does not mean "represent."

Next he made the astonishing statement: God does not ask us to believe what we cannot understand.

Like the Virgin Mary, he asked, "How can these things be?" Luke 1:39.

On this Melanchthon comments to the elector: "Such inept speeches escaped him [Zwingli], though Christ's teaching has much more incomprehensible, higher articles, as that God became man, that the same person, Christ, who is true God, died."

Luther simply pointed to his text, which was quite plain; it must not be explained away, but simply accepted in faith.

Zwingli said it was unworthy of Christ to be in the Lord's Supper. Luther replied it was just the glory of Christ that He humbled

THE CONFERENCE AT MARBURG   EWING GALLOWAY

Himself to become a slave and die on the cursed cross in order to serve and save sinners.

Zwingli ever came back to his "brazen wall," John 6, and cried, "This passage breaks your neck, Herr Doktor!"

The Herr Doktor was not familiar with the Swiss phrase, took it literally, flared up, and fired back, "We are here in Hesse, not in Switzerland, and the neck is not so soon at stake!"

The Landgraf explained the phrase, the misunderstanding was cleared up, and all was lovely again.

Saturday afternoon Zwingli held it offensive to believe wicked pastors could turn bread into the Lord's body.

That was a dirty dig, for Luther fought the Romish transubstantiation. We here marvel at Luther's great patience.

Luther replied it was not man's worth, but God's word that guarantees the presence. "God speaks, and it is done."

Zwingli held Luther's teaching strengthened the papacy.

Luther was no friend of the papacy, not that the pope could notice it, but he would do no violence to the clear words of Christ, though it helped Luther and weakened the papacy.

What a gallant, honorable, knightly stainless fighter, this man Luther! He disdained to take an undue advantage, he would not strike below the belt.

Zwingli said Christ was locally in heaven, therefore it was impossible for Him to be in the Lord's Supper.

Luther joked about the impossibility and said he did not care about mathematics in this matter, but relied on the plain words of Scripture.

Sunday morning Luther preached justification by faith. "I gladly make this sermon that you may see the concord of our doctrine with the doctrine of your preachers."

He tactfully avoided touching on the matter under debate. This was resumed even before breakfast, when the Swiss at last gave in it was possible for Christ to be in the Lord's Supper, but asked for proof.

Luther lifted the velvet table cover and simply pointed to the words of Christ, "This is My body."

The Swiss quoted Church Fathers.

Luther replied, Church Fathers are no authority; the only authority is the clear text of Scripture.

Oecolampadius thought if these quotations from the Fathers did not impress Luther, it was useless to go on debating. Zwingli also thought so.

Osiander says the dreary discussions about the Fathers greatly bored the hearers.

Chancellor Feige appealed to both parties to break the deadlock.

Luther — "The only way to reach an understanding is for you to honor the Word of God and believe as we do."

The Swiss — "As you refuse to bend to our explanation of the text, so we refuse to accept yours."

Luther — "Well, then we commend you to God and His judgment."

He thanked them for their courtesy and asked Zwingli's pardon for any harsh words he might have used, being only flesh and blood.

Zwingli also begged Luther's pardon for any harsh words that might have passed and wished for peace and union; all noticed the tears in his eyes.

Bucer tried to defend the Strassburgers.

Luther said they had tried to pass off their teaching under his name — "You have a different spirit," or, "Your spirit and our spirit do not rhyme." For there cannot be the same spirit where one simply believes the words of Christ and the other fights them and makes them lies. They might teach as they could answer to God.

This was the end of the official talk on Sunday afternoon, October 3. But the Landgraf would never say die; he pleaded with both parties to find a formula both could accept.

ZWINGLI REJECTS LUTHER'S OFFER

Luther drew up a statement asserting "the body of Christ is truly present in the Sacrament, and not merely in the remembrance of the partaker," and not insisting on saying, "whether bodily or spiritually, naturally or supernaturally, spatially or non-spatially."

If the Zwinglians accepted that, the Lutherans would receive them as brethren and do everything to please them.

James Mackinnon says this "final concession represents a real stretch of principle for the sake of union," for which Luther was "genuinely desirous."

And yet the Zwinglians spurned this outstretched hand.

Bucer offered to accept the real presence, but only for the believers. Even to this the Swiss would not agree.

THE MARBURG ARTICLES

In order that there might be some result of the meeting, the Landgraf still insisted on some statement on which both could agree.

Luther Monday morning based on the recent pointed misnamed Schwabach Articles and quickly drew up the mild fifteen Marburg Articles. Fourteen were adopted. The last declares the spiritual eating chiefly necessary for every Christian.

"And though we have at this time not agreed whether the true body and blood of Christ are bodily present in the bread and wine, still each part is to show the other Christian charity as far as conscience permits, and both are to pray God through His Spirit to confirm to us the right understanding."

Signed by the ten official participants. They also agreed to stop the press war.

The Zwinglians learned how unjust they had been in cruelly calling the Lutherans *"carnivorae,"* cannibals, etc., ignorantly accusing them of teaching a Capernaitic, coarse, physical, biting, chewing, and eating of the Lord's body.

Justus Jonas found a certain boorish and arrogant manner in Zwingli and a foxiness in Bucer.

John Brenz praised the "humane and mild" manner of the discussion; yes, one could have taken Luther and Zwingli for brothers.

NO BROTHERHOOD

The Landgraf now worked on both parties to receive each other as brethren.

Zwingli said, "There are no people on earth with whom I had rather be at one than with the Wittenbergers" and most earnestly begged for fellowship in Holy Communion.

Luther expressed surprise they should wish to be brothers with people whose teaching they condemned, and refused the outstretched hand because it was not the hand of brotherhood — "You have a different spirit than we."

Luther's companions strengthened him in this refusal, and especially the peaceful and gentle Melanchthon, as Bucer complained.

Luther wrote Agricola: "We gave them the hand of peace and charity, agreeing that bitter words and writings be stopped and each teach his own opinion without invective, but not without argument and defense. So we parted."

Why did Luther refuse the hand of brotherhood?

First, because there was no brotherhood as long as Zwingli condemned Luther's most holy faith.

Second, because he did not wish to be responsible for everything Zwingli might have up his political sleeve against the government.

Why would Zwingli not give in? Professor Walther Koehler of Zurich blames Zwingli for the split and blames it on his politics. He dared not go home and be accused of "Luthering," of giving in to Luther, who was considered too "papistic"!

Zwingli was a politician and somewhat of a demagog.

Why did Zwingli sign fourteen of the "Articles"? Politics, he wished to win Luther for his scheme, says August Lang.

HOME!

Since no more could be hoped for and the new deadly "English Sweat" had broken out, everybody hurried home.

So they parted, and they are parted to this day.

Who split the Protestants?

James Mackinnon declares Luther's "final concession represents a real stretch of principle for the sake of union," for which Luther was "genuinely desirous."

Von Schulte calls Luther's offer "this mildest and broadest form," and it is a fact that it was Zwingli who rejected it.

The *Cambridge Modern History II* states: "As the German Reformer grew more conciliatory, the Swiss became more uncompromising."

Walther Koehler of Zurich wrote *Martin Luther and the German Reformation* in 1916; *Zwingli and Luther* I, 851 large pages, 1924; and *The Marburg Religious Conference* in 1929.

This expert declares: "Uncontested the fact must remain that by the Lutherans a formula of union was proposed, but by Zwingli and Oecolampad in the end rejected...."

"The planned Marburg union was wrecked on Zwingli and not on the Wittenbergers.... Zwingli refused. He could not. Personally he could have agreed, but home politics forbade it.... Zwingli would lose everything did he in the Lord's Supper in the least 'lutherise'; the Zurich public opinion in that saw 'popery,' the abandonment of the Reformation."

At Worms Luther defended the authority of the Bible against the fallible human pope; at Marburg he defended the authority of the Bible against fallible human reason. Dr. Hans Preus declares both times Luther saved Christianity.

MARTIN LUTHER

Chapter Fourteen

LUTHER SAVED FROM BURNING

I. BY KING FRANCIS

Kaiser Karl, in 1521, by the Edict of Worms doomed Luther to death. Who saved the friar from the fire? "The Most Christian" King Francis I of France. Well!

Fearing the power of Hapsburg, Francis made war on the "Most Catholic" Kaiser, and so Karl had troubles of his own and could not trouble the troublesome monk, and so turned the heretic over to brother Ferdinand, Archduke of Austria.

Ferdinand called the *Reichstag* to Nuernberg in December, 1522, but he also could not do a thing to the lone Luther.

Why not?

"We know that at our holy chair for some years many abominations have happened — and no wonder the disease went from the head to the members; we all, prelates and clerics, have turned off to our own ways; for a long time there was not one that did good. Luther was God's punishment for the sins of the clergy."

Who's that talking?

The Vicar of Christ, His Holiness Pope Adrian VI, is making this most amazing confession of sins.

To whom?

To the Holy Roman Empire of the German Nation.

And then the Vicar of Christ demanded this worse than Mohammed be burned, like Hus.

The pope's spokesman was Francesco Chieregati. The *Reichstag* told their Holy Father to sweep before his own door, correct the corruptions he had admitted, then the heretic Luther would cease from troubling and the weary be at rest.

Instead of burning the heretic, they trotted out their "Hundred Grievances of the German Nation" against the pope.

They demanded a free Christian council in Germany within a year and — O horrors! — seats and votes for laymen to reform the corrupt Roman Church. So deep, so high, so wide in so short a time had spread Luther's teaching.

Chieregati was dazed; he asked that the matter be taken up again. They told him they had no time for that. He demanded prison for the Lutheran preachers at Nuernberg. Nothing was done. Aldermen Holzschuher and Jerome Baumgaertner, Katharina von Bora's erstwhile lover, were ordered to take Luther's polemical writings from the book dealers, which did not amount to much.

On January 27, 1523, brother Ferdinand reported to brother Karl: "The doctrine of Luther has taken such deep root throughout the Empire, that today among every thousand persons there is not one who is not touched by it to some extent."

On February 16 Nuncio Francis Chieregati took French leave. He reported Luther's arguments were held unanswerable at Rome, but the heretic had to be resisted to uphold authority, says Sarpi. It was even said Chieregati, Cajetan, Contarini, and Pole believed in justification by faith.

Though Karl's arm was not long enough to reach Luther in Germany, it was strong enough to get some Lutherans in the Netherlands. On July 1, 1523, Heinrich Voes and Johann von Esch, two young Augustinian monks of Antwerp, were burned for Lutherans at Brussels, chanting the *Te Deum* in the flames. They were the first Lutheran martyrs. Heinrich Moeller of Zuetphen, who had studied at Wittenberg, was done to death on December 11, 1524. At Vienna, Caspar Tauber was beheaded; at Pesth a man was burned for selling Luther's books. When Luther heard of the heroic death of the first two Lutheran martyrs, tears started to his eyes as he murmured he had not been found worthy to die for Christ. That blow opened the hidden poetic vein, and he wrote his first poetical work, the rousing ballad in honor of them, "Ein neues Lied wir heben an."

Some Catholics are ashamed of the persecutions. Alfred Baudrillart, rector of the Catholic Institute of Paris, says in *The Catholic Church, the Renaissance, and Protestantism:*

"Some Frenchmen adopted the dogma of justification by faith, which Luther proclaimed. This formidable doctrine had its martyrs. They were persecuted without pity, and with invincible fortitude they endured horrible tortures, similar to those the followers of the Crucified suffered at the hands of expiring paganism; their blood bore new children to the Reformation. The stake was the attraction that held or drew towards it the holiest souls and the most generous consciences.

"We speak of them with respect, because human interest had no part in determining their resolve.

"When confronted by heresy, she [the Roman Catholic Church] does not content herself with persuasion; arguments of an intellectual and moral order appear to her insufficient, and she has recourse to force, to corporal punishment, to torture. She creates tribunals like those of the Inquisition; she calls the laws of the State to her aid; if necessary, she encourages a crusade or a religious war, and all her 'horror of blood' practically culminates into urging the secular power to shed it, which proceeding is almost more odious — for it is less frank — than shedding it herself. Especially did she act thus in the sixteenth century with regard to Protestants.

Not content to reform morally, to preach by example, to convert people by eloquent and holy missionaries, she lit in Italy, in the Low Countries, and, above all, in Spain the funeral piles of the Inquisition. In France under Francis I and Henry II, in England under Mary Tudor, she tortured the heretics, whilst both in France and Germany during the second half of the sixteenth and the first half of the seventeenth century, if she did not actually begin, at any rate she encouraged and actively aided, the religious wars. No one will deny that we have here a great scandal to our contemporaries.

"Mgr. d'Hulst remarked on this fact in his *Careme* of 1895: 'The intervention of the secular power in the cause of heresy has left memories which haunt the imagination of our contemporaries like a nightmare. Many men of divers opinions find in this the great scandal of ecclesiastical history. . . . Even among our friends and our brothers we find those who dare not look this problem in the face. They ask permission from the Church to ignore or even deny all those acts and institutions in the past which have made orthodoxy compulsory. And when the Church refuses this right, when she condemns the thesis of absolute liberalism, when she defends, if not in its detailed application, at any rate in principle, a legislation belonging to the great centuries of faith, then a dread fear seizes them and leaves them with halting faith or saddened by the sight of ironical or triumphant impiety.'"

The Catholic Lord Acton wrote Mary Gladstone: "The Inquisition is peculiarly the weapon and peculiarly the work of the popes. . . . The distinctive feature of papal Rome. . . . It is the principal thing with which the papacy is identified and by which it must be judged. The principle of the Inquisition is murderous, and a man's opinion of the papacy is regulated and determined by his opinion about religious assassination." P. 298, ed. H. Paul, 1914.

If need be, the Romans could put up with a saint; but a barbarian? Never! The epigram on Alexander VI was revived —

"The Sixth Tarquin, the Sixth Nero, and that Sixth: Rome always was ruined by Sixths." On September 14, 1523, Adrian VI died suddenly. In death they still pursued him. He was buried between Pius II and Pius III, and at once Pasquino quipped, "The Impious between the Pious."

HANS SACHS

To his physician, Macerata, the happy Romans built a statue: "To the Liberator of his Country" — meaning he had poisoned the Vicar of Christ.

At the second *Reichstag* of Nuernberg, in 1524, Ferdinand again could do nothing against Luther. The new pope was Julius de Medici, Clement VII, a bastard who had his bathroom decorated by Perino del Vaga with scenes from the life of Venus in the licentious manner of Giulio Romano.

The worthy Holy Father sent a legate worthy of him, Cardinal Campegi. One of his wenches stole his gold cardinal's ring, so the virtuous Cardinal Aleander reports.

Campegi was caricatured; the Augsburgers hooted at his blessing. Nuernberg was turning Lutheran under his very nose. Albrecht Duerer, one of the world's greatest painters, Hans Sachs, Germany's most famous shoemaker-poet, Lazarus Spengler, the city secretary, and others were leading Lutherans. Andrew Osiander from the pulpit called the pope the Antichrist, and the pope's legate couldn't

ALBRECHT DUERER

do a thing. Four thousand took the Lord's Supper in both kinds, the Lutheran way, even members of the kaiser's government. On Maundy Thursday, in the old Zollern Castle, Osiander gave the Lutheran Lord's Supper to Queen Isabella of Denmark — the kaiser's own sister.

Campegi sneered at the "Hundred Grievances of the German Nation," and haughtily told the *Reichstag* to expect no answer to the complaints of the year before.

The kaiser demanded Luther be burned and Lutheranism crushed. The *Reichstag* promised to do so "as far as possible" — meaning nothing.

They again demanded a free general council in Germany. In the meantime a national German assembly was to meet at Speyer in November to see what was right and what was wrong in Luther's teaching and so advise the next council. This was passed over the head of the pope's legate.

The kaiser denounced the *Reichstag* for meddling with his rights and denounced Luther as a worse enemy of the faith than Mahomet; the pope denounced the *Reichstag* for insulting him; Luther denounced the *Reichstag* for making a fool of itself — "the drunken and crazy princes" promising to burn him and at the same time promising him a fair trial. A fine set to war on the Turk, who was ten times as godly as they!

And the kaiser he calls a poor mortal "maggot sack." James Mackinnon can hardly help thinking of "Imperial Caesar dead and turned to clay" or wondering whether William Shakespeare might not have borrowed something from Martin Luther.

The Catholic princes broke faith; they did not go to Speyer in November, as they had resolved. Campegi bribed them with a reduction of papal taxes to meet at Regensburg on June 24, where he organized them into the Southern Catholic Confederacy to execute the Edict of Worms to execute Luther and crush Lutheranism.

This is historic, it is the first wedge driven to split Germany into the Catholic South and the Lutheran North.

The Catholics at once persecuted their Lutheran subjects in the most cruel manner. Bibles were burned, the printers were drowned, women and children were forced to kneel in burning ashes. In one district no fewer than forty Lutheran pastors were hanged. The pope urged the kaiser to depose the Saxon elector and put the Lutheran cities under the ban.

II. SAVED BY POPE CLEMENT VII

George von Frundsberg's German *Landsknechte* in 1525 in the Battle of Pavia captured King Francis I, and in the Peace of Madrid on January 14, 1526, Kaiser Karl forced him to swear to help crush the Lutherans.

Kaiser Karl did not crush Luther. And who, think you, saved Luther? Of all men under the sun, it was — the pope!

When the *Reichstag* met at Speyer on June 25, 1526, the Lutheran princes blazoned their slogan V. D. M. I. E., "Verbum Dei Manet In Eternum, The Word of God Remains in Eternity."

All the churches were closed to the Lutherans. They preached in the open, daily, twice on holidays, to large numbers, many princes and clerics attending. Faber in the Dome was almost forsaken.

A committee of the princes proposed the marriage of the clergy, Communion in both kinds, abolition of private masses, reduction of the number of begging monks and of fast and festival days, the use of German as well as Latin in Baptism and Communion, the interpretation of Scripture by Scripture — not by popes, priests, and professors.

On orders by the kaiser, Ferdinand vetoed all changes and demanded the Lutherans be put under the yoke of the pope by force.

The *Reichstag* replied by trotting out the famous "Hundred Grievances of the German Nation" against Rome. "Never before at any *Reichstag* was there such free and independent and outspoken criticism of the pope, the bishops, and clergy as at this one," Spalatin reports.

In addition, Sultan Solyman the Magnificent in the battle of Mohacz defeated King Louis of Hungary, who lost his life in flight. His widow, Kaiser Karl's sister Mary, favored the Gospel, and Luther dedicated to her "Four Comfort Psalms" — 37, 62, 94, 109.

Having troubles of his own, the kaiser could not afford to trouble the Lutherans; he needed them in his business. If he enforced the Edict of Worms, the Lutheran princes would not aid him in his wars; if he did not, the Catholic princes would desert him — as a result the *Reichstag* of Speyer, in 1526, promised a general council — "every state in the meantime to live, rule, and bear itself as it shall be ready to answer for to God and his Imperial Majesty."

Now the Lutherans cheerfully poured out their blood and treasure to save the kaiser against the pope, the king of France, and the Turk before the walls of Vienna.

Luther held the *Reichstag* gave a legal basis for the princes to reform their lands and called on Elector John to do so. Leopold von Ranke and Theodor Brieger agree.

No wonder Luther boasted he was no longer a heretic! The excommunicated monk, cursed by the pope, and the outlawed monk, hounded by the kaiser, certainly triumphed gloriously.

Why did brother Ferdinand give in? He had to.

Fearing for his lands from the kaiser's growing power, the pope simply loosed Francis from his solemn oath just made to the kaiser. The pope, you see, can do things that men of honor cannot do.

When Benvenuto Cellini, the famous artist, reproached this same pope for breaking his word, the Holy Father smilingly said he had power to bind and loose! Witty and wicked.

On May 22 Pope Clement with King Francis of France, the Swiss, Venice, Florence, Milan, and the good will of King Henry VIII of England formed the Most Holy League of Cognac to war on the kaiser.

Of course, the kaiser was not especially pleased with the pope's treachery, and so he made up his mind to teach his brother ruler and Holy Father a little lesson in common honesty. "I shall go into Italy and revenge myself on those who have injured me, especially on that poltroon, the pope. Someday, perhaps, Martin Luther will become a man of weight." Karl had "poured out streams of gold" for the election of the pope, now the election was attacked because the pope was a bastard.

On September 17, 1526, Karl addressed a letter to his Holy Father in language "of which no follower of Luther need have been ashamed," as Ranke writes, and Ehses thinks: "The imperial state paper is perhaps the most violent document addressed in that century by a Catholic sovereign to the pope."

Don Hugo de Moncada, the kaiser's envoy, and Pompeo Colonna, the pope's cardinal, let loose their troops on the pope. Not a Roman hand was raised to help the pope, who had taxed his people almost to starvation. The kaiser's eagle floated over the Vatican. Imprisoned in St. Angelo, the pope could watch the plundering of his palace. Relics, crosses, sacred vessels, and vestments were stolen, and even the altar of St. Peter's was robbed. Soldiers wore the white garments and the red cap of the pope and in mockery gave the papal blessing. The host was profaned.

A cardinal driving the Holy Father from the Vatican and looting his furniture — what a sight!

On Holy Thursday, April 18, 1527, after the reading of the bull *In Coena Domini,* when the pope was giving the blessing, a man dressed only in a leathern apron clambered onto the statue of St. Paul in front of St. Peter's and shouted to the Holy Father: "Thou bastard of Sodom, for thy sins Rome shall be destroyed.

Repent, and turn thee! If thou wilt not believe me, in fourteen days thou shalt see it."

Pretty good prophet! Only four days out of the way.

Cheer up, Holy Father, the worst is yet to come! Georg von Frundsberg pawned even his beloved castle of Mindelheim, the cradle of his race, and the jewels of his wife, to raise 38,000 gulden to gather an army of lusty young men. He held it would be pleasing to God and mankind that the pope should be hanged, should he have to do it with his own hand.

On May 6, 1527, the *Landsknechte* of the deceased Frundsberg, with the Spaniards under Bourbon, stormed the city. Bourbon was killed, and Benvenuto Cellini claimed credit for firing the fatal shot.

The pope with some cardinals barely escaped from the Vatican into the Castle of St. Angelo. Dressed like cardinals, the soldiers marched to the castle, proclaimed Luther pope, and threatened to hang Pope Clement VII. Hunger forced the imprisoned pope and cardinals to surrender. The pope bought his life from the good Catholic army for 400,000 ducats. To raise the cash, he auctioned off crucifixes and Communion vessels and even put his triple crown into the melting pot. Cardinal Cajetan was dragged through the streets in a disgraceful procession.

An officer reports to Karl: "Having entered, our men sacked the whole Borgo and killed almost everyone they found [even the sick in the hospital and the children in the orphanage]. . . . All the monasteries were rifled. Every person was compelled by torture to pay a ransom. . . . The ornaments of all the churches were pillaged, and the relics and other sacred things thrown into sinks and cesspools. Even the holy places were sacked. The Church of St. Peter and the papal palace, from basement to the top, were turned into stables for horses [even the glorious Sistine Chapel]. . . . Everyone considers it has taken place by the just judgment of God, because the court of Rome was so ill-ruled."

Cardinal Como writes: "The sacking and taking of prisoners continued for 12 days, and it would have lasted longer still if there had been anything to sack, or any more prisoners to take. . . . The fight raged in his [the cardinal of Sierra's] palace for more than four hours; it was entirely gutted, and the cardinal himself was made prisoner, together with all that were within. He was dragged through the streets without his biretta, with a sorrowful visage, and many kicks and blows, and made to pay 50,000 ducats; and after he had paid them, he was tied to a stable, and his head would have been cut off if he had not paid 50,000 ducats more. . . . Many friars were beheaded, even priests at the altar; many old nuns were beaten with sticks; many young ones violated, robbed, and made prisoners; all the vestments, chalices, silver, were taken from the churches. The tabernacles in which were contained the *Corpus Domini* [Body of God] were broken, and the host itself was thrown, now on the ground, now into the fire, now trampled underfoot, now put into a frying pan to roast, now broken into a hundred pieces. All the silver reliquaries were scattered about. The head of St. John Baptist at San Silvestro was spoiled of its silver and thrown on the ground. . . . There is not a house in Rome, either of cardinals or others, not a church or monastery, either of the Romans or foreigners, great or small, which has not been sacked; even the houses of the water carriers and porters. . . . Many of the private soldiers have made as much as 25,000, 30,000, or even 40,000 ducats each. Fancy what the captains have made! — Civita Vecchia, 24 May 1527."

Soldiers put on the vestments, officiated at the altar in derision, substituting for prayers the most horrible blasphemies. Others put the Cardinal Ara Coeli on a bier and sang the office for the dead; before a church they made a funeral oration with the most revolting obscenities. Then they forced him to serve them with the choicest wines in the holy vessels.

Some were hanged in the air by their arms; others were dangled over wells with the threat of drowning if they would not give up their treasures.

A soldier had trouble stripping a diamond ring from the finger of a prelate. The corporal cut off the finger and gave it to the soldier. He pulled off the ring and flung the finger into the face of the prelate.

Russell writes: "They have burned houses to the value of two hundred millions of ducats, with all the churches, images, and priests that fell into their hand. They compelled priests and monks to violate the nuns. . . . They did not spare the boys, and carried off the girls; and whenever they found the host in the church they threw it into the river, or the vilest places they could find."

On June 17 Theodorich Vater, *alias* Gescheid, a clerk of Speyer, wrote in a letter: "We have profaned all the churches of Rome; men and women have been slain over the altar of St. Peter's; the tomb or coffin inside which the remains of Peter and Paul had been laid to rest has been broken open and the relics scattered."

On September 25 Rome was pillaged again, in some ways worse than before. "Hell has nothing to compare with the present state of Rome," reports a Venetian.

Drunkenness and debaucheries brought on dreadful diseases. Famine and pestilence cut down the population and the soldiers. 13,000 houses were destroyed, 33,000 people were killed, the population reduced from 85,000 to 32,000, says Gregorovius.

The Catholic Professor Ludwig Pastor writes: "The Spaniards committed the worst abominations. . . . The excesses of the German *Landsknechte* were not marked by such inventive cruelty. . . . Since the *Landsknechte* were for the most part Lutherans, they did not neglect this opportunity of heaping scorn and ridicule on the papacy."

The pope and his court deserved the scourge.

Bishop Stafileo said to the Rota on May 15, 1528, God's punishment had come "because all flesh has become corrupt, because we are not citizens of the holy city of Rome, but of Babylon, the city of corruption." He called Rome the whore of Babylon and said the Lord had driven the buyers and sellers from His temple. Cardinal Sadoleto said the same. A Spaniard wrote: "Now I recognize the justice of God, who forgets not, even if His coming tarries. In Rome all sins are openly committed — sodomy, simony, idolatry, hypocrisy, fraud. Well may we believe, then, that what has come to pass has not been by chance, but by the judgment of God." The pope spoke of the *sacco di Roma* as a chastisement for their sins.

Did they repent? A Venetian reported: "The court here is bankrupt; there is no improvement in morals; men here would sell Christ for a piece of gold."

Lope de Soria, Karl's ambassador to Genoa, advised him to end the temporal power of the popes, who were the causes of all the wars he had seen during his residence of twenty-eight years in Italy. Chancellor Gattinara's nephew awaited the kaiser's decision whether any sort of apostolic chair were to remain at Rome or not! Macchiavelli desired the end of the papacy as the root of all evil. The historian Guicciardini, after having served Leo X and Clement VII faithfully for long years, broke out into violent accusations against Rome and cherished the hope that Luther might bring about the destruction of the ecclesiastical polity. The Florentine Bartolomeo Cerretani, though an adherent of the Medici, places his hopes of salvation in no other than Martin Luther. In him he hails a man distinguished equally for morals, learning, piety, whose views are penetrated by the ideas of the Ancient Church, and whose writings are marked by a true and solid learning. In spite of the pope's bull *Exsurge* he still believed that from Luther would come the ardently desired reform of the Church.

An English envoy, who could speak plain English, called Karl's confessor Quinones "a whoresun flatteryng fryar"; but this worthy now told the kaiser, if he did not undo the wrong to the pope, he should not call himself the kaiser, but Luther's captain.

When so many good Catholics were rejoicing over the sack of holy Rome, did Luther shout with glee?

"Christ so orders that the kaiser, who for the pope persecutes Luther, for Luther must destroy the pope."

To Jonas in November: "I am sorry Rome was sacked."

What a tender heart in that "German beast"!

READING THE AUGSBURG CONFESSION

Chapter Fifteen

THE FIRST PROTESTANTS THEIR FIRST CONFESSION AND THE FIRST RELIGIOUS PEACE

I. THE FIRST PROTEST

As Clement had broken his papal word of honor to the kaiser, so Karl now broke his kaiserly word of honor to the Lutherans. In 1529 he was at peace with the pope and the king of France and so had his hands free to use force against the "pestilential disease of Lutheranism" at the second *Reichstag* of Speyer.

In the cathedral John Faber preached hymns of hate against the Lutherans, "worse than the Turks, for these fast, and the Lutherans do not." He would give up the Gospel rather than the Church, for this cannot err. He tried to exploit the difference between the Lutherans and the Zwinglians — "having oppressed the one the easier to oppress the other," as Jacob Sturm wrote to Strassburg.

He also wrote: "Christ is again in the hands of Caiaphas and Pilate. . . . It is only a small number that wishes to remain with God's holy Word, but they are unafraid."

King Ferdinand forbade the Lutherans to preach, but they preached daily in the open. On Palm Sunday Elector John of Saxony wrote his son: "About eight thousand people were present today in my chapel at morning and evening services."

The Lutherans again blazoned their slogan, V. D. M. I. E. — Verbum Dei Manet In Eternum — The Word of God endureth forever. A fellow with a merry, scoffing wit thought the letters stood for Verbum Diaboli Manet in Episcopis, The Word of the Devil remains in the Bishops.

Through brother Ferdinand, since 1526 king of Bohemia and Hungary despite the opposition of the Catholic Duke of Bavaria, the kaiser told the *Reichstag* at Speyer on March 15, he had in virtue "of his Imperial and absolute power annulled" the resolutions of 1526, he forbade leading anyone to a wrong faith, he ordered the *Reichstag* to put his will into its resolutions.

If the kaiser could simply tear up the resolutions of the *Reichstag* and, instead, enforce his own personal will, why a *Reichstag?* Even Catholic princes felt this.

On April 19 the Catholic majority signed on the dotted line and adopted most of the kaiser's commands.

Until the general council, promised for the next summer by the papal legate, John Thomas Picus, Count of Mirandola, or a national German assembly, the Catholic princes were to enforce the Edict of Worms, that is, crush Lutheranism in their lands. In Lutheran states, however, it was forbidden to turn Lutheran; it was forbidden to abolish the mass, which might force Lutheran pastors to celebrate the Romish mass. And the Romish bishops might be restored where their jurisdiction had been practically abolished. The Anabaptists were to be punished with fire and sword, and the Zwinglians, who denied the real presence in the Lord's Supper, were not to be tolerated.

Jedburgh justice — first hang a man and then try him. Lutheranism was to be crushed, and then discussed in a free Christian general council in a German city!

The Romanists demanded toleration in Lutheran lands, but refused toleration in Catholic lands.

The Lutherans promptly protested against the brutal tyranny of the majority, and on the 25th put their formal protest into legal form on thirteen sheets of parchment.

They stood on the legal and constitutional ground that the unanimous and ratified agreement of the *Reichstag* of 1526 could not be broken by one part without the consent of the other part. They stood on higher and stronger ground when appealing to conscience in the dynamic principle — "We fear God's wrath more than we fear the kaiser's ban. *In matters pertaining to God's honor and the soul's salvation everyone must stand for himself before God and give account,* so that in this matter no one can excuse himself by the doing or resolution of others.

"Up to this time the decree (of 1526) has maintained the peace, and we protest against its abrogation."

When the heroic Lutherans signed this protest, they did so at the risk of their lands and their lives, for the lowering clouds of civil-religious war were coming over the Alps.

In the very same month that the Romanists were trampling on the conscience of the Lutherans at Speyer, Luther wrote *On the War Against the Turk,* his patriotic call to all to haste to help the kaiser against Sultan Solyman, who was planting his victorious banners under the walls of trembling Vienna. Some patriot, this Luther. He comes mighty near turning the other cheek and loving his enemy, for Karl seemed more set to fight Luther than the Turk. Philip von Hesse and others refused help to the kaiser.

In July the kaiser threatened the Lutheran princes with the severest penalties, and in September cast into prison at Piacenza the messengers that brought the protest.

In case the kaiser really warred on the Lutheran religion, were the Protestants to resist with arms? Luther said the kaiser must first be deposed for violating the Constitution.

Disdainfully ignored by the *Reichstag,* haughtily set aside by King Ferdinand, ungraciously rejected by Kaiser Karl, this protest stands for all time a shining milestone in the history of civilization.

From this protest the Lutherans were contemptuously nicknamed

Protestants, but the name became a highly characteristic badge of honor. From this protest all Protestants the world over take their name.

Archbishop John Bramhall of Armagh in Ireland, 1663, says truly: "The name Protestant is one to which others have no right but by communion with Lutherans."

The American Methodist Bishop Hurst writes: "The ages past did not make him; rather did he make the ages which were to come. Luther has influenced the Protestant world without regard to type."

The Catholic von Schlegel writes: "The Protestant religion is solely the work and deed of one man, unique in his way, Martin Luther." W. S. Lilly, secretary lawyer of the Catholic Union of Great Britain, says in his "Renaissance Types": "Evangelical Protestantism . . . is Luther's creation."

The Very Reverend Principal John Tulloch writes in *The Nineteenth Century* of April, 1884: "All modern Christian liberty may be said to be the outcome of the protest taken at Speyer and Augsburg by the Evangelical members of the German Empire. The attitude of these Christian princes and others was again only possible in the light of the great struggle which had been maintained during the twelve previous years by one man. The Diet of Worms and Luther's memorable words there alone explain the subsequent diets at Speyer and Augsburg. The courage of a single man as he faced on that great occasion the mailed chivalry of Germany — a pale and slight figure, as yet without any of the brave rotundity of his later years — gave the courage which inspired the famous protest, and laid the foundation of all Christian and ecclesiastical liberties."

II. THE FIRST CONFESSION

What is a pope's treacherous perjury and a kaiser's sack of Rome between — rogues? Mere trifles. Rogues fight, rogues unite. The pope and the kaiser made the Peace of Barcelona in 1529. From November, 1529, to March, 1530, they lived together in the Palazzo Pubblico at Bologna. "Behold, how good and how pleasant it is for brethren to dwell together in unity!" Ps. 133:1.

On February 24, his birthday, the thirty-year-old kaiser swore on the Gospels to be the faithful champion of the Holy Roman Church, i. e., to crush "the pestilential disease of Lutheranism." The "God on earth" placed on his head Charles the Great's golden crown of the Holy Roman Empire — "neither holy nor Roman nor an empire," sneered Voltaire.

The kaiser offered the usual three pieces of gold and served as deacon, bringing the wafers to the altar and pouring water on the pope's hands "in so seemly and devout a fashion, as one long accustomed to fulfill such services, that all standing around were filled with wonder and joy." The kaiser of the Holy Roman Empire kissed the "god's" toe, held his stirrup, and led his horse by the bridle — a goodly stable boy.

Karl called his *Reichstag* for April 8 to Augsburg, the burg of the great Caesar Augustus, and promised "to hear, understand, and consider everybody's view, opinion, and meaning in love." He cooed as gently as any sucking dove, and the simple soul of the honest German Luther rejoiced with great joy over these honeyed phrases of the crafty Spaniard. Cardinal Wolsey called him a liar, and Wolsey had a right to do so.

At Innsbruck Karl "made as if he would kiss the young ladies, but disengaged himself as soon as might be from those of riper years," observes the observant chronicler, likely a reporter for the yellow press.

In the Kaiser's train was the "god's" legate, Lorenzo Campegi, who had paid the pope 24,000 ducats for the red hat. He was a bribe-taking, gambling, drinking, immoral cleric — Cardinal Aleander tells us.

Though a high official in the pope's court, Campegi blames the pope's court for the corruptions in the Church — just as Pope Adrian VI had done. He denounced the abuses of the indulgences, especially in connection with the building of St. Peter's — just like Luther. He called the officials of the Dataria "bloodsuckers." How do we know? The *Catholic Cyclopedia* tells us so. This Campegi kept on urging Karl to execute the Edict of Worms, to crush the Lutherans with fire and sword.

"The Messiah of the priests" came on June 15 and was received with proper pomp.

The kaiser asked the Lutherans to march in the Corpus Christi procession next day. This they resolutely refused; it was not a matter of courtesy, but of conscience. Margrave George of Brandenburg, grown gray in the kaiser's service, with deep emotion cried out, "Before I would refrain from God's Word, I would rather kneel on this spot and let my head be chopped off." The kaiser replied, "Dear Prince, not head off, not head off."

Candle in hand, the kaiser walked behind the host for two hours in the blazing sun. Though the city council had appealed from house to house, not a hundred Augsburgers followed the kaiser.

Karl had promised in writing to settle the religious question "in a spirit of love." In the opening speech the papal nuncio Vincenzo Pimpinella had a lengthened contrast between the Turks and many Germans (Lutherans), and the Turks were much better than many Germans. "The truest and most revered teachings of Christ they by devilish inspiration turn into farces and shameful things. If Peter's keys will no longer open and unlock the marble hearts of the German princes, then Paul's sword must help and smite."

And then he begged for help against the Turk! The nerve! No wonder even the Cardinal-Elector-Archbishop of Mainz was furious—"What does he mean by calling on St. Paul to cut down the Germans with his sword?" Yes, what?

The princes replied by again presenting the historic "Hundred Grievances of the German Nation Against the Corruptions of the Papacy." "Rebellion" in the own camp, cried the frightened Campegi.

The speech from the throne was cold and severe. It complained that the Edict of Worms to crush Lutheranism had not been executed. The Lutherans were pretty plainly held responsible for the outrages of the Peasants' War and the fanaticism of the Anabaptists.

John Eck printed 404 heresies of the Lutherans, classing them with the condemned old and new heretics.

Melanchthon took the Saxon Visitation Articles, the misnamed seventeen Schwabach Articles, the fifteen Marburg Articles, and the Torgau Articles, and these cubs he licked into shape, as Vergil would say.

PHILIP
MELANCHTHON

On May 11 a draft of some of the articles was sent to Luther, who endorsed the work. But more articles were added, and "daily we change much," wrote Melanchthon to Luther.

Luther! Where was Luther all this time? He was left high and dry in the elector's *Veste* (Fortress) Coburg, 500 feet above the town and 1,500 feet above the sea.

Why? Cardinal Sforza Pallavicini, the Jesuit historian, thinks it would have been an unpardonable insult to the kaiser to bring the damned and banned heretic into the kaiser's own city of Augsburg. Luther had a hunch he had "too coarse a voice" for the *Reichstag;* likely he had something there.

At the Coburg Luther grew a beard, just as at the Wartburg; he complained about his spectacles; he received a sword from Abbot Friedrich Pistorius of Nuernberg; he shot at bats with a crossbow and hit one in the heart — always a straight shooter. He enjoyed the wonderful month of May and the woods in leaf and the singing of the larks and everything on God's green earth.

The Coburg was an ideal summer resort, but Luther just simply did not know what to do with a vacation. "I have come to my Sinai, dearest Philip, but I shall soon make it a Zion and build three tabernacles, one for the Psalter, one for the Prophets, and one for Aesop." Aesop! in this company and in these times!

Hearing of his father's death in May, Martin took his Psalter and went to his room and wept so much that for two days he couldn't work. Since then he didn't give way to grief any more.

"I am now old Luther; soon I shall follow him to that kingdom which Christ has promised. I rejoice that he lived long enough to see the light of the new Gospel."

He wrote Melanchthon: "It is my pious duty to weep for him, whom the Father of mercy destined to give me birth — for him, by whose labor and sweat God nourished me and made what I am, such as that is."

He was sickly himself.

"At Coburg I sometimes felt that death was not far off, and would look around in the place, where I might bury me; there, in the chapel under the cross, I said to myself, I shall likely be laid to rest."

Melanchthon wrote: "Oh, that with my poor life I could buy his, for earth has nothing diviner than him!"

Kate sent him a picture of their little Magdalene by Cranach. The fond father hung it on the wall opposite the dining-room table, and it helped him forget his cares.

He wrote home about the crows having a *Reichstag;* the wise and witty letter to Teutleben; the letter of sublime faith to Brueck; the letter to the Catholic Bavarian court musician Senfl for music for Ps. 4:9; the Christmasy letter to four-year-old Haenschen.

At the risk of their lands and of their lives the Lutheran laymen signed the Augsburg Confession.

The *Reichstag* met in the large Gold Room of the town hall, but in order to reduce the number of hearers as much as possible, Karl ordered the meeting on the 25th to be held in the bishop's palace, in the chapter room holding only about two hundred, and it was cleared of visitors. Karl was the ruler of two worlds — also a peanut.

The *Reichstag* was a brilliant affair. On a throne under a canopy of cloth of gold sat the greatest ruler of the world. He was attended by his brother, Ferdinand, king of Bohemia and Hungary, to be invested with the Austrian hereditary lands on September 5, soon to be elected king of the Romans and then kaiser. There were six electors of the German Reich, forty-two dukes, ninety counts, ninety-eight deputies of cities, doctors of divinity and doctors of laws, six cardinals, and the ambassadors of foreign courts. Imagine the picturesque cut and the dazzling color of their clothing!

At three in the afternoon the two Saxon chancellors stepped into the middle of the hall, Dr. Gregor Brueck with the Latin copy of the Confession and Dr. Christian Beyer with the German, which he read, read from four to six. The kaiser did not understand German and so fell asleep — asleep at the switch at a most critical and dramatic moment in modern history. But Beyer read so clearly that the throng outside could understand every word. It seemed we could hear every word when we stood on the historic spot after almost four hundred years.

The Confession is so mild Luther called it "The Pussyfoot." "Too strong," said Alfons Valdez, the secretary of Karl, making the timid Melanchthon still more timid.

What a change! At Worms, in 1521, the boyish kaiser forbade the lowly and lonely Luther to say a single word in defense of his teaching; nine years later the mighty ruler, on whose lands the sun never set, was forced to listen to the German reading of a formal confession of the Lutheran teaching of princes and lords and cities in the public *Reichstag!*

"I will speak of Thy testimonies also before kings!" Ps. 119:46.

On June 26 Melanchthon sent a copy to Luther and, "almost in constant tears," asked what more could be conceded. "More than enough has already been conceded. . . . Please God, nothing more shall be wrung from me, let matters go as they will. . . . May Christ heal you!" was Luther's answer on the 29th, and the next day he wrote again: "I would rather fall with Christ than stand with the kaiser. . . . Let us pray with the Apostles: 'Lord, increase our faith.'" Luke 17:5.

Cardinal Campegi collected a committee of twenty to concoct a Confutation of the Confession. But they dipped their pens in stinkpots and the kaiser rejected the savage slanders. Five times — yes, the Romish historian Johannes Janssen says so — five times it had to be shortened and somewhat disinfected. At this Eck is reported to have been very much hurt.

While the Catholic committee was concocting its Confutation, Luther, on July 6, sent his work on Psalm 2 to Albrecht of Mainz and urged a political peace, religious liberty for Lutherans and Romanists. And, would you believe it? Albrecht granted religious liberty at Hammelburg to Erfurt; as long as they paid taxes, he did not bother about their religion.

In 1930 they celebrated the four hundredth anniversary of their separation of Church and State. Would to God the kaiser had done likewise!

On August 3 the Catholic Confutation was read, and the kaiser impartially fell asleep.

A committee of fourteen — princes, councilors, and theologians — from August 16 to 21 tried to concoct a compromise. Luther jeered: "I hear you have undertaken a weird work, to unite the pope and Luther. But the pope will not be willing, and Luther forbids it. If you bring it about, I'll reconcile Christ and Belial."

Another committee of six — Melanchthon and five Romanists with Eck — made another effort. Fearing war, the timid Melanchthon made dangerous concessions, egged on by Erasmus. The crooked Cardinal Campegi even offered him four hundred scudi and two hundred scudi a year to betray the Lutheran cause. Osiander heard Melanchthon remark it was not wrong to keep peace by wrong means. Melanchthon would sacrifice all for the cup for the laity and marriage for the priests. Cardinal Campegi would not grant even wine and wives, and Cardinal Aleander blames him for the breach.

"There is a tide in the affairs of men."

Melanchthon became a leader without followers. Jerome Baumgaertner, Kate von Bora's erstwhile lover, wrote home to Nuernberg that Melanchthon was "more childish than a child. . . . No man to the present day has harmed the Gospel more than Philip." Lazarus Spengler, secretary of Nuernberg, and Landgraf Philip wrote Luther to write to Augsburg and bolster up the waverers.

Luther to the rescue! Roused, he wrote: "Should you, what you, please God, will not do, make concessions that clearly oppose the

Gospel and so thrust the eagle into a sack, well, then Luther will come, do not doubt it, he will come and gloriously free this eagle. As true as Christ lives, that will happen."

"All treaty about harmonizing our doctrine displeases me, for I know it is impossible to unite Luther and the pope, unless the pope will abolish the papacy. I am almost bursting with anger and indignation. Break off the conferences and go home!" If there must be war, then let there be war. "Let them go to their own place."

Luther hurled his thunderbolts from the Coburg to Augsburg. With God-given courage he heartened the disheartened. With God-given power he cheered and steered those helplessly and hopelessly floundering in the bog. He quoted Vergil's Aeneas: "Friends, worse have ye endured, a God will end this also; hold out and save yourselves for better times."

Justus Jonas called him the Elijah who drove the chariot of Israel, 2 Kings 2:12. Melanchthon declared his willingness to follow the lead of Luther. And please make this memorandum — while this Atlas was carrying this modern world, he was often a sick man.

Marvelous man! "We ne'er shall see his like again."

Urbanus Rhegius found him the mighty theologian whose like would not again be seen. "This judgment flows not from love, but the love from the judgment."

Bucer found him a man who truly feared God and heartily sought the glory of God.

Princes and preachers made pilgrimages to the Coburg as to the shrine of a saint or to the voice of an oracle. "I shall soon have to go elsewhere if the pilgrimage hither continues," he wrote Kate.

On September 14, the Kurprinz John Frederick came to the Coburg and presented to Luther a gold ring with the celebrated coat of arms; it was too large and fell to the floor. Luther joked he was born for a bullet or a halter, rather than for gold.

All work and no play makes Jack a dull boy.

A Venetian visitor wrote that Karl and Ferdinand enjoyed themselves vastly in banqueting, dancing, and shooting; they seemed to care little who was Lutheran and who was Catholic; indeed, a great Lutheran gave a dinner party to Karl, who could see on the walls the portraits of Luther and his wife. The kaiser and all his court were the guests of the great banker, Fugger, who entertained them in more than princely style. In one pantomimic comedy there appeared Reuchlin, Erasmus, Luther, the pope, and the kaiser himself.

The Venetian ambassador Badovaro says: "He was addicted to vulgar and miscellaneous incontinence."

His former confessor, Cardinal Garcia di Loaysa, charged him with indolence and sensual pleasure and wasting precious time; in that way he would never win "the crown of the world."

On September 22 the kaiser loftily declared "his creed" had thoroughly confuted the Lutherans "out of Scripture," and they were to return under the pope by April 15, 1531, or else their heresy was to be rooted out by force!

Brenz gloomily forecast "the end of Germany." Bucer wailed and whined about "the massacre of the saints worse than that of the time of Diocletian." Luther scoffed at these dangers. He was clear-eyed when others were blear-eyed. He was willing to lose an ear and an eye if Venice, the pope, and the Frenchman would heartily become good kaiser men; for they are three persons in one essence in their incomprehensible anger and hate of the kaiser with their hypocrisy, lies, and fraud.

That man Luther had an uncanny way of being right. He was a better statesman than the professional politicians. He said there would be no war, and there was no war.

The Kurfuerst and Melanchthon came to the Coburg on October 4, and next day all started for home.

On June 15 Kaiser Karl had been received as a conquering hero; on November 24 he left — defeated. After nine years of brilliant victories, the most powerful ruler of the world was defeated by the damned and banned "devil in a monk's cowl," as Karl called him.

Edward Armstrong, the latest writer on Karl, says: "It was the Emperor's first real check.... It may be admitted that the Diet of Augsburg was one of the supreme moments of Lutheranism — that princes and towns did indeed sacrifice something for conscience' sake."

Preserved Smith writes: "Luther was right."

The kaiser forbade the printing of the Augsburg Confession; kaiser or no kaiser, somehow, in Carlylese, it got itself printed. The kaiser himself sent copies to the kings of France, England, and Portugal. Even during the *Reichstag* the Confession was translated into French, Italian, English, Dutch, Spanish, and Portuguese — the best seller of the year. Lutheran publicity!

In the same year it was accepted 'way up in Riga. 'Way down in Venezuela the Welser Augsburg merchants had founded a colony in 1529, and in 1532 the Confession was adopted — if Von Kloeden can be trusted.

Melanchthon sent the Confession to King Henry VIII, and it formed the basis of the Episcopalian Thirty-Nine Articles and the creed of the Methodists.

The Congregationalist Professor Williston Walker, in his *Church History,* says "the Augsburg Confession is one of which the Lutheran Churches of today may well be proud." Well, they are; they placed it and its Apology at the head of their Confessions in the *Book of Concord* of 1580.

Professor Curtis of Aberdeen, in his *History of Creeds,* calls it "the model as well as the mother of later confessions. . . . No subsequent confession has been drawn up without regard to its teaching and beyond the circle of its direct or indirect influence."

Dr. Philip Schaff, of Union Seminary, thinks "The Augsburg is the first and most famous of all the Evangelical Confessions — the most churchly, the most catholic, and the most conservative creed of Protestantism. . . . It furnished the keynote to similar public testimonies in faith and strengthened the cause of the Reformation elsewhere."

The Reformed church historian Gieseler says: "If it be a question which of the Protestant creeds is best adapted to become a basis of union for all evangelical churches, I would pronounce unhesitatingly for the *Confessio Augustana.*"

Well, you unionists, if you really want a real union, come and welcome.

President Herbert Hoover sent "cordial greetings to the Americans of the Lutheran faith who are celebrating on October 31 the anniversary of the Protestant reformation and the 400th anniversary of the reading of the Augsburg confession. . . . The effects of these historical events are reflected in our national life and institutions — in Government through the principle of separation of Church and State. It is fitting that we should commemorate the persons and events from which mighty forces have sprung." — *Milwaukee Sentinel,* October 14, 1930.

III. THE FIRST RELIGIOUS PEACE

The whole Sacred College at Rome urged Karl to use force. "Force would certainly get the best results," he wrote to Rome, "but the needed weapons are not forthcoming." He wished for 3,000 trusty troops to war on the Lutherans.

When the jurists declared this against the constitution, Luther, Melanchthon, and Jonas advised to meet force with force, which would be according to civil law and also according to duty and stress of conscience.

On Christmas Day the Protestant princes formed the *Bund of Schmalkalden* to defend their Lutheran religion. The strict Romish dukes of Bavaria joined, and the Most Christian King Francis and the English "Defender of the Faith" sent friendly letters. They were afraid of the growing power of the kaiser and of the pope. Fighting Henry of Brunswick told his Lutheran neighbors Germany should have political peace — just what Luther had demanded from the Coburg. And if the Holy Father dillydallied and shilly-shallied much longer about calling a general council, they would with the Lutherans call a German assembly to settle the church affairs to suit themselves.

Came April 15, 1531, the date set by Karl for the Lutherans to return to the pope or he would force them.

They didn't — and he didn't.

Instead of executing the Edict of Worms, the noble kaiser executed a turn-about-face. Why?

In June Luther wrote Amsdorf an enormous Turkish army was marching against Germany and he thought it an enormous outrage that the Catholic king of France and the pope refused to help the Catholic kaiser against the Turk.

What's that? Isn't Luther misinformed? Not at all.

Solyman the Magnificent was again waltzing up the blue Danube to the walls of Vienna, and he was backed by "the Most Christian King" Francis, and he was backed by "the God on earth" Clement VII! And the Catholic dukes of Bavaria would not help the Catholic kaiser, and "the Defender of the Faith" would not defend the faith.

Biographer Edward Armstrong writes: "From every quarter clouds were gathering around Charles." Vol. I, p. 260.

"In his dire distress Charles found a staunch ally in his capital enemy. Luther's patriotism saved the emperor's cause, and perhaps that of Christianity.

"In 1530 the Spanish Cardinal Loaysa, the kaiser's confessor, had advised force as the best rhubarb for German as for Spanish heresy.

"On June 8, 1532, the confessor's 'elastic conscience' advised the kaiser either a truce between Lutherans and Catholics, which would leave each party to believe as they pleased, or else an agreement that until the future council they should all live under their respective rites without molesting one another; if, by fault of the pope, the council should not meet within three years, henceforth the Lutherans might live freely, and continue in their own form of belief, without hindrance from princes or diets: all this Charles might grant without blame on the sole condition that they served against the common enemy. Pp. 263—264.

"Let Your Majesty be satisfied that the heretics serve you and prove faithful, even if against God they are worse than devils. If dogs they will be, let them be. Close an eye, since you have not the power to chastise them."

That certainly is "to maken vertue of necessite," as old Chaucer has it. The pope also wrote Karl, "although their opponents were Lutherans, they were yet, for all that, Christians," and he was to get their help against the terrible Turk.

When Ferdinand's agents would bluff the Turk by saying Karl had all his people back of him, Solyman sarcastically asked had the kaiser yet made peace with Luther?

And then, while the kaiser promised a general council, the pope tried all tricks to hinder the council. He hated the very name of council worse than the devil in hell, said Cardinal Loaysa, the kaiser's former confessor, for he feared his own Catholic bishops more than all Lutheran heretics. He would rather allow wives to the priests and the cup to the people and even swallow the Augsburg Confession than let a council reduce his income, or even depose him for being a bastard.

Armstrong writes: Karl was disheartened and disgusted by the champions of his own religion. Living from hand to mouth, he must conciliate the Lutherans who would feed his army which was to fight the Turks. The Protestants intensified his confidence. P. 265.

The pious persecutors of poor Lutherans in their dire distress asked for help from the "pestilential Lutherans."

On July 23, 1532, the Religious Peace of Nuernberg was made, which bound the Catholics and the Lutherans to respect the faith of each other — until the next council. The high words at Augsburg only two years ago, and now a dish of crow!

Brother Ferdinand sighed and cried as he told the pope's legates, and these remarked such a truce would strengthen the Lutherans till they would be invincible.

Aleander wrote Rome, the papacy, while not endorsing, must shut its eyes to concessions as dangerous as they were unavoidable. "If in these evil times we had for an emperor a Frederick Barbarossa or the like, we Catholics would soon have little or nothing of a great part of Christendom."

The lone Luther victorious over pope and kaiser!

Burckhardt observes: "The moral salvation of the papacy was due to its mortal enemies."

Wilhelm Walther of Rostock agrees "Luther saved Christianity for the world."

Alfred Baudrillart, rector of the Catholic Institute of Paris, shows that in Pope Nicholas V paganism took possession of the chair of St. Peter. So the infidel Nietzsche says truly: "Christianity no longer sat in the chair of St. Peter." And then he adds with disgust or a smothered curse: "Luther restored the Church." — *Der Antichrist,* page 61.

ELIZABETH, WIFE OF ELECTOR JOACHIM I OF BRANDENBURG,
secretly receives the Lord's Supper in both kinds according to the Lutheran way at Easter, 1527

Anatole France wails: "The star of the God of the Christians paled and began to set. Already the comely Graces and the Nymphs and Satyrs danced in merry choir; at last the earth rediscovered joy. But, Oh horrors! Oh ill fortune! Oh fatal event! A German friar, swollen with beer and theology, set himself against this renascent paganism, threatened it, fulminated against it, prevailed alone against the princes of the Church, and rousing the people, led them to a reform which saved what was about to be destroyed. ... This robust sailor repaired, caulked, and relaunched the derelict bark of the Church. Jesus Christ owes it to this scamp of a friar that his shipwreck was put off for perhaps more than ten centuries."

The English Catholic Hilaire Belloc admits "Luther generously protested — against the Catholic enemies fighting the Catholic kaiser."

Biographer Edward Armstrong, always rather frigid toward Luther, judges "Luther's conservative common sense and his German patriotism saved the emperor's cause, and perhaps that of Christianity."

Thomas Mann, rated by *Time* "the greatest living German author," writes: "I frankly confess that I do not like the Lout of Wittenberg; I would have gotten along much better with the amiable humanist Pope Leo X." Yet he also frankly admits Luther saved Christianity.

Germans, English, French — Protestants, Romanists, infidels — Jews and Gentiles — all agree Luther saved Christianity.

Not a bad day's work — for a damned and banned "devil in a monk's cowl."

Margrave George of Brandenburg was deeply impressed by Luther at Worms in 1521 and soon made his land Lutheran. His brother Albrecht, Grand Master of the religious Order of the Teutonic Knights, on Luther's advice turned his land into the Lutheran duchy of Prussia, which became the kingdom of Prussia and the head of the German Reich.

Joachim I of Brandenburg could not attend a *Reichstag* without taking his mistress in male attire, but he was so good a Catholic that he would fling into prison his wife Elizabeth for taking the Lord's Supper in the Lutheran way. When he died between two of his mistresses, his son Joachim II, in 1535, made Brandenburg Lutheran, and his brother, John of Kuestrin, made his Neumark a Lutheran land.

In 1534 Philip of Hesse wrested Wuerttemberg from King Ferdinand and restored it to Duke Ulrich, who made it a Lutheran land.

Lutheranism was growing in England.

The king of France was flirting with the German Lutherans and sent an embassy to invite Melanchthon to France, which Luther seconded, but the elector forbade.

On May 21, 1536, the "Wittenberg Concord" united all Protestants of Germany. Denmark, Norway, and Sweden were turning Lutheran.

ST. THOMAS CHURCH
IN LEIPZIG

Chapter Sixteen

MORE TALK OF A COUNCIL

When Clement VII died in 1534, his loving Romans plunged daggers into the corpse of their Holy Father and were hardly kept from dragging it through the streets.

Talk of poison. Pasquino wrote under the portrait of the pope's doctor, Matteo Curtius:

"Curtius has killed our Clement — let gold, then, be given to Curtius for thus securing the public health."

Again:

"Behold the Lamb of God, which taketh away the sin of the world!"

Historian Guicciardini calls Clement a good pope, but hastily adds: "I mean not goodness apostolical, for in those days he was esteemed a good pope that did not exceed the worst of men in wickedness."

Alessandro Farnese was called "Cardinal di gonella — of the petticoat" — because he had given his married sister, the bella Julia, to be mistress of Pope Alexander VI in order to become a cardinal; he now became Pope Paul III. He had astrologers, whom he consulted before every important step; also three sons and a daughter. Small wonder, for he said: "Men unique in their profession, like Benvenuto Cellini, are not subject to the law."

At once the Holy Father, rather grandfather, was to make cardinals of grandsons, 16 and 14.

Pasquino quipped: "Let us pray for Pope Paul, for the zeal for *his* house is eating him up."

When the kaiser was surprised, he was coolly told boys in the cradle had been made cardinals.

Kaiser Karl in a fury reproached this Holy Father, old as he was, with having contracted a venereal disease, with being neither an honest man nor a good shepherd, caring only for earthly pleasures and the enrichment of his children, and not for the service of God.

This god on earth sent Peter Paul Vergerius to win Luther for the next council. On November 6, 1535, he rode into Wittenberg with twenty-one horses and one mule, lodged in the Castle, and at once invited Luther and Barnes to bathe and sup with him. Luther declined to be surveyed so closely, but promised to dine with him on the morrow, Sunday.

Luther sent for Master Heinrich, the barber, to be dolled up. He dressed in his best and put on rings and a gold chain with a locket.

"What's the big idea?"

Luther roguishly said he wished to look young in order to make the Roman think: "Oh, the devil! Is Luther still so young and has done so much damage, how much more will he do?"

The ruse worked well. The legate reported Luther looked like a man under forty, "pleasant and serene."

But, of course, he never wrote his books without the help of the devil.

As Luther and Bugenhagen drove off to the Castle, Luther joked: "There go the Lutheran pope and his cardinal!"

(Robert Barnes did not go.)

Luther was in a regular carnival spirit, and he tells us he acted the most Lutheresque Luther before the great dignitary of the pope. The legate was certainly impressed with the quick and fiery eyes of Luther, just as Cardinal Cajetan at Augsburg had been impressed with the demonic eyes of this "German beast."

Vergerius was quite sure this beast never had the ability to write his books except with the aid of the devil. He told the pope a high authority — King Ferdinand? — had told him it wanted only a hint, and all Germany would rush greedily on the Church and pour into Italy, craving as the sole reward the overthrow of the pope and all his crew.

Later this cardinal studied the Bible and was accused of "Lutheranism." He fled and in 1553 gladly accepted a call from Duke Christopher of Wuerttemberg and worked for the Gospel, helped Primus Truber put the Bible into Slovenian.

Pope Paul III, on June 9, 1535, appointed a committee of cardinals to propose reforms for the Church — "When our own house is cleansed, we more readily take in hand the cleansing of others" — Lutherans. Not a bad idea.

In 1537 they reported:

"Flattery has established in the Roman Curia the doctrines which reign therein, to wit, that the pope is the owner of all dignities, that he can sell them, that the acts of the Sovereign Pontiff are not subject to the laws of the Church." Contarini adds: "It is *idolatrous* to pretend that the pope has no rule but his own will to establish or abolish positive rights." So writes President Alfred Baudrillart of the Catholic Institute of Paris.

In their *Consilium* they advised about thirty reforms. What did the pope do? The pope did nothing. Why?

The Venetian ambassador Soriano in 1535 said the removal of the abuses meant robbing the pope of his means of living, and a cardinal told Vergerio, before any reform could be begun, the whole church system had to be broken in pieces.

When the Holy Father called a council for May, 1537, to root out the "pestilential Lutheran heresy," the Elector John Frederick asked Luther to write articles to be considered by the Protestant princes at a conference at Schmalkalden in February of 1537. The result was the famous Schmalkald Articles, in which Luther calls the papacy the Antichrist of 2 Thessalonians 2.

Though the roads were rough, and the cold severe, and he not well, Luther, on December 31, set out for Schmalkalden in his own wagon and arrived on February 7. His quarters were wretched, the bed damp, and the food heavy, and he had a severe attack of the stone for fourteen days and wished himself dead.

Since the 11th he could not take part in the talks; on the 18th he preached, "not so much speaking as thundering from heaven in the name of Christ." He was seized with violent pains. Doctors poured in vile stuff. — "They made me drink as if I were an ox." Melanchthon suspected the doctors worsened matters; we suspect that is correct. The abused body no longer functioned, and since the 24th Luther prepared for the end.

Like carrion crows waiting for the carcass, the papists hovered around the house to view the remains and report to Rome.

Even at death's door the irrepressible humor cropped out, and in an epigram Luther warned all travelers to beware of the Hessian beds. Seeing Melanchthon in tears, the sick man whimsically said: "Hans Loeser says it's no trick to drink good beer, but to drink sour beer, that's a trick." Again: "Have we not received good at the hand of the Lord, and shall we not receive evil? The Jews stoned Stephen; my stone, the villain, is stoning me." He did not rue the game he had played with the pope and the devil; he had done right to do up the pope. "I depart," he cried with sublime boldness to his Maker, "a foe to Thy foes, cursed and banned by Thy enemy, the pope. May he, too, die under Thy ban, and we both stand at Thy judgment bar on that day."

The elector visited him twice and promised to care for the family as if they were his own.

In the company of friends Luther left on the 26th in a wagon of the elector. On leaving, he made the sign of the cross over the assembly and said: "God fill you with His blessing and with hate of the pope!" That strong blessing points to Rome as the source of all corruption, and it was to stiffen the backbone of those left behind.

The jolting of the wagon gave such severe pain that Luther cried out aloud, but it brought relief. At Tambach, two miles away, the body began to function, the gathered mass of water passed away and one gravel after another. Schlaginhaufen galloped back shouting, "Luther lives!" to the papal legate looking out of the window.

At Gotha he had a relapse and felt he would die after all and made his so-called first will — "I know, praise God, I did right to attack the papacy, which is a slander on God, Christ, and the Gospel," etc. He made confession and received absolution from Pastor Bugenhagen. He preached at Easter.

When outsiders doubted his recovery, Luther with great good nature made a written confession that he was still living, to the great disgust of the devil, the pope, his enemies, and his own.

Though Luther and Melanchthon advised against it, the princes refused to attend the pope's council, and Melanchthon was asked to write the reasons to the kings of England and France.

This was a new departure. So far they had appealed to a council, now they proclaimed themselves a communion distinct from Rome.

When the Catholics threatened war in 1538, Luther called on the Protestants to fight the kaiser as a common robber.

Discretion is the better part of valor. Karl made no war; he made the Frankfurt Recess — on April 19, 1539, he promised protection to the Protestant princes for fifteen months. Then the religious question was to be settled by a German national synod, which was to take in laymen.

A most notable victory for Luther.

Even the good old Catholic Duke George longed for peace and for the second time called a conference with the Lutherans at Leipzig in January, 1539. Counselor Carlowitz advised him to reform things himself, since the pope's policy was simply to rule all nations, otherwise he did not much care "whether we go to the devil or to God."

Duke George died the same year, and Luther accompanied his elector to Leipzig and drew the people's attention more than all the princes. Twenty years before, when he disputed with Eck, all pulpits were forbidden him, now he preached the Gospel in

St. Thomas' Church, as he had prophesied, and George's brother Henry made the duchy Lutheran.

The plague drove the *Reichstag* of Speyer to Hagenau, where many Catholics would give up the Catholic ground to unite with the Protestants. In this way, thought Cardinal Morone, Germany might certainly be united, but the unity would be Lutheran.

To this papal legate King Ferdinand said hotly he could not find a confessor who was not a fornicator, a drunkard, or an ignoramus, owing to the evil example of the pope's court, and insisted the pope must allow marriage to the priests, the cup to the laity, and a change in doctrine.

In January, 1540, the Wittenbergers calmly declared the kaiser and bishops had simply to renounce "their idolatry and error"; the *Augsburg Confession* and its *Apology* must be upheld in their entirety.

At the religious conference at Worms in January, 1541, Melanchthon and Eck debated four days — "a duet between a nightingale and a crow," said the people. When the legate Morone saw the Lutherans were getting the best of it, he got Chancellor Granvelle to defer the matter to Ratisbon, where Karl would be present in person.

While De Soto was discovering the Mississippi River, the pope's legate Contarini was discovering how hard it was to unite the papists and Protestants at Regensburg in 1541, for Melanchthon stood fast by the Gospel.

Granvelle asked the Pope for 50,000 scudi to bribe the Protestants. His Holiness was willing to spend that sum for the good cause if his name were not mentioned.

Aleander wailed the news from Germany was "enough to give the stomach-ache to a statue."

In June the great German Kaiser Karl sent a special princely embassy over the head of the elector to the great heretic Luther in order to win him over where Philip had balked.

Sure enough, Luther was quite peaceable and willing to bear with certain ceremonies if only justification by faith were preached "pure and clear."

Melanchthon was astonished at Luther's mildness, but Luther

knew full well the papists would never, could never, accept justification by faith. Luther was right, as usual.

Led by Leonhard von Eck, the Catholic Dukes of Bavaria would war on Lutheranism, "not for zeal of religion, but for greater political power," as the Catholic Pastor writes. Contarini had to keep them from plunging Germany into war, which would give the impression the Catholics shunned the light of reason. He wrote bitterly: "There is scarcely a man, or very few, who serve God with an honest heart. . . . Everyone sought his individual interest." Again: "Would to God many had never taken up their pens on behalf of the Catholic cause, doing thereby more harm than good."

The Bavarians wrecked Karl's plans for peace; the pope wrecked Karl's plans for a council; the Turk, on July 29, took Buda-Pesth—the poor kaiser was beaten all along the line. "Uneasy lies the head that wears a crown."

Duke Heinrich von Braunschweig announced the death of his prostitute, Eva von Trott, and buried a large doll with all churchly honors and ordered masses for the repose of her soul, and the duchess wore mourning for her. At the same time Eva bore one child after another to the noble Duke of Brunswick. Such was the man who also fiercely attacked Luther, who at last settled with him in the notoriously fierce book *Against Hans Worst*. On re-reading it, Luther, like Warren Hastings, was astonished "how I could have been so moderate. I attribute it to the sufferings of my head, which did not permit my mind to display a more upright and stronger vehemence." In 1542 Henry was expelled, and Brunswick became Lutheran.

In 1542 Luther ordained Amsdorf the first Lutheran Bishop of Naumburg. In like manner Duke Moritz of Saxony took Merseburg in 1544 and made his brother August the bishop.

Hermann von Wied, the venerable Archbishop of Koeln, said the study of Scripture convinced him the Lutheran teaching was right, and he wished his priests to preach the pure Gospel. Melanchthon helped evangelize the elector's land in 1542.

Alfieri of Venice in 1542 wrote "To the most excellent and most upright doctor and master in the Holy Scriptures, Martin Luther, our chief and brother in Christ, the brothers of the church of Venice, Vicenza, and Treiso, wish health.

"We humbly confess our great fault and our ingratitude, in having so long delayed to recognize and acknowledge how vast a debt we owe to thee, who hast opened unto us the way of salvation. . . ."

On November 20, 1544, the people of Heidelberg in Holy Ghost Church of their own accord sang Speratus'
> Salvation unto us has come
> By God's free grace and favor,

and the elector introduced the Reformation in his Palatinate, the Pfalz.

In Hungary and in Siebenbuergen, or Transylvania, a Lutheran church was organized; and in Venice there were Lutheran preachers.

Archbishop-Elector Albrecht had one of his many prostitutes carried into his castle in a box of holy relics, but her untimely sneezing betrayed her presence, and his prostitutes were called "the bishop's holy relics." The resentment against him rose so that he moved himself and his relics to Mainz. Through his fault, Erfurt, Magdeburg, and Halle became Lutheran.

In 1545 Albrecht died and was succeeded by Sebastian von Heusenstamm, who leaned toward the Gospel, and so the majority of the Electoral College was now Protestant, and Karl's son Philip II would surely not be elected the next German kaiser. The next German kaiser was William I, King of Prussia, that same Prussia that had become secular on the advice of Luther!

At the *Reichstag* of Speyer, in 1544, the Bund of Schmalkalden gained a triumph. Karl promised peace to the Protestants till a free German national council could settle the question of religion, pope or no pope. He needed Lutheran help against Catholic France. Of course, he did not intend to keep his pledge, and at the Peace of Crespy in September he forced King Francis to promise help to crush the Lutherans.

Morone wrote the pope the bishops cared only for drink and women; they had no interest in theology, no respect for the pope; their only aim was to be rid of the pope.

In March, 1545, Luther received an Italian pamphlet with a German translation. It told the dying Luther asked for the Holy

Sacrament and that his body be placed on the altar and worshiped as a god; but he went to hell.

Luther published both versions. "It soothes my right knee and left heel that the devil and his gang, pope, and papists, hate me so heartily."

And then? And then he prays for his enemies!

Pope Paul III wrote the kaiser a letter lecturing him like a naughty boy for meddling with affairs of the Church, especially since he had called a council to Trent for March 15, 1545.

It is held Karl's chancellor Granvelle played this letter into the hands of Luther, and the dying lion roared his final defiance with youthful vigor in his classic hymn of hate and swan song, *Against the Papacy at Rome, Founded by the Devil,* published in March of 1545. He "used the ax, for which by the grace of God he had a higher spirit than other men," as Chancellor Brueck wrote. King Ferdinand also judged the rough words had to be put out, "but otherwise the work is not badly written." A case of good judgment.

Calvin also wrote a vigorous pamphlet against Paul III, and Sleidan, the historian of the Bund of Schmalkalden, published two addresses calling on the kaiser to depose the Antichrist, and end the pope's temporal power.

The *Reichstag* lasted from March to August and promised a conference and another *Reichstag.* As Hamlet said, "Words, words, words!"

The leaders at the Council of Trent were the Jesuits, founded by Ignatius Loyola. The Catholic Baudrillart writes: "In 1540 Cardinal Guiddaccioni, who was deputed to examine the first constitutions of the Society of Jesus, was strongly opposed to the order. 'In the beginning,' he said, 'all orders are full of fervor, but they relax in time, and when they grow old, the harm they do to the Church is greater than the good they did her at first.'"

The Archbishop of Toledo forbade his clergy to have anything to do with the Jesuits; they were excommunicated by the Vicar-General of Saragossa; the Dominicans suspected their orthodoxy; Melchior Cano called them the forerunners of Antichrist; the universities of Salamanca and Alcala were foremost in denouncing them; at Salamanca Loyola was for a time in chains.

LUTHER AT HOME

Chapter Seventeen

LUTHER AT HOME*

I. MARTIN AND KATE

"This is my wife, with whom I now wish to celebrate the engagement" — meaning marriage in those days. So said Luther to Pastor Justus Jonas of All Saints, the Castle Church, Pastor John Bugenhagen of St. Mary's, the City Church, Lawyer John Apel, Lucas and Barbara Cranach, whom he had invited to the Black Cloister about 5 P. M. on Tuesday, June 13, 1525. Lawyer Apel and Pastor Bugenhagen performed the ceremony in the manner then usual, followed by a light lunch. The same guests were invited to the

---

* For more details see the writer's *Kate Luther*. Northwestern Publishing House, Milwaukee.

wedding breakfast at ten, for which the city council sent the "wine of honor."

A lucky time for weddings was the old god Ziu's day, and so Tuesday, June 27, was set for the church wedding.

The wedding breakfast was served at ten. The elector sent venison and the city council the liquid refreshment. — "2 shock 16 groschen 6 pennies." John Pfister was the toastmaster. The elector and Graf von Mansfeld sent best wishes. The professors and city officials paid their respect. The groom's aged parents were the guests of honor.

PRESENTS

"The University of the Electoral City of Wittenberg presents this bridal gift to Herrn Doktor Martino Luther and his virgin Kethe von Bore. Anno 1525." What is it? A goblet ¾ ell high of solid silver heavily plated with gold and exquisitely decorated. It held 2½ noesel, weighed 84 lot, and cost 23 gulden, when three gulden bought a cow.

The elector gave 100 gulden and free rent in the cloister; the city council 20 gulden; Spalatin a portugaleser — a Portuguese gold coin worth 28½ marks.

Albrecht von Brandenburg, a prince of Hohenzollern, Cardinal-Archbishop of Mainz, Primate of all Germany, at the same time elector and keeper of the Great Seal of the Reich, the mightiest man of Germany of his day, by Councilor Ruehel sent 20 gulden to the runaway nun!

Bishop Matthew Lang of Salzburg in 1525 "sent one of his doctors to my house with 20 gold florins, which the man slipped into Katherine's hand; but as soon as I found the matter out, I returned him the money."

"To Dr. Martin, Catharina V. Boren 13 Jun. 1525" — a gold ring worked in filigree and relief, showing a ruby, the Crucified with the instruments of torture and the dice of the soldiers.

Cranach painted the newlyweds — he, forty-two, she, twenty-six.

THE MOST FAMOUS WEDDING

Everything that Midas touched turned into gold; everything that Luther did turned into history. Though the wedding was that of a simple monk and a poor nun in an obscure dorp "on the edge

THE WEDDING OF MARTIN LUTHER — BROWN BROTHERS

of civilization," all the world and his wife sat up and took notice, and many are still talking about it after four hundred years.

Luther knew for the marriage of monks and nuns the punishment was death, and Lawyer Jerome Schurf opposed the step, because against the laws of Church and State, and so Soeren Aabye Kierkegaard remarks on Luther's great boldness. It is under these conditions that Luther became the "founder of the Protestant minister's home . . . the creator of Protestant morality," in the words of Otto Pfleiderer of Berlin. And Philip Schaff of Union judges: "Viewed simply as a husband-father, and as one of the founders of the clerical family, Luther deserves to be esteemed as one of the greatest benefactors of mankind."

SLANDERS

"Perhaps the cleanest and surely the most momentous of historic love affairs was that of Friar Martin and Sister Catherine," says Preserved Smith of Cornell. And yet none has ever had such a foul epithalamium. King Henry VIII, his chancellor Sir Thomas More, England's greatest wit, Duke George of Saxony, joined a horde of poets and professors in the world's vilest chari-vari of gutteral pornography.

KEEPING HOUSE

Kate had no gold, but she was better than much fine gold. Martin had next to nothing — a few pots and pans and spits, hardly worth 20 gulden. Thus furnished, they began to keep house.

Kate began her day's work at four. Lovers love to rib, and Lover Luther loved to rib his rib and promptly conferred on her the first honorary degree of "Morning Star of Wittenberg."

"Cleanliness is next to godliness." Kate enjoyed her honeymoon by a thorough housecleaning so dear to the heart of all good housewives. Did the old bachelor's quarters need it? "Before I was married, the bed had not been made for a whole year. I worked all day and was so tired at night that I fell into bed without knowing anything was amiss."

The rough stone walls received a coat of whitewash instead of Gobelin tapestry. A bathroom came later. The kitchen, laundry, etc., were on the ground floor. Going up the circular stone stairs, we find the 24×24 living room looking north over the yard and step on the bare deal floor. In the center a heavy pine table, over it in season a branch full of cherries; in one corner a large green tile stove; in another, a chest for valuables — in the sweet by and by; in another, a clothes chest, sent by Gabriel Zwilling. It was so worm-eaten that the clothes did not keep clean. Link of Nuernberg was to get another, one with a shelf for the linen to keep free from rust spots. Kate seemed to be particular about the price, twenty florins! The timbered ceiling was decorated, as were the paneled walls. Benches and a plate rail for mugs, cups, plates, and pegs for hats and coats. A portrait of Kate done by Master Lucas Cranach; a picture of the Virgin with her Babe; another of the Crucified. Aromatic and decorative plants on the window sills. At one window were two settees, on which Martin and Kate would sit and look out into the yard. In 1927 the writer and his Lulu sat on these same settees and looked out upon the same yard.

Abbot Friedrich Pistorius of Nuernberg sent an artistic clock,

Link a second, another a third. The Doctor admired that miracle of the human mind, which put the flight of time before the eyes of the thoughtless and careless.

Gerhard Wilskamp of Herford sent cloth and two lamps. "Catherine and I use your lamps every night. We reprove each other with having nothing to send you."

Hausmann sent a very fine Venetian glass, which Kate greatly admired.

In order to get her Martin the three square meals a day, Kate kept five cows; her cheese was better than that on the market. Kate kept chickens, ducks, geese, pigeons; and bees improved each shining hour. More ornamental than useful, a peacock proudly paraded about the place, from which we get this interesting bit of natural history: "The peacock dresses like an angel, walks like a thief, and sings like the devil."

Martin liked pork. Kate started a piggery, for which she got her second degree, the prosaic title "My Lord Kate, Mistress of the Pigsty."

Some say fish is good brain food. Kate bought a fish pond near the Sow Market — "Sow Market Woman" was the third honorary degree Martin gave his able Kate. "The Archcook" fairly beamed when serving these denizens of the deep. "Kate, you get more fun out of these few small fishes than many a nobleman when he fishes a large lake."

Vegetables are also good for a bookworm. Link of Nuernberg and Lang of Erfurt had to send seeds, and Kate raised peas, beans, cabbage, carrots, beets, cucumbers, lettuce, radishes, pumpkins, and melons. What about potatoes and tomatoes? Not yet known in Europe!

He boasted the giant Erfurt radishes had been raised by himself! No, everything wasn't lovely. There ought to be a law "against the nuisance of sparrows, crows, and woodpeckers that spoil everything!"

A year after marriage the happy Benedick wrote Spalatin: "I have planted a garden, dug a well, both with good success. Come, and you shall be crowned with lilies and roses." Can Horace or Omar equal that? We trow not. Here is the same love of simplicity, the same love of nature, the same joy of living, but all sanctified by Christianity.

The French Catholic Audin writes: "Rather than bend the knee before the pope or the emperor, he would have preferred to die; but when descended from his high position which he had so long occupied, he forgets himself and his past elevation and, after having ruled men's minds, becomes obedient as a child to the humors of a woman of thirty, plays with his children as he had played with crowned heads, and cultivates his little garden at Wittenberg. . . . A curious spectacle to observe the monk, whom Charles V had been unable to subdue, losing, in the bosom of his family, all the memories of his past renown, and concealing himself from the world to surrender himself to . . . the culture of his garden. . . .

"These modest virtues — we have no interest in concealing them — are like the flowers in the solitude of that cloister in which the obedient son of the Church dwelt so long."

Hedge of Harvard calls Luther "a leader in the way of tenderness for the brute creation, a lover of nature, close observer of the habits of vegetable and animal life, the first naturalist of his day."

Why did they drink wine and beer?

First good reason — In those days they did not have coffee, tea, cocoa, and Coca-cola.

Second good reason — "If our Lord makes big pike and Rhine wine, I may eat and drink. It is all right with the Lord if you once in a while laugh and enjoy yourself from the bottom of your heart."

Third good reason — Doctor's orders for Martin's painful gravel, or stone.

What about beer — buy it? Not Kate! She repaired the little brewery where the monks had brewed their *Klosterbraeu* and learned to brew; and Martin praised her brand as the "Queen of Beers." Even from the famous beerville of Torgau he wrote in 1534: "If only I had some of your beer! Have I not at home a fair wife, or shall I say boss?"

Martin found it to be a diuretic, a purgative, and a soporific, certainly a good triple alliance for a constipated bookworm.

Martin Goerlitz of Torgau sent some beer, and after some time

Luther wrote: "I forgot it at the bottom of my cellar, where it would have remained unknown had not my servant reminded me of it."

Chancellor Brueck calls Kate "very sparing in eating and drinking," and Kraus tells us she gave beer "with a sparing hand" to her husband and his companions.

"With what philosophic calmness Luther speaks of his poverty. Amidst all those vain triumphs which might have puffed up a mind less worldly than his, he is always the same as we have seen him at the beginning of his contest with the pope. Now he who had opposed the emperor and the Orders of Germany at Worms; who had roused with his anger all the princes of Germany against the peasants; and had bandied controversies with crowned heads, cannot find anyone to lend him ten florins. It is certain that had he wished to sell his silence, he would have found more than one monarch to be its purchaser. This poverty is noble, and Luther bears it with courage."

Early on July 6, 1527, he had a severe heart attack and at 8 sent for Pastor Bugenhagen, confessed, and desired absolution and comfort from God's Word, and commended himself and his family to God.

"Because in my outward life I sometimes am jolly, many think I always walk on roses; but God knows how it stands as to my life. I have often resolved to show myself more serious and holy — don't know how to call it — but God did not give it to me to do so. If the Lord wills to call me now, then His will be done." He begged all to testify he died in the faith he had preached.

At 5 P.M. he fell on the floor unconscious. Jonas poured cold water on his face and back. When he came to, he prayed to God and regretted not having been found worthy to shed his blood for Christ, and called on those present to witness his confession. He could say with a good conscience he had taught rightly and helpfully the chief articles of God's Word according to the command of God, who had led him into this business, drawn and forced him without his will. He had never regretted his violence of speech or writing, since he had never sought anybody's harm, but everybody's salvation.

LUTHER'S DAUGHTER
MAGDALENE

Doctor Augustine Schurf rubbed him with hot cloths and produced circulation and perspiration, and the danger passed over.

On August 2 he wrote Melanchthon: "For a week I was thrown back and forth in death and hell." Every limb of his body was still trembling.

II. LUTHER AND HIS CHILDREN

"I am a happy husband, and may God continue to send me happiness, for from the most precious woman, my best of wives, I have received, by the blessing of God, a little son, John Luther, and, by God's wonderful grace, I have become a father." June 6, 1526.

What awe in that word *father!* Peter Bayne, LL. D., remarks: "Martin Luther, housefather, with little Johnny on his knee, as Mr. Spurgeon loves to picture him, is regarded as the world's defender against monkish ideals." This chap became "loquacious, voracious, and bibacious" — also "howlacious," for the father made

LUTHER'S SON PAUL

this great speech: "Why do I love you so? What cause have you given me that you have deserved to be called my heir? By making yourself a general nuisance? And why aren't you thankful instead of filling the house with your howls?"

That should have held the lad a while.

Elizabeth came on December 10, 1527, and left in August. "She has left me wonderfully sick at heart and almost womanish, so grief for her moves me. I would before this never have believed a father's heart could become so tender for his children. Pray for me to the Lord!" After four hundred years the heart is still touched by these words of that strong man.

Magdalen came in 1529, Martin in 1531, Paul in 1533, Margaret in 1534.

Luther was a fond father. His letters to Kate never fail to have a few words for them. In 1530 Kate sent a portrait of little Magdalen to the Coburg, but it just wasn't a masterpiece. "I don't know the lassie, it's mighty black." By and by he made out the features and placed the picture on the mantel and feasted his eyes on it.

Kate had Tutor Jerome Weller write the fond father how the four-year-old Hans was wrestling with his Latin and making good progress. This brought what Principal John Tulloch of St. An-

LUTHER'S DAUGHTER MARGARET

drew's in Scotland calls "that most beautiful and touching of all child letters that ever was written."

In 1532 Luther writes: "Kiss young John for me and bid Johnny, Lennie, and Aunt Lena pray for our dear prince and for me. Though a fair is on, I cannot in this town find anything for the children. Should I not bring anything decent, then you attend to it for me."

In her fourteenth year in September, 1542, Magdalen fell asleep in her father's arms. As they laid her in the coffin, he said: "Darling Lena, you will rise and shine like a star, yea, like the sun. I am happy in spirit, but the flesh is sorrowful and will not be content, the parting grieves me beyond measure. I have sent a saint to heaven."

Coming from God's acre, Luther said: "My daughter is now well cared for, both as to body and soul. Now we Christians are not to mourn. We know that thus it must be, for we are most sure of eternal life!"

W. Baur muses: "What a loss for Christendom had this man not become a father! The hugging, kissing, and blessing of children done by the Savior is here translated into the German of a father whose love of children goes through his inmost soul."

George L. Prentiss of Union judges: "Luther stands alone of all public men in history for his tender sympathy with childhood."

When Sir Knight George left the Wartburg, Keeper Hans von Berlepsch gave him a dog, which spent fifteen years of its life at the feet of the Doctor while he worked and also studied "dogology" till it died of old age. What a human man! That faithful dog was also a pet of the children.

Fond father that he was, he was no Eli; especially would he not brook disobedience. Once Johnny was banished from his father's face for three days, and it took all the eloquence of Kate and friends to bring the father around.

He wrote Marcus Crodel, the Torgau schoolmaster, to spank Kate's nephew, Florian von Bora, three days running for stealing a knife and lying about it.

A HOLY FAMILY

Kate pulled together with her husband in the rearing of their children.

"For making a home you need a believing man and a believing woman."

"The greatest work you can do is to train your child in the fear and knowledge of God. Do it on pain of losing God's grace. If Christendom is to grow strong, you must begin with the children."

In 1529 Luther wrote the Small Catechism, "the gem of the Reformation," as Professor McGiffert of Union Seminary called it. "When I get up [at six], I pray with the children the Ten Commandments, the Creed, the Lord's Prayer, and some Psalm." When older, the children read a Bible chapter after grace before meals. Lectures at seven; dinner at ten; writing; supper at five; to bed at nine.

"I have to hurry all day to get time to pray. It must do me if

I can say the Ten Commandments and one or two Petitions besides, thinking over which I fall asleep."

Luther went to church regularly; when he could not walk, he was taken in his wagon; when not well, he preached at home; Veit Dietrich took notes, published as Luther's *House Postil*.

Kate also taught the Catechism to the household.

The Catholic Audin writes: "Catherine was fond of reading the Scriptures, especially the Psalms, in which she found great comfort; but often also many obscure passages which puzzled her, and which the doctor endeavored to explain, frequently admitting that 'there were some which he could no more comprehend than a goose.' "

A SINGING FAMILY

Next to theology Luther loved music. The singing David drove the evil spirits from King Saul, and singing drove the evil spirit of depression from Luther many a time. He could never get enough of music and singing, folk songs and Gospel hymns, especially the ones he sang as a boy chorister from door to door for a loaf of bread or a sausage.

Extra busy on Christmas Eve, 1533, Kate brought the baby to the father, who then and there made a brand new "rockaby, baby": "From heaven above to earth I come." Competent critics call it the world's greatest Christmas hymn. When they sang it for him the first time Christmas Eve, 1535, tears started to his eyes. "O we poor people, so cold and lazy toward this great joy!"

III. LUTHER'S CHARITIES

1. Luther started the first Lutheran orphanage. He took in no fewer than thirteen orphaned nephews and nieces!

2. Luther started the first Lutheran old folks' home. He gave a home to Kate's old aunt Lena. He invited Else von Kanitz, who had fled the convent with Kate. "With me you are to be at home and at table, that you shall have no danger nor worry. So I beg you now not to refuse me this."

He wrote his father: "I should prefer that you and my mother would come to me; my Ketha desires it with tears."

Wolf Sieberger could not make the grade for the ministry, and so Luther gave him a home. What would he do when Luther died? The poor soul did not want to live any longer, but be buried with Luther.

Seems to have been a pretty good housefather, that man Luther.

3. Luther started the first Lutheran hospital. "My house has become a regular hospital. The wife of George, our chaplain, died of the plague; everybody seemed afraid to have any contact with the poor fellow; so we took him and his children into our house." The university moved to Jena, and the elector himself urged Luther to flee, for he could not be spared. Luther flee? The hireling fleeth, the good shepherd lays down his life for the sheep. "The fear is worse than the pest," and he fearlessly went out to comfort the stricken. The wife of Mayor Tilo Dene died almost in the arms of Luther, and Mrs. Roerer died in Luther's house.

Bugenhagen with his wife and two children fled from the parsonage into the Luther hospital. Magdalena von Mochau caught the plague; Kate witnessed the pest boil lanced and the poison pressed out; she daily dressed the wound. "Her escape from death seems an absolute miracle." The family doctor's wife, Hannah Schurf, took sick and was nursed by Kate. Two nieces were down. Little Johnny "is too ill to speak. For the last three days he has not eaten a morsel. He would be as gay and joyful as ever were it not for excess of weakness. Remember us all in your prayers." To Melanchthon Luther wrote that he was "a poor sick servant of Christ, who can hardly keep life within him. It seems God would overwhelm me with all the waves of His displeasure at once."

"Brave in faith and sound in body," Kate managed everything in the home, hotel, hospital, orphanage. Five precious pigs died. Kate could take it. She praised God that "the devil had entered the swine" as once among the Gadarenes, Matt. 8:32.

In 1529 from Marburg he wrote Kate: "We are all hale and hearty and live like princes. . . . They are crazy with fear of the sweat; yesterday fifty took to bed, of whom one or two died," and mocked at the "new-fangled disease."

King Henry did not mock, he confessed himself every day. And it was not a time for mocking, for Du Bellay wrote: "One has a little pain in the head and heart. Suddenly a sweat begins; and a physician is useless, for whether you wrap yourself up much or little, in four hours, sometimes in two or three, you are dispatched without languishing."

The "English Sweat" came to Wittenberg, and many died. Many thought they had caught it. Luther drove Chancellor Brueck and others out of bed into the fresh air, and then they laughed at themselves.

So in 1532, and in 1534, and in 1538.

In 1539 Cosmographer Dr. Sebald Muenster, Melanchthon's brother-in-law, his wife, and three others in the same house died. Kate took in the four orphans and nursed them, although about to become a mother.

This time it was too much even for her iron constitution. For a long time she hovered between life and death. Martin nursed and prayed her back to health — God's miracle to all friends.

"The doctors give me one year to live."

In 1540 ten down at once in Luther's hospital.

In 1541 the inflammation of his left ear pained him so that for two weeks he could neither eat nor sleep, and at times he was deaf. The elector sent two doctors, but no relief. "The pain attacked my life. The unbearable pains pressed tears out of me — something I don't easily do; and I said to the Lord, 'Either put an end to the pain or put an end to me.'" The next day the ear opened to the outside. In time he could hear again.

When the Franciscans left their cloister, Luther led in the work of turning it into a hospital and old folks' home. He went to Leisnig and helped them start the first "Community Chest."

4. Luther started the first Lutheran asylum, refuge for refugees. He wrote in 1539: "I was utterly overwhelmed by the crowds of poor people who come here from far and near as to an open house."

When the wedding guests were gone, Luther opened the door for his enemy Carlstadt, who fled for his life from the Peasants' War, and fled to Luther, who saved his life.

Conrad Cordatus preached the Gospel at Ofen in Austria, was flung into prison, escaped, fled to Luther in 1526, and later boarded with Kate again for almost a year.

Michael Stiefel, chaplain in the noble family of Joerger von Tollet in Austria, had to flee on account of his Lutheran preaching, went to Luther, and lived there seven months in 1528.

The Austrian Kummer was persecuted for his Lutheran preaching and escaped in disguise as a woman to Luther's home, where he lived during 1529.

Wolfgang Schiefer, tutor of the future Kaiser Maximilian II, had to leave court for his Lutheran teaching and fled to Luther.

The noble lady Rosina von Truchsess sought shelter in the Luther house, saying she had left a nunnery for the sake of conscience. Kate heeded the piteous pleading. Soon one thing was missing, then another. Hm! Then it was the talk of the town that the visitor was immoral. Luther called her on the carpet. She broke down, confessed her whole story was a lie, pleaded for forgiveness. She was forgiven. She kept on in her evil course, and so, while Luther was on a trip, Kate put her out. When Luther returned, he was put out with Kate — Rosina should have been drowned in a sack.

"A burned child dreads the fire" — the Luthers didn't. The widow of Wolf of Worms, called Dalberg, ran off with a rich Jew, who was lynched, Southern style. The poor woman roamed about the country. About to become a mother, she desperately fled to the Luther house. Despite the bitter experience with Rosina, they took her in. Luther baptized the child and stood sponsor for it. When Knight Hartmut von Cronberg came looking for his sister Lorichia, Luther knew this time he had not been bitten. And he got the brother to be reconciled to his sister.

When the Agricolas moved to Wittenberg in 1536 and could find no house, Kate took them in, with their nine children for months. And this is what Agricola wrote: "Domina Ketha, regent in heaven and on earth, Juno, wife and sister of Jupiter, who rules the man as he wills, spoke a good word for me."

Ursula, Duchess of Muensterberg, a relative of the grim Duke George of Saxony, was a guest.

The wife of Elector Joachim I of Brandenburg, Elizabeth of Denmark, took the Lord's Supper in the Lutheran way, but her fourteen-year-old daughter Elizabeth tattled, and the Elector Joachim promptly clapped his wife into prison; she escaped and lived with the Luthers for three whole months, and Kate carefully nursed her during her illness. The daughter that had betrayed her mother came to visit now and turned Lutheran and later introduced the Reformation in Brunswick.

The same elector wanted the wife of John Hornung and drove him out of Berlin. Whither? To Luther! "Myself a poor man, I have received this poor man and given shelter to the pitiful exile. Stone and rock should take pity."

Whenever he thought of Luther, the noble Duke George of Leipzig saw red, and in a towering rage wrote: "You have opened an asylum so that all monks and nuns robbing our cloisters have with you a refuge and abode, as if Wittenberg were, to speak politely, a den of rogues for all reprobates of the country."

Dispraise from Duke George is praise indeed.

Another snapshot of the same cave of Adullam. 1 Chron. 11:15.

When Prince George of Anhalt thought of taking lodgings with Luther in 1542, George Held warned: "In the house of the Doctor there lives a wonderfully mixed company consisting of young people, students, young girls, widows, old women, and children, for which reason there is a great noise in the house, wherefore many pity Luther."

It seems every unfortunate saw a sign over Luther's open door: "Come unto Me, all ye that labor and are heavy laden, and I will give you rest." Matt. 11:28.

Luther was an attorney for the poor and friendless and persecuted.

About 1534 he told a judge: "You know Doctor Martinus is not only a theologian and defender of the faith, but also a counsel at law for the poor, who flee to him from all parts to find redress against injustice."

He became interested in the case of Hans von Schoenitz, who had been a favorite of Elector-Cardinal-Archbishop Albrecht and suddenly hanged in a suspicious manner.

He became a defender of respectable men and women who had been slandered in vicious epigrams by Simon Lemchen, Lemnius.

He showed sympathy for Hans Kohlhase, who had received a raw deal, etc., etc.

5. Luther started the first Lutheran hospice for visitors and guests.

Luther had a great head on his shoulders; in fact, his mental powers were so varied that John Cochlaeus cartooned him with seven heads. Kate was like unto him. "I must divide myself into seven parts, be at seven different places at the same time, and attend to seven kinds of duties, for I am 1. farmer, 2. brewer, 3. cook, 4. nurse girl, 5. gardener and vintner, 6. comforter and almoner of all beggars in Wittenberg, 7. the Doctorissa who is to prove herself worthy of her celebrated husband and entertain many guests on a salary of 200 gulden."

She did all that — and more!

For three weeks in October, 1525, John Walther and Conrad Rupf were at Kate's table and helped Luther with the musical part of the hymnal and sang and sang, and Luther couldn't get enough of singing.

Elizabeth von Meseritz, an escaped nun, married Caspar Cruciger, and wrote the hymn "Lord Christ, the only Son of God, the Father's in eternity" and also helped Luther with the first hymnal.

Matthias Weller, an organist, came often, and the three Wellers sang with the Luthers. John Joeppel was "a jolly, welcome guest, who showed much pleasant friendship with his music."

Peter Weller came in 1530 and stayed till 1538. There came Hyneck Perknowsky, a nobleman of Berckhani, one of the first to bring Luther's Gospel to Bohemia. He and Peter died of a fever in the Holy Land. With Hyneck came Count Borziwog of Dohna in Bohemia, fourteen years old, who stood sponsor for Martin Luther, Jr., in November, 1531. Count Frederick II lettered his warmest thanks to Luther for the great happiness of having his boy at Kate's table.

Hans Honold of Nuernberg in 1540 willed Luther a costly cup for the kindness shown his son.

Recommended by Dr. Justus Jonas and Master George Roerer, John Mathesius was admitted to Kate's table in 1540, "for which I must thank God all the days of my life."

In 1543 Jerome Bezold became Kate's boarder; after Luther's death he wrote: "My grief grows by thinking of the very sweetest life with him, who was so full of friendliness, love, and fatherly goodwill. Never will I let this time of my life get out my heart, and in that eternal companionship, where we shall see him again, will I thank him eternally for his fatherly love."

Adam Krafft, Crato von Crafftheim, was at Kate's table from 1534 to 40, on the recommendation of the Breslau reformer John Hess. Luther found "his complexion too weak for preaching" and advised him to study medicine. He became the very famous physician of Kaisers Ferdinand I, Maximilian II, and Rudolf II — in spite of his firm Protestantism.

The famous Matthias Flacius Illyricus was Kate's guest, and Luther became his wedding guest.

Martin's sister was a visitor in February, 1534, and Kate served pike — sent from the elector's pond! In March Kate repaid the debt by serving lunch to the elector behind the city wall.

An Italian of Siena took all his meals at Kate's table for several weeks, and the Hungarian noble Matthias Dévay was another guest.

Thomas Dusgate, or Bennet, "feeling himself much cumbered with the concupiscence of the flesh and too weak to overcome it — he departed from Cambridge and went to Luther in Germany."

After he had declared his great frailty, Luther advised him "that if by no lawful means he could not live chast, that he should take a wif and lyve a meane lyfe."

On January 15, 1532, he went up in flames for his Lutheran heresy.

Prior Robert Barnes[*] of Cambridge became a Lutheran, escaped from prison in 1528, fled to Luther, and "that Black Englishman" became Luther's table friend.

On January 1, 1535, Bishop Edward Fox of Hereford, Archdeacon Heath, and Robert Barnes, King Henry's chaplain, trotted into Wittenberg with forty horses and stayed till April 8. Luther would not agree to the king's divorce, but they agreed to "The

---

[*] For details see the writer's *Robert Barnes*. Third edition. Concordia Publishing House, St. Louis, Mo.

Wittenberg Articles of 1536" — "A Repetition and Explanation of the Augsburg Confession," according to Seckendorf. These went into "The Ten Articles" of 1536, the first Protestant confession of England.

When King Henry's committee left, came Bucer, Myconius, Capito, Musculus, Menius, and Mathew Alber to agree with Luther on the Lord's Supper in the "Wittenberg Concord."

They must have fared well, for at the farewell Capito wrote: "I hereby say farewell to your wife, Frau Katharina, the best wife. After my return I'll send her something she is to wear to remember me. I love her with all my heart. For she has been created to keep up your health so that you may serve the Church born under you, that is, all that hope in Christ. She is deservedly esteemed because as *Hausfrau* she cares for our common teacher with gentleness and diligence."

He sent a ring.

On May 12, 1538, Remige, Remigius, a servant of Dr. John Thixtoll, a prominent reformer, told Luther England with great desire hoped for the Gospel and even some of the bishops frankly opposed the horrible abomination of the pope. The names of Wittenberg, Luther, and Melanchthon were held in high esteem, and even those who had been at Wittenberg were held in honor. He related the wiles of the monks of Canterbury, who had made a crucifix which could move its face and lips and nod its head by means of cords and keys in the back. The king's visitation had laid bare the fraud, and the image was torn apart in London.

Thomas Minturn repeatedly tried to meet Luther in his garden but refused to appear at his table. Suspected of designs on Luther's life, he was arrested on July 22. All they found was notes of sayings of Luther, Melanchthon, and Myconius. He said twenty-four people had lost their lives at Paris for eating meat on a fast day, and he had saved his by flight. On Luther's request he was freed on August 31.

On November 4, Edwardus Morus was at Luther's table. Under date of November 4 Anton Lauterbach entered in his *Diary:* "A certain Englishman, a learned man, sat at table, who did not understand German. Said Luther, 'I'll give you my wife for teacher;

she is quite eloquent, so expert she surpasses me by far.'" Likely the man with whom Luther joked was Dr. Edwardus Morus Anglus, warden of Winchester College, who registered at the university in April, 1539.

On the 14th, Edward Morus and Basil Monner, a lawyer of the consistory, were at Luther's table.

On the 25th, Edward Morus and Aurogallus.

On January 21, Edward Morus.

On February 1, Basil Monner.

On April 8, Lucas Cranach.

And so forth and so on.

Bluebeard Henry on July 30, 1540, burned Barnes at Smithfield for his Lutheran preaching. His glorious confession of faith at the stake was at once put into German and printed at Wittenberg. In the introduction Luther flays the murderous king and erects a beautiful monument to "our good, pious table companion and guest of our home ... this holy martyr, St. Robertus."

In 1541 an Englishman with an introduction from Osiander was Luther's guest. On leaving he left his boy and never came back. Kate got Luther to write Jerome Baumgaertner at Nuernberg to place him in an orphanage.

Luther made Wittenberg the greatest university of the world.

He wondered a university should be built "on a dump on the border of civilization," which was despised by others. But things which are despised hath God chosen to confound the wise and the mighty. 1 Cor. 1:27-28.

The Lord puts down the mighty from their seats and exalts them of low degree. Luke 1:52.

Luther was the magnet that drew students from many parts of Europe and filled them with the Gospel and with his spirit. They went back and preached the Gospel, and thousands sealed their faith with their blood.

"Guilielmus Daltici ex Anglia" registered at the University of Wittenberg on May 27, 1524 — William Tyndale.*

---

* For details see the writer's *William Tyndale*. Fourth edition. Concordia Publishing House. St. Louis.

On the 30th, Matthias von Emersen of Hamburg, nephew of widow Margaret von Emersen, who had befriended Tyndale.

On June 10, 1525, "Guilhelmus Roy ex Londino" — William Roy, Tyndale's helper.

James Anthony Froude says Tyndale translated his New Testament under Luther's "immediate direction." Historian Richard Green speaks of "Tyndale's Lutheran translation."

According to Knox, Patrick Hamilton * came to Luther in 1527; he became the first Lutheran preacher and martyr of Scotland. He converted Canon Alexander Alane, who fled to Wittenberg, where Melanchthon dubbed him Alesius, Wanderer. In 1539 came John Wedderburn, who with two brothers put hymns of Luther into *The Gude and Godlie Ballatis,* the first Scotch hymnal, sung to the Lutheran tunes.

Then came Fyffe, M'Alpine, and others. And so to Wittenberg, says Prof. A. F. Mitchell, "our native country owes a debt of gratitude which its historians have hitherto been slow to acknowledge."

And so Luther radiated the Gospel to all other Protestant countries. Lawyer William Samuel Lilly, secretary of the Catholic Union of Great Britain, in his *Renaissance Types:* "Of the greatness, the titanic greatness of the man, there can be no question. The greatness of the revolution wrought by him is manifest to all. We may, with strict accuracy ascribe to him the Protestant reformation and all that came of it. Evangelical Protestantism . . . is Luther's creation."

That is much; there is more: "Luther's revolution was the salvation of the Papal Church. A Catholic historian has called the Council of Trent the greatest thing effected by him."

In other words, it was Luther who compelled the Papal Church to clean house and sweep out at least the most disgraceful public scandals in morals. On December 4, 1563, the Bishop of Nazianzus said: "Holy things will no longer be bartered, for the scandalous traffic of professional collectors is at an end." He thereby admits the truth of the sharp saying of Erasmus: "Christ drove out of the Temple those who bought and sold; but those who buy and sell

---

* For details see the writer's *Patrick Hamilton.* Third edition. Concordia Publishing House, St. Louis.

have driven Christ out of the Church." When Carafa became Pope Paul IV in 1555, a medal was struck showing Christ driving the thieves out of the Temple. Quite interesting, this papal medallic admission that there were thieves in the Temple, just as Luther had charged. If the pope did the driving, it was Luther who forced him to do the driving.

And yet still more!

The Catholic Lord Acton, professor of history and member of Gladstone's cabinet: "Luther broke the chain of authority and tradition at the strongest link. . . . It was an awakening of new life; the world revolved in a different orbit, determined by influences unknown before. After many ages, persuaded of the headlong decline and impending dissolution of society, and governed by usage and the will of masters who were in their graves, the sixteenth century went forth armed for untried experience, and ready to watch with hopefulness a prospect of incalculable change." — *Lecture on the Study of History,* 1895, pp. 8-9.

Luther set off an A-bomb, and in all the world it is still radioactive — and it will be.

Professor Peter Guilday of the Catholic University at Washington writes: "There is no doubt that the religious problem today is still the Luther Problem. . . . Every Catholic should acquaint himself with the life story of the man."

Historian John Richard Green writes: "The little town had suddenly become the sacred city of the Reformation."

Why?

The Reformed Abraham Scultetus, Schulz, in his *Annals* tells us students on getting sight of the town fell on their knees, for "from Wittenberg, as heretofore from Jerusalem, the light of Gospel truth had spread to the uttermost parts of the earth."

Christ prepared Christianity: Luther restored Christianity.

IV. LUTHER'S TABLE TALK

Old Samuel Johnson had one Boswell who made himself immortal by painting the gruff Doctor, warts and all, but Luther had a round dozen who jotted down every word more or less correctly and gave us an insight into this most wonderful soul as has been done to no other human being. Augustine's *Confessions,* Eckermann's *Talks with Goethe,* and the *Talks with Bismarck* fall far short of Luther's *Table Talk.*

In the summer of 1540 Kate looked at the men busily taking notes and wished her Martin would charge them a fee for his table talk.

At another time, as they were all busy talking, she remarked sharply, "What's all this talking about? Your supper is getting cold!" Martin meekly fell to with knife and fork.

Sometimes Luther was so busy that he wrote during meals. "Figure it out whoever will if I must write three letters in one hour when each one requires an hour — isn't that a pastime of a life?" But as a rule the meal was not a silent food funeral as in the days of monkery and nunnery. They talked about everything under the sun and points beyond — 7,075 items, the news, proverbs, stories, anecdotes, jokes, Aesop's Fables, "Reynard the Fox," laughter loud and long.

A SAMPLE SUPPER

John Mathesius wrote the first Lutheran Life of Luther in sermons for his silver miners at Joachimstal in Bohemia, from which we got "Taler" and our "dollar." He gives a very vivid account of a supper in 1540: "Though our Doctor often came to the table with heavy and deep thoughts and sometimes kept his cloister silence during the whole meal so that not a word was spoken at the table, at a fitting time he let himself be heard very joyously, and we used to call his talks 'Table Sauce,' which we loved more than all spiced and choice foods. When he wished to get talk out of us, he used to start the ball arolling: 'What's the news?' The first call we'd pass up. When he started again, 'You Prelates, what's the news?' the old ones at the table began to talk. Doctor Wolf Severus [Schiefer], who had been preceptor of the Roman Royal Majesty, sat towards the head, and, clever courtier that he was, started some subject when no stranger was present.

When the talk became lively, though with proper manners and respect, others would also give their share, till we had the Doctor agoing. Often we would ask good questions out of Scripture, which he answered, short and snappy. And if one would hold his own, the

TAKING DOWN LUTHER'S TABLE TALK
After Leys

Doctor could take it, and refute him with a clever reply. Often there came to the table honored people from the university and from abroad; then came very fine talks and histories.

"Of wedlock he often made very fine talks and as a chaste husband spoke very highly of womanhood and was an enemy of immorality and smutty speech. As long as I was around him, I did not hear one indecent word out of his mouth. He cut out the nasty stuff from stories and proverbs.... He was very angry with Sebastian Franck for printing many nasty proverbs in which wedlock and the female sex were disgraced and called him 'a dirty bug.' 'He that speaks evil and nasty of women, young women, government, and pastors is not honorable.'"

Luther was no prude, but he hated the nude. No "art for art's sake" hypocrisy about the sturdy man.

In 1545 Cranach caricatured the pope with the head of an ass and the body of a woman indecently exposed. Though no friend of the pope, Luther faulted his friend. "Master Lucas is a coarse painter; he might have spared the female sex because God created woman and for the sake of our mothers. He could have depicted the pope in other forms worthy of him, even more diabolical."

Dr. Crotus wrote that a bishop of Mainz spoke vile words of women. Luther flared up and fiercely denounced the dirty bishop.

The refined, classical, scholarly Erasmus published his *Colloquia,* which was used as a schoolbook for children, though so coarse that we stand aghast. The "coarse, crude, vulgar peasant" Luther declared none of his children should read the book, "for Erasmus teaches in them much ungodly stuff."

Though an enemy of Luther and a close friend of Sir Thomas More, the elegant Erasmus had to admit the saintly and courtly and gentlemanly More was coarser than the peasant Luther; in fact, he was unprintably filthy.

The age was certainly one of "free speech"; everybody spoke in the most natural manner of what was quite natural and what everybody knew about. Gladstone says: "Boccaccio's extremely indecent *Decameron* was published in 1573 with express approval from the Roman Inquisition and with a brief from Pope Gregory XIII." Margaret of Navarre was one of the most devout and refined women of the sixteenth century, and yet she wrote a series of stories that no decent woman can now read with pleasure.

England's Virgin Queen Elizabeth used language shocking to us. Her dress was cut so low in the back that the French ambassador made note of it. And to make both ends meet, she "danced very high," as the Scotch ambassador noted.

Luther was offended at such things, and when the styles of the Italian harlots came in, he thundered: "The women and the girls have begun to go bare before and behind." "The race of girls is getting bold and run after the fellows into their rooms and offer them their free love."

Shakespeare's men and women certainly used the Queen's English. People spoke plain English — emphasis on "plain." But in all of Luther's works of more than one hundred volumes in the Erlangen edition you cannot find anything frivolous or lascivious. At times he is as rough as a scaly bark hickory, but always sound to the core and pure at heart; as a matter of downright fact, he is more refined than his age.

Dr. John Aurifaber, Goldsmith, writes in the first published edition: "These most profitable discourses of Luther, containing such high spiritual matter, we should in no wise suffer to be lost, but worthily esteem them, out of which all manner of learning, joy, and comfort may be received."

Selnecker sensibly says a few weeds in a large fine meadow should not offend us.

Many eminent scholars agree with great enthusiasm, from whom we quote only a few Catholics.

The Catholic Joseph Sonntag in his *Green Letters* (1931, 262) writes: "Luther began one of his great deeds only with doubts and misgivings, namely, the founding of the evangelical pastor-wedlock. He could not imagine its blessed results. The Thirty Years' War had made wide stretches of Germany and the German people a moral, intellectual, and economic desert. In the degenerated and corrupted rural population the parsonage was the only place of morality, education, and culture. Without Luther's Bible the German language would scarcely have become the language of Goethe and Kant, scarcely again a cultural language. The pastor at that time was the educator, director, and leader in almost all departments. Streams of blessings went out from him at that time. Perhaps the greatest gift to the German people was the countless number of eminent men that came out of the evangelical parsonage."

The Catholic Mrs. Jameson says: "In modern times ill-paid Protestant ministers are noted for their large families, and *also* for the surprisingly large percentage of their sons in *Who's Who.*" — *The Reader's Digest,* December, 1943.

The French Catholic Audin writes: "The Reformer was temperate; he drank little and brought to table agreeable conversation, expansive gaiety, sarcastic sallies, and the treasures of his exhaustless memory. Every subject was discussed there."

Jules Michelet, member of the Institute of France, in his *Luther:*

"Luther showed himself to the world as of the very highest power; an individual who was at once a real personage and an idea; a man perfect in thought and action; a man whose life was known in fullest detail, whose every word, whose every deed, had been marked and treasured up. . . .

"Among these joys Luther had those of the heart, of the man, the innocent happiness of the family and home. What family more holy, what home more pure? Holy, hospitable table, where I myself, for a long time a guest, have found so many divine fruits on which my heart yet lives. Yes, the happy years I spent reading Luther have left me a strength, a vigor, which I hope God will preserve to me until death. . . .

"Let us seat ourselves at his own table, surrounded by his wife and children and his intimate friends; and let us listen to the solemn and memorable sayings of the pious, the tender father of the family" — nearly 100 pages of the "genuine confessions of Luther, confessions all the more true, that they were not deliberately drawn up by the confessor, but are collected for the most part from the words which fell from his lips from time to time, in open, honest, heedless intercourse with his friends and family. Those of Rousseau are beyond question, far less honest; those of Augustine less complete, less various. . . . It presents in combination the two aspects which they exhibit separately. . . . In Luther we see not the equal balance of grace and nature, but their fierce and painful struggle. Many other men have undergone the trials of the flesh and the still higher and more perilous temptations of doubt; Pascal manifestly so: he stifled them in his own breast and died in the contest. But Luther has concealed nothing, he kept nothing to himself, he fought the battle out openly, and he thus enabled us to see and sound in him this deep and awful wound in our nature. He, indeed, is perhaps the only man in whom we can fully study this terrible anomaly. . . . Amiable and winning individuality. . . . 'The Arminius of modern Germany.' . . .

"It is not inexact to say that Luther was, in point of fact, the restorer of liberty to the ages which followed his era. . . . To him it is, in great measure, owing, that we of the present day exercise in its plenitude that first great right of the human understanding, to which all the rest are annexed, without which all the rest are nought. We cannot think, speak, write, read, for a single moment, without gratefully recalling to mind this enormous benefit of intellectual enfranchisement. The very lines I here trace, to whom do I owe it that I am able to send them forth, if not to the liberator of modern thought?

"This tribute paid to Luther we the less hesitate to admit, that our sympathies are not with him in the religious revolution he operated. . . . We shall not, after the example of so many others, lay bare the sores of a church in whose bosom we were born and which is still dear to us."

How did we get the *Table Talk?*

"It fell out that . . . Pope Gregory XIII . . . did fiercely stir up and instigate the Emperor Rudolphus II to make an Edict that Luther's Divine Discourses should be burned; and also that it should be death for any person to have a copy thereof. . . . Yet it pleased God that, anno 1626 . . . Casparus Van Sparr found a copy in a deep obscure hole, without any blemish. [Digging a foundation for a house over an old one.] For fear of Emperor Ferdinandus II the finder sent the book to his friend Captain Henry Bell, who had the High Dutch Tongue very perfect. I was ten whole years in prison, where I spent five years thereof about the translating of the said book.

"Archbishop Laud of Canterbury heard of this, sent for it, studied it for two long years, said I had performed a work worthy of eternal memory, he had never read a more excellent divine work. He would make it known to His Majesty (Charles I) what an excellent piece of work I had translated, and that he would procure an order from His Majesty to have the said translation printed, and to be dispersed throughout the whole kingdom, as it was in Germany.

"The House of Commons appointed a committee, Sir Edward Dering, Chairman, who had Mr. Paul Amirant, a learned minister, who had lived long in England, but was born in High Germany, in the Palatinate, compare the translation with the original. His report satisfied them, yet they desired two of the Assembly, Mr. Charles Herle and Mr. Edward Corbet, to peruse the same, and to make report if they thought it fitting to be printed. They made report, dated the 10th of November, 1646, that they found it to be an excellent Divine Work, worthy the light and publishing. . . . Whereupon the House of Commons, the 24th of February, 1646, did give order for the printing thereof, given under my hand the 3rd day of July, 1650. Henry Bell."

"24th February, 1646.

"It is Ordered and Ordained by the Lords and Commons assembled in Parliament, that the said Henry Bell shall have the sole disposal and benefit of Printing the said book . . . for the space of fourteen years. (Vera Copia.) Henry Elsyng."

"Books have their fates." This one surely had.

A second edition came out in 1791 with a preface by John Ryland of Northampton and a life by Dr. John Gottlieb Burckhardt, minister of the German Lutheran church at the Savoy, London, a large folio of 502 pages, with XXIV of prefatory matter. Another translation was made by William Hazlitt.

Editor Macaulay of *The Leisure Hour* edited a selection in 1883. Cassell published a selection in 1892. Preserved Smith edited a selection in 1915.

THE AGE OF THE REFORMATION
After Kaulbach

Chapter Eighteen

LUTHER'S DEATH

Luther himself wrote his so-called second will. Because legal proceedings might be raised upon his marriage, he left his wife to the special protection of the elector. His children, friends, servants, were all remembered. "Finally, seeing I do not use legal forms, I desire all men to take these words as mine. I am known openly in heaven, on earth, and in hell also; and I may be believed and trusted better than any notary. To me, a poor, unworthy, miserable sinner, God, the Father of mercy, has entrusted the Gospel of His dear Son and has kept me therein true and faithful. Through my means many in this world have received the Gospel and hold me as a true teacher despite popes, emperors, kings, princes, priests, and all the devils' wrath. Let them believe me also in the small matter of my last will and testament, this being written in my own hand, which otherwise is not unknown. Let it be understood that here is the earnest, deliberate meaning of Doctor Martin Luther, God's notary and witness of His Gospel, confirmed by his own hand and seal. — January 6, 1542."

Do you know the like? Neither do we.

In 1545 a report was printed at Rome that Luther had died. It told how he demanded his body be placed on an altar and receive divine worship, but the devil got his beloved son, damned in body and soul.

Luther simply reprinted his death notice and said he enjoyed it hugely. He thus practically cracked Mark Twain's famous joke hundreds of years before the funny American was born, *viz.*, that his death was "greatly exaggerated." And then? And then he prayed for his enemies.

On November 10 he celebrated his birthday for the last time. The elector had sent some wine, a score of carp, and a hundredweight of pike — "fine fish." The old warrior was very jolly with Melanchthon, Bugenhagen, Cruciger, Major, and Eber; but at parting he solemnly said: "During my life, please God, there will be peace in Germany; but when I am dead, there will be great need of praying. Our children will have to grasp the spear; there will be dreadful times in Germany." He earnestly begged his guests to be faithful to the Gospel.

A week later he closed his last lecture at the university — "This is the dear Genesis; God grant others do better with it after me; I can do no more, I am weak. Pray God to grant me a good, blessed hour."

He said: "If I die in my bed, it will be a grievous shame to the pope. Popes, devils, kings, and princes have done their worst to hurt me; yet here I am. The world for these two hundred years has hated no one as it hates me. I, in turn, have no love for the world. I know not that in all my life I have ever felt real enjoyment. I am well tired of it. May God come soon and take me away."

In December Luther went a second time to Mansfeld to settle a quarrel between the counts. The work was broken up by the sickness of Melanchthon, whom Luther personally took home.

In January, 1546, Luther calls himself "old, worn-out, sluggish, weary, cold, and now even one-eyed," and yet the old warrior, on the 23d, again put on the armor of peace and set out for Eisleben. On the 25th the flooded Saale halted them at Halle. Likely it was at this time Luther gave Jonas a goblet with this inscription:

> To Jonas, a glass, gives Luther a glass, himself but a glass,
> That each may know he's like breakable glass.

On the 28th they left, escorted by a guard of honor of one hundred and thirteen heavily armed horsemen. On February 1 he wrote Kate: "As I drove through the village [Nissdorf], such a cold wind blew from behind through my cap on my head that it was like to turn my brain to ice. M. L., Your old lover."

Kate was worried, and Martin wrote her loving letters of comfort with the characteristic Lutheresque combination of serious humor or humorous seriousness. The aged couple were as devoted to one another as young cooing lovers — it is touching. And yet some people can see no romance in their marriage!

On the 14th the great preacher preached in St. Andrew's on Matt. 11:25 ff., his last sermon. He had to cut it short — "Much more might be said on this Gospel, but I am too weak; let this suffice."

At table there was much talk of sickness and death, and Luther said: "When I get home again, I will lay myself in my coffin and give the maggots a fat doctor to eat."

On the 17th, peace was made, and Luther signed it. They begged him to spare himself and rest in his room. In the forenoon he walked up and down or lay on a leather couch. In the afternoon he felt a sharp pain in the chest and was rubbed with hot cloths. At supper he was cheerful and spoke with wonted vigor of death and the resurrection. He soon went upstairs to his bedroom and prayed at the window. Another severe pain in the chest. Count Albrecht of Mansfeld came and himself scraped some of a tooth of a narwhal in wine and gave this precious remedy to the patient. He felt relieved and slept gently from 9 to 10 on the couch, surrounded by his sons Martin and Paul, their tutor Rudtfeld, Jonas, and Coelius. He awoke and said: "Are you still up? Don't you want to go to bed?" Still thoughtful of others.

He went to bed, shook hands with all, as usual, and bade them

WHERE LUTHER DIED

good night. He slept with regular breathing till 1 o'clock. Then he asked Rudtfeld to heat the room, though it was heated. He said: "O my God, what a great pain! O dear Dr. Jonas, I reckon I'll stay in Eisleben, where I was born and baptized."

Without help he went into the room, walked up and down a few turns, repeating: "Into Thy hands I commend my spirit." Then he lay down on the couch and complained of a severe pain in the chest, though it did not yet touch the heart.

They called the host, the city clerk John Albrecht, and his wife, also the two doctors of Eisleben. The doctors found him as lifeless; they could not feel his pulse. Soon Count and Countess Albrecht of Mansfeld arrived, and Count and Countess of Schwarzburg.

ST. ANDREW'S CHURCH

While they were applying all kinds of remedies, Luther said: "Good God, I am in great pain and anguish; I am passing away!"

When Jonas and Coelius tried to cheer him, telling him a wholesome sweat had broken out, Luther said it was the cold sweat of death.

His last prayer was: —

"O my heavenly Father, one God, and Father of our Lord Jesus Christ, Thou God of all comfort, I thank Thee that Thou hast given for me Thy dear Son Jesus Christ, in whom I believe, whom I have preached and confessed, loved and praised, whom the wicked pope and all the godless shame, persecute, and blaspheme. I pray Thee, dear Lord Jesus Christ, let me commend my little soul to Thee. O heavenly Father, if I leave this body and depart, I am

253

certain that I will be with Thee forever, and can never, never tear myself out of Thy hands. God so loved the world that He gave His only-begotten Son, that whosoever believeth in Him should not perish, but have everlasting life." Then three times quickly: "Father, into Thy hands I commend my spirit. Thou hast redeemed me, Thou faithful God."

"When he became so still," Jonas and Coelius "called strongly into him: 'Reverend Father, will you stand steadfast by Christ and the doctrine you have preached?'"

He answered, "that you could hear it distinctly"—"Yes."

He turned on his right side and slept a quarter of an hour. The Countess of Mansfeld and the doctors rubbed his pulse with *aqua vitae* and rose vinegar. The feet and nose grew cold. Luther fetched a deep, gentle breath and departed this life in peace at 2:45 in the morning of February 18, 1546.

When the Catholic apothecary, John Landau, came, his efforts were in vain; the Prophet of Germany had already gone to the saints' everlasting rest.

One of the doctors said the immediate cause of death was a stroke of apoplexy come during a fainting spell.

An hour after, Justus Jonas wrote out a careful account of Luther's last hours. Another interesting account has been found in the United States in an old book from Germany; likely it was written by John Albrecht, the city clerk, in whose house Luther died.

The corpse was dressed in a long white linen shroud, placed in a zinc coffin, and in the afternoon of the 19th it lay in state in St. Andrew's Church, where Jonas preached from 1 Thess. 4:13-18 and ten citizens of Eisleben kept the dead watch.

In the morning an Eisleben artist painted the features of Luther, and the next day Lucas Furtenagel did the same at Halle, and the Duchess of Mansfeld had a death mask taken.

On the 19th the news of Luther's death was brought to Wittenberg by an electoral messenger, and Melanchthon told the students:

"Gone is the chariot of Israel and the horsemen thereof [2 Kings 2:12], who has ruled the Church in this last age of the world. For not human wit has discovered the teaching of the forgiveness of sins and trust in the Son of God, but God has revealed them through this man, whom God has raised up. So, then, let us keep in love the memory of this man and the teaching in the manner in which he handed it to us."

On the 20th Coelius preached from Is. 57:1, and then the body was taken to Wittenberg.

Greater throngs than had followed the bier of even the elector now honored Luther as the coffin was carried from dorp to dorp till it came to Wittenberg on the 22d, at 9 A. M.

The corpse was received at the Elster Gate, where Luther had burned the papal bull, and the procession wended its way through the town to the Castle Church.

Mathesius gives us the funeral procession —

The counts of Mansfeld with about forty-five horsemen.

The corpse.

Kate Luther.

The three sons, brother Jacob, nephew Cyriacus Kaufmann, and other relatives.

The Rector Manificus of the university, student princes, and counts.

Chancellor Gregory Brueck, Melanchthon, Justus Jonas, Pomeranus, Kreutziger, Jerome Schurf, and others.

The city council.

The student body.

Citizens.

Bugenhagen preached in German from 1 Thess. 4:13-18, and then Melanchthon in Latin.

"In our time through the mouth and writing of the venerable Dr. Martin Luther the pure teaching of the Gospel has been rekindled and brought to light much brighter and purer. . . . Especially raised by God. . . . Taught of God. . . .

"There is no doubt pious Christian hearts will ever and ever until eternity praise the divine benefit He has given His Church through this Dr. Luther. Then they will confess publicly before all the world that they have been much bettered through this dear man's faithful diligence and work in writings and preachings. . . .

"Not human power, but divine grace and gifts were needed to bridle a fiery nature like Dr. Luther's. . . ."

He referred to Luther's human weaknesses, especially his violent temper, but, as Erasmus said, the diseases of the times demanded a severe physician. "With all his great dignity he was gracious, affable, and friendly, not storming and quarrelsome; he had a heart without guile, was all that Paul demanded in Phil. 4:8. His violence flowed from his zeal for the truth, and in all his battles he had kept a conscience void of offense. We are as poor orphans, who had an excellent man for a father, and are now bereft of him."

The corpse was buried near the pulpit. The monk damned by pope and banned by kaiser had a princely burial.

At once there came *The true Hystorie of the Christian Departynge of the Reverend man Doctor Martyne Luther,* Collected by Justus Jonas, M. Coelius, and John Aurifaber, which were present thereat; translated into English by Johan Bale, 1546. 18mo.

Dymmock sent Lord Paget, Secretary of State, who had visited Luther, a colored woodcut of the Reformer.

"If you look for a monument, look around you." The modern world of liberty in Church and State is his product and his monument. This truth is brought out forcefully in Kaulbach's great painting of "The Age of the Reformation." Here are gathered all the great ones of the modern world; in the center, holding aloft the open Bible, stands the master of them all, Martin Luther.

In 1927 two hundred Lutheran pilgrims from the United States laid a large wreath on his grave, and we preached to them in German and in English from his pulpit, thanking God for restoring His pure Gospel through His servant Martin Luther.

INDEX

Aachen, 115.
Abelard (1100), against indulgences, 66.
Adrian VI, Pope, 104, 111; his confession of sins, 181; death of, 183.
Agricola, Johann, 178.
Alber, Matthew, 238.
Albrecht, Duke of Prussia, 210.
Albrecht von Brandenburg, 62, 63; gets the 95 Theses from Luther, 69, 72; Elector-Archbishop of Mainz, 82, 114, 131, 135, 145, 202, 218, 221.
Aleander, Hieronymus, papal legate, 79, 105, 114 ff., 118, 121, 122, 125 f., 130, 184, 208, 216.
Alexander VI, Pope, 5, 35 f., 37, 212. (On page 35 read Alexander VI.)
Amsdorf, 57, 119, 135, 206, 217.
Anhalt, a prince of, Barefooter, 6; Adolf von Anhalt, 23, 71; Georg von A., 235.
Anselm, Saint, 14.
Antichrist, 94, 100, 102, 219.
Apology of the Augsburg Confession, 215.
Aristotle, 57 f., 76.
Arnoldi, Bartholomaeus, 12.
Audin, French Catholic, tributes to Luther, 141, 142 f., 149, 170, 225, 231, 245.
Augsburg Confession, 193, 196 ff., 205.
Augsburg Reichstag called, 197.
Augustine, 242, 246.
Augustinian Cloister, Wittenberg, 42.

Augustinian order, 23.
Aurifaber, Dr. John, 244, 256.
Aurogallus, 154, 239.

Barnes, Robert, Luther's table friend, 237; martyred, 239.
Baumgaertner, Jerome, alderman, 181, 202, 239.
Behaim, Martin, 124.
Bellarmine, Cardinal, Jesuit, 89; "the fine songs of Luther," etc., 162.
Berlepsch, Hans von, captain of the Wartburg, 132, 230.
Bernard, Saint, 14.
Berthold von Regensburg, preached against indulgences, 66.
Beyer, Dr. Christian, at Augsburg, 201.
Bible reading forbidden, 156.
Boniface VIII, Pope, 61.
Bora, Florian von, 230.
Bora, Katherine von, see Katherine Luther (von Bora).
Braun, John, 8, 21.
Brenz, Joh., 76, 204.
Brueck, Dr. Gregory, famous chancellor, 45, 99, 200, 201, 219, 226, 233, 235.
Bruno, Giordano, 43.
Bucer, Martin, 76, 121, 177, 203, 204, 238.
Bugenhagen, Johann, "Pomeranus," 105, 152, 213, 220, 226, 232, 250, 255.
Bull of Leo X, 108.
Bunyan, John, praises Luther's *Galatians*, 78.

257

Cajetan, ordered to arrest Luther at once, 80, 84 ff., 102, 213.
Calvin, 219.
Campegi, Cardinal, 89, 166, 184, 185, 186, 197, 198, 201, 202.
Capito, Wolfgang, 93, 142, 238.
Carlstadt, 47, 57, 77, 85; Leipzig Debate, 95 f.; uproar at Wittenberg, 139 ff., 159, 233.
Carlyle, Thomas, 1.
Castle Church "All Saints" at Wittenberg, 67, 70, 71.
Cato, 4.
Cellini, Benvenuto, artist, 188.
Clement VI, Pope, *Unigenitus,* 86, 109.
Clement VII, Pope, 10, 148, 172, 184; he saved Luther from burning, 186; Clement driven from the Vatican and placed in captivity, 188 ff.; backs the Turk, 207; died, 211.
Cochlaeus, Johann, 48, 147, 153, 236.
Coelius, Michael, 251, 253, 254, 255, 256.
Columbus, 124.
Constantine's Donation, 100.
Contarini, 213, 216, 217.
Cordatus, Conrad, 233.
Cortez, 124.
Cotta, Ursula, 8.
Coverdale, Miles, 160.
Cranach, Lucas, 67, 143, 152, 200, 220, 223, 239, 243.
Cranmer, Thomas, Archbishop of Canterbury, 164.
Cruciger, Kaspar, 152, 250, 255.
Cum postquam, papal bull, 88.

De Soto, 216.
Diaz, Bartholomaeus, 3.
Dietenberger, John, a Dominican, 155.
Dietrich, Veit, 231.
Doellinger, Ignaz von, 164.
Duerer, Albrecht, 67, 71; meets Luther, 89, 91, 122, 123, 144, 153, 161, 184 f.

Eber, Paul, 250.
Eck, John, 41, 67, 72; in debate, 95 ff.; his pen portrait by Peter Schade, 98, 102; chief author of the bull *Exurge, Domine,* 108, 116, 155; at Augsburg Reichstag, 198, 202, 215.
Ecken, Johann von der, spokesman for Karl V at Worms, 125, 127, 129.
Eisenach, 8, 121, 132.
Eisleben, 1, 250, 251, 252, 254.
Elisabeth of Brandenburg, 209, 210, 234.
Emser, Jerome, 14, 153 f.
Erasmus, 48, 54, 56 f., 63, 66, 72, 74, 77, 78, 93, 94, 104, 108, 110 f., 118, 123, 135, 155, 163, 169 ff., 202, 240, 244, 256.
Erfurt, 10.
Esch, Johann von, martyr, 182.
Esch, medicinal doctor, Luther's physician, 107.

Faber, John, 193.
Ferdinand and Isabella, Spain, 5.
Ferdinand, king of Bohemia and Hungary, 180, 184, 194 f., 200, 208, 216, 219.
Flacius Illyricus, Matthias, 237.
Fleck, Dr., 43, 71.
Forsyth, P. T., principal of Hackney College, London, 5.
Francis I of France, 114; how he saved Luther from burning, 180, 186.
Franck, Sebastian, 243.
Frederick, Elector, 45, 53, 67, 68, 90, 91, 92, 93, 99, 113 f., 129, 141; Peasants' War, 145; 168, 237.
Froben, Johann, scholarly printer of Basel, 93.
Frosch, John, Augustinian prior, 85, 90.
Frundsberg, George von, captured Francis I, 186
Fuggers, 63; Jacob Fugger, papal banker, 83, 204; a Fugger agent, 92.

George, Duke of Saxony, 95, 96, 102, 148, 166, 215, 235.
George, Markgrave of Brandenburg, 210.
Gerson, John, 85.
Gladstone, 244.
Glapion, Jean, 117, 122.
Granvelle, 216.

Gregory the Great, introduced instrumental music and choir singing into the Church, 159.
Gregory XIII, Pope, 244, 247.
Grisar, Jesuit Hartmann von, gives Luther's treatise on Christian Liberty high praise, 107, 144 f., 157.
Gurk, Raymond von, seller of indulgences, 12.
Gutenberg, Johann, inventor of printing, 156.

Hamilton, Patrick, 240.
Hausmann, Nicholas, 140, 224.
Henry VIII of England, how he gained the title "The Defender of the Truth," 105, 110, 114, 205; burned Barnes, 239.
Hessus, Eobanus, poet, 120.
Hilton, John, 8.
Holzschuher, Jerome, alderman, 181.
Hoogstraten, Jakob, terrible inquisitor, 94.
Hus, John, 18, 21, 101, 103.
Hutten, Ulrich von, poet laureate, 82, 86, 100, 102, 112, 117, 118, 121, 122, 135.
Hutter, Conrad, 8.

Indulgences, 30, 31, 65 ff.; fell through at Leipzig Debate, 96; King Henry's argument, 167.
Innocent IV, Pope, 23.
Innocent VIII, Pope, 3.
Inquisition, 183.

Janssen, Johannes, Romish historian, 201.
Jerome (Hieronymus), translated the Bible into Latin, 155.
Jesuits, lead Council of Trent, 219.
Joachim I of Brandenburg, 62, 117, 119, 210.
Joachim, II, made Brandenburg Lutheran, 210.
John Frederick of Saxony, 203, 213, 214, 215, 221.
Jonas, Justus, 53, 57, 122, 123, 163, 192, 203, 220, 226, 236, 251, 252, 253, 254, 255, 256.
Julius II, Pope, 37 f.

Karl V, Emperor, 62, 63, 110, 113 ff.; crowned at Aachen, 115, 118, 123 ff.; the edict against Luther, 130 f.; Peasants' War, 145, 170; war with France, 180; Nuernberg Reichstag, 184 f.; Karl's sister favored the Gospel and is comforted by Luther, 187; his troops storm and pillage Rome, capture Clement VII, 189 ff.; rejects protest of Speyer, 195; Clement crowns Karl, 197; the Kaiser at Augsburg, 197 ff., 212, 216, 217, 218, 219.
Kaufmann, Cyriacus, 255.
Kessler, John, 141.
Koeln Cathedral, 45.

Lang, John, 54, 56, 57, 75, 76, 94, 97, 102, 224.
Lauterbach, Anton, 238.
Leipzig Debate, 94 ff.
Lena, Aunt, 229.
Link, Wenzeslaus, 83, 87, 38, 102, 223.
Lollards, Brethren of the Common Life, 6.
Lotther, Melchior, printer in Leipzig, 94, 153.
Lufft, Hans, Luther's printer, 143.
Luther, Elisabeth, 228.
Luther, Hans, 2, 19.
Luther, Jacob, Martin's younger brother, 2, 255.
Luther, Johannes (Haenschen), 200, 227, 229, 230.
Luther, Katharina (v. Bora), 181, 200, 203, 237, 238, 242, 251, 255.
Luther, Magdalen, 200, 227, 228.
Luther, Margaret, Luther's mother, 2.
Luther, Margaret, Luther's daughter, 228, 229.
Luther, Martin, 1; studies at Erfurt, 12; his love of music, 12; professor, 13; begins to see errors in papacy, 13; receives a Bible from Staupitz, 17; L. the cleric, 17; his first mass, 19; authors he studied, 20; ordered to Wittenberg, 21; trip to Rome, 23; nothing to do but see the sights, 25; the Church of Saint Paul, 26;

catacombs, 27; St. John Laterman, etc., 28; levity of priests at Mass, 34; Roman fables, 34 f.; leaves the city of Rome, 40; his conversion, 42 ff.; called to Wittenberg, 44; becomes Doctor of Theology, 45 f.; "The just shall live by faith," 49; Grace Alone, 50; Scripture Alone, Faith Alone, 51; lectures on Romans, 54; L. as lecturer and preacher, 54; burdened with work, 55 f.; bodily ills, 56; sermons on the Lord's Prayer, 56; the *Seven Penitential Psalms,* 57; theses *Against the Scholastic Theology,* 57; the Ninety-Five Theses, 58 ff., 70; nailed them to the door of the Castle Church, 69; his *Resolutions* on the Theses, 71; meeting of the Augustinians at Heidelberg in April, 1518, 74 ff.; his *Commentary on Galatians* (spring, 1519), 77; writes *Tessaradecas Consolatoria,* to comfort the sick elector, 78; controversies about the Theses: Luther and Cajetan, 80; *Appeal from the Pope Ill-Informed to the Pope Better Informed,* 88; leaves without leave, 88; L. and Miltitz, 91 ff.; L. and Eck, 94 ff.; Sermon on Good Works, 94; first pen portrait of Luther, 98; prepares to leave the country, 99; *To the Christian Nobility,* 100 ff.; the greatest statesman of his day, 101; *Babylonian Captivity of the Church,* 102 ff., 117; pastor of the City Church at Wittenberg, 105; *The Liberty of a Christian Man,* 105 ff.; writes letter to Leo X, 105 ff.; the bull *Arise, O God,* 108 ff.; sale of his books, 112; at Worms, 113 ff.; entering, 122, 125; before the Reichstag, 126; his speech, 127 ff.; the edict of the Kaiser, 130 f.; at the Wartburg, 132 ff.; Junker Joerg, 133; *On Monastic Vows,* 134; *Church Postil,* 134; Translation of the New Testament, 135; *Against the Idol of Halle,* 135 f.; riots in Wittenberg, 139 ff.; Peasants' War, 144; the Anabaptists, 150 f.; Luther's Bible, 152 ff.; L.'s hymns, 161 ff.; L.'s Catechism, 162 ff.; *Letter to the Aldermen and Cities of Germany to Erect and Maintain Christian Schools,* 162 f.; visitation of the churches, 163; L. and King Henry VIII, 165 ff.; *On the Unfree Will,* against Erasmus, 171; L. and Zwingli, 173 ff.; his hymnbook, 158 ff.; *On the War Against the Turk,* 195; at Coburg, 199; his patriotism, 207; sickness, 214; his so-called first will, 215; *Wider Hans Worst,* 217; *Against the Papacy at Rome, Founded by the Devil,* 219; Luther at home, 220 ff.; heart attack, 226; violence of speech, 226; *House Postil,* 231; Christmas hymn "Vom Himmel hoch," 231; first Lutheran orphanage, 231; old folks' home, 231; hospital, 232; asylum, refuge for refugees, 234 ff.; hospice for visitors, 236 ff.; Catholic tributes, 241; Luther's Table Talk, 241 ff.; he was no prude, but he hated the nude, 243; more refined than his age, 244; his family, 246; his death, 249 ff.; last sermon at Eisleben, 251; his last prayer, 253.

Luther, Martin, Jr., 228, 251.
Luther, Paul, 33, 228, 251.
"Lutheran," the term first used by Eck, 98.

Magdeburg, 6.
Magellan, 124.
Major, George, 250.
Mann, Thomas, tribute to Luther, 158.
Mansfeld, Albrecht of, dines Luther, 89, 250; peace made, 251; gives Luther medicine, 251, 252; Countess of Mansfeld, 254.
Mansfeld, George of, 3.
Marburg, 173 ff.; Marburg Articles, 177 f., 198; no brotherhood, 178, 232.
Martin of Tours, 2.

Martyrs, the first Lutheran, 182.
Mathesius, Johann, on L.'s Small Catechism, 156, 163, 236; his *Life of Luther*, 242 f., 255.
Maximilian, Emperor, 71, 80, 82, 114, 145.
Melanchthon, Philip, 3, 44, 77, 83, 91, 94; wedding of M. and Kate Crapp, 108, 109, 110, 140, 152, 153, 170, 171; at Marburg, 154, 173 f., 178; at Augsburg, 198 ff., 205, 210, 214, 215, 216, 217, 227, 232, 233, 238, 240, 250, 254, 255.
Menius, Justus, 238.
Michelangelo, 39, 49, 152.
Milan Cathedral, 41.
Miltitz, Karl von, 91 ff., 105, 113.
Milton, in defense of Luther's fierce language, 102.
Milvian Bridge, 40.
More, Sir Thomas, 166, 169, 170, 244.
Moritz of Saxony, 217.
Morone, Cardinal, papal legate, 216, 218.
Mosellanus (Peter Schade), professor of poetry, gives pen portraits of Luther and Eck at Leipzig, 98, 169.
Mosshauer, Dr. Paul, 6.
Muenzer, Thomas, 140, 147, 148.
Murner, Thomas, 110, 168.
Musculus, Wolfgang, 238.
Myconius, 45, 70, 79, 238.

Nero's burial place, 35.
Nicholas V, Pope, 85, 208.

Obscure Men, Letters of, 54.
Oekolampad, John, 98; at Marburg, 173, 179.
Oemler, Nicolaus, 4.
Osiander, Andrew, 184, 185, 239.

Pappenheim, Ulrich von, 124.
Parsonage, the evangelical, 245.
Pascal, 246.
Paul III, Pope, 212, 213, 219.
Peter Lombard, 22.
Peutinger, Dr. Konrad, Augsburg patrician, 85, 88.

Philip of Hesse, Landgraf, 148, 173, 177 f., 195, 202; restored Wuerttemberg to Duke Ulrich, 210.
Pilate's staircase, 32.
Pirkheimer, Willibald, dines Luther, 89, 94, 97, 111.
Pistorius, Friedrich, 223.
Pius II, Pope, 58, 66, 164.
Pius III, Pope, 183.
Plato, 57, 76.
Platter, Thomas, 4.
Pleissenburg at Leipzig, 80, 95.
Pollich of Mellerstadt, Martin, 45, 53.
Popess Joanna, 30.
Porta del Popolo, 25, 26, 59.
Prierias, 72, 73 f.
Printers of Luther's early books, 93.
Proles, Andreas, Augustinian, 7.
Protestants, the first, 193, 195 f.
Purgatory, at Leipzig Debate, 96.

Ranke, Leopold von, 70; *To the Christian Nobility* "world-historic pages," 102; on L.'s Small Catechism, 163;
Reichstag of Speyer, 187.
Regensburg, 1541 convention, 216.
Reinecker, Peter, 6.
Relics at Rome, 26, 28 f., 30 f.; at All Saints' Church, 67; at Aachen, 115; at Halle, 135.
Rennebecker, Bartholomaeus, 2.
Reuchlin, John, 14, 22, 53 f., 94.
Rhegius, Urban, 203.
Rinkart, Martin, 1.
Roerer, George, 154, 232, 236.
Roman's, Epistle to the, 49; Luther's Preface to Romans, 55.
Rome, sights of, 26.
Rudtfeld, Ambrosius, tutor of Luther's sons, 251, 252.

Sachs, Hans, 184.
St. Ann, 5, 14.
St. George, 5.
St. John Lateran, 29, 32.
St. Peter's Cathedral, Rome, 30.
St. Thomas' Church, Leipzig, 211, 215 f.
St. Veronica, 31.
Santa Maria dell' Anima, German church in Rome, 35.

Santa Maria del Popolo, 35.
Santa Maria Maggiore and its relics, 30.
Savonarola, Jerome, 36, 120.
Schalbe, Heinrich, consul in Eisenach, 8.
Scheurl, Christopher, 43, 45, 54, 57, 91, 93, 109.
Schlaginhaufen, Johann, one of Luther's table guests, 215.
Schmalkalden, Bund of, 206; Schmalkald Articles, 214.
Schnepf, Erhard, 76.
Schurf, Dr. Augustine, 227.
Schurf, Jerome, 45, 57, 70; 541 f., 222, 255.
Scultetus (Schulz), Hieronymus, Bishop of Brandenburg, 94.
Senfl, Ludwig, Bavarian court musician, 200.
Sickingen, Franz von, 112, 117, 121.
Sieberger, Wolf, 232.
Sixtus IV, Pope, 66.
Spalatin, reforms Augustinian order, 23, 43, 53, 54, 75, 77; asks Luther to comfort the sick elector, 78, 89; Antichrist letter, 94, 99, 102, 109, 119, 121 f., 129, 154; at Speyer, 187; sends wedding present, 221, 224.
Spengler, Lazarus, famous secretary of Nuernberg, 79, 91, 99, 184, 202.
Speratus, Paul, "Es ist das Heil uns kommen her," 218.
Speyer, Reichstag of, 187 ff.; second, 193.
Sprenger, Jacob, 3.
Staupitz, Johann, 7; exhorts his monks to read the Bible, 17, 18, 21, 45, 46, 48, 54; on the lookout for relics at Antwerp, 67, 68, 72, 73, 76, 81, 85, 87, 88; again urges Luther to stop, 102, 115, 142.
Sturm, Kaspar, emperor's herald, 119, 122.
Sylvester II, Pope, 30.

Tetzel, John, 63 ff., 68 f., 72, 73 f., 92, 97.
Thomas Aquinas, 14, 85.
Trebonius, John, 9.
Tritheim, Johannes von, 3.
Trutvetter, Jodocus, 10, 12.
Turks, 206; backed by Francis I and Clement VII, 207.
Tyndale, William, registered at the University of Wittenberg, 239, 240.

Ulrich of Wuerttemberg, made his land Lutheran, 210.
Usingen, Bartholomaeus Arnoldi von, 20.

Valla, Lorenzo, proves the Constantine Donation a huge forgery, 100.
Vatican, 31.
Verbum Dei Manet in Eternum, 186, 194.
Vergerius, Peter Paul, 212 f.
Voes, Heinrich, martyr, 182.

Wartburg, 132 ff.
Welsers of Augsburg, 118, 205.
Wesel, Johann von, 66.
Wesley, Charles, converted by Luther's *Romans*, 78.
Wesley, John, and Luther's Preface to *Romans*, 55.
Wiclif, 101.
Wimpheling, good Catholic, 39.
Wittenberg, 8, 44; University of, 44 ff., 239; St. Mary's, or City Church, 46.
"Wittenberg Concord," The, 210, 238.
Wolsey, Cardinal, 72, 89, 93, 115, 166, 197.
Worms, the diet, 113 ff.; the edict, 130 ff.

Zwickau "prophets," 140, 142.
Zwilling, Gabriel, 139, 142, 158, 223.
Zwingli, Ulrich, Luther and, 173 ff., 177.